CW00968337

IT MADE YOU
THINK OF HOME

For Ted, Sid, Gord, Art, and Bill:
Warriors for the working-day.

IT MADE YOU THINK OF HOME

The Haunting Journal of Deward Barnes, Canadian Expeditionary Force: 1916–1919

Bruce Cane

THE DUNDURN GROUP
TORONTO

Copyright © Bruce Cane, 2004

All rights reserved. No part of this publication may be reproduced, stored in a retrieval system, or trans-mitted in any form or by any means, electronic, mechanical, photocopying, recording, or otherwise (except for brief passages for purposes of review) without the prior permission of Dundurn Press. Permission to photocopy should be requested from Access Copyright.

Editor: Ward McBurney
Copy-Editor: Andrea Pruss
Design: Jennifer Scott
Printer: Transcontinental

Library and Archives Canada Cataloguing in Publication

Barnes, Deward
    It made you think of home : the haunting journal of Deward Barnes, CEF 1916-1919 /
[edited by] Bruce Cane.

Includes bibliographical references.
ISBN 1-55002-512-0

1. Barnes, Deward--Diaries. 2. World War, 1914-1918 — Personal narratives. 3. Canada. Canadian Army. Canadian Expeditionary Force — Biography. 4. Soldiers — Canada — Diaries. 5. Executions and executioners — Canada — History — 20th century. I. Cane, Bruce II. Title.

D640.B35 2004   940.4'8171   C2004-903715-3

1   2   3   4   5   08   07   06   05   04

Conseil des Arts du Canada   Canada Council for the Arts   Canada   ONTARIO ARTS COUNCIL
CONSEIL DES ARTS DE L'ONTARIO

We acknowledge the support of the Canada Council for the Arts and the Ontario Arts Council for our pub-lishing program. We also acknowledge the financial support of the Government of Canada through the Book Publishing Industry Development Program and The Association for the Export of Canadian Books, and the Government of Ontario through the Ontario Book Publishers Tax Credit program, and the Ontario Media Development Corporation's Ontario Book Initiative.

Care has been taken to trace the ownership of copyright material used in this book. The author and the pub-lisher welcome any information enabling them to rectify any references or credit in subsequent editions.

J. Kirk Howard, President

Printed and bound in Canada.
Printed on recycled paper.

www.dundurn.com

Dundurn Press
8 Market Street Suite 200
Toronto, Ontario, Canada
M5E 1M6

Gazelle Book Services Limited
White Cross Mills
Hightown, Lancaster, England
LA1 4X5

Dundurn Press
2250 Military Road
Tonawanda NY
U.S.A. 14150

This story shall the good man teach his son ...
King Henry V, act IV, scene iii

My nerves were always good untill I was wounded I had my last leave from France Sept 1918 & maybe on account of the War lasting so long & the thought of what was in front of us. I then started to ... over it. Since I came home I have always tried to work hard & steady to get over this three years experience, but could never do it, so I class myself as a war wreck, which people will never under- stand

TABLE OF CONTENTS

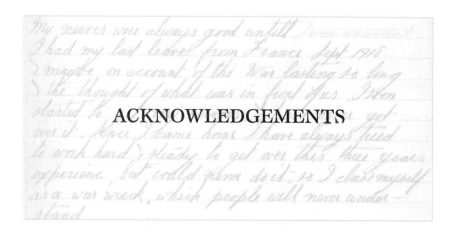

ACKNOWLEDGEMENTS

To paraphrase John Donne, the seventeenth-century English writer and cleric, "No *author* is an island entire of himself."

What Donne meant to say in his original meditation was that no human life can exist in isolation, just as I have discovered that no author can write a book in isolation. As a result (contrary to another of Donne's assertions, that we are all "of one author") this book has many authors.

Deward's son, George, who foresaw that someday the diary might be published and so preserved it, has played a vital role in bringing this book to the shelves. His enthusiasm for the venture was infectious, and a driving force behind its completion.

My long-time friend Ward McBurney has spent almost as much time working on this project as an editor and proofreader as I have as a researcher (a task made much easier by Ward's access to the University of Toronto libraries) and author. Ward's clarity of thought and gentle, timely advice have made this an infinitely better book for you, the reader, than anything I could have done on my own. I have learned much about the lively art of writing from him, for which I will always be grateful.

Many other friends also helped to interpret Deward's story by lending their expertise or resources: Edward Anderson helped me figure out the riddle of Deward's paper ammunition; Brian Cox provided valuable information on the Lewis gun; Laure France was of great assistance in locating and standardizing the names of the French villages that Deward chronicles; Kevin Hebib shared his encyclopaedic knowledge of the small-box respirator; and Chris Laverton gave me open access to his research library. Thank you to all.

Special thanks, too, must go to Kirk Howard and Beth Bruder of Dundurn Press for the support and encouragement they provided to me.

The Argyll and Sutherland Highlanders of Canada perpetuate the memory of the 19th Canadian Infantry Battalion and made many of their resources and personnel available to me. In particular, I would like to thank Dr. Robert Fraser, the regimental historian, and Richard Seager, curator of the regimental museum, for their support; and Taber James for providing me with generous access to the electronic database of 19th Battalion personnel that he is creating. Through Dr. Fraser, I also met David Campbell, who is currently writing a history of the 19th Battalion and who freely shared with me his research and was tremendously giving with his time.

During the research phase of this book, I stumbled down many unanticipated paths. Along the way, I benefited from meeting many kind people who were only too happy to share their hard-won knowledge. I would like to thank specifically Mr. John Endicott of the Kent Police Museum and Mr. Robert Mee, of Derbyshire, England for helping make sense of the lights that Deward saw on top of police helmets while he was in England.

Closer to home, too, people proved generous with their expertise. In particular, Mike Filey and Barbara Forsyth were a great help with my research on Bayside Park, Toronto.

I also wish to thank Mr. John Koopman, president of the Empire Club of Canada, for permission to quote from several of the club's wartime speeches.

There are also many institutions that provided invaluable help and research material. Of course, these organizations are only as good as the people that run them — and they are very good organizations indeed. The following is a list of those bodies: the Canadian Agency of the Commonwealth War Graves Commission; the Canadian National Exhibition Archives; the Canadian War Museum;

the City of Toronto Archives; the Imperial War Museum; the National Archives of Canada; and the Whitby Public Library.

A word of thanks must also go to John Badowski, who several years ago spent a great deal of time and care creating a typed copy of Deward's 1926 diary.

Before closing, I must take a moment to thank Carl Benn, Chief Curator, City of Toronto Museums and Heritage Services. It was Carl who encouraged me originally to write about history and gave me the opportunity to take my first, halting steps into the world of publishing many years ago. Thank you Carl.

Finally, and most importantly, I want to thank my family for doing without me for the year and a half it took to write this book. My wife, Dana, gallantly stepped into the breach made by my absence and assumed an unequal share of the household chores so that I could have time to write. And for my children, Patrick, Aidan, and Catrina: I hope I have given them a means to access the legacy of sacrifice, dedication, and determination that was left to them by Deward, their great-grandfathers, and all of the Canadians who left the comforts of home for an uncertain fate and who laboured in the birthplace of our nation.

My nerves were always good untill I [?] I had my last leave from France Sept 1915 & maybe on account of the War lasting so long & the thought of what was in front of us. I then started to get [?] never got over it. Since I came home I have always tried to work hard & steady to get over this three years experience, but could never do it, so I class myself as a war wreck, which people will never understand

INTRODUCTION

We don't know very much about the early life of Deward Barnes. A glance through his army service record reveals that he was born in Toronto on September 2, 1888; that his father, who was from Bristol, England, died before Deward volunteered for military service; and that his mother, Eliza, married again. But beyond this, his childhood exists today only in family stories and what we can reconstruct from the pages of his diary.

It appears Deward's family — which included three sisters, Beatrice, Norah, and Dorothy — lived comfortably enough, probably in central Toronto, where it is thought Deward attended Jesse Ketchum elementary school. However, he withdrew from the public educational system before reaching high school, and chose instead to work. It was likely then that Deward found a job in the workshop of National Casket, a coffin factory located just north of the old fort that marks the site of Toronto's birthplace. There, he worked as an apprentice machinist, grinding profiles into the steel blades used to shape the decorative wood mouldings and panels on the coffin lids and sides.

One other detail from Deward's pre-war life is certain: he met and fell in love with a young woman, Lucy Field, and the two became engaged.

In 1839, the Treaty of London recognized the newly independent kingdom of Belgium and declared it would remain a neutral state.

The key to this declaration was Article 7, which guaranteed Belgian neutrality by obliging the signatories, which included Great Britain and, paradoxically, Germany, to help defend the smaller nation in case of attack. Nevertheless, on August 4, 1914, thirty-eight German divisions, three-quarters of a million men, came crashing over the Belgian border and churned across the Flanders plain in a race to outflank the French army and then push on to Paris. When Britain's ultimatum to Germany demanding a withdrawal from Belgian soil expired at 11:00 p.m. London time on August 4, Great Britain, as well as her dominions and colonies, was at war. This implementation of imperial policy sent Canada to war by default and without consultation, although it did give the Dominion government the right to decide how it would support to the war. The decision came swiftly and was resounding. Canada would raise and equip an infantry division for service at the front, for which the Canadian Privy Council authorized a twenty-five-thousand-man expeditionary force. Over time, the government raised and equipped a total of five divisions, four of which saw active service at the front.

A force of this size required a continuous flow of new recruits to replace those men who were killed or wounded. Patriotic posters and military rallies, with their earnest appeals for recruits, became common throughout the land. The winter of 1916 proved the most productive recruiting period of the war up to that time, when almost ninety thousand men answered the call to arms between January 1 and March 31, Deward among them. On February 26, he enlisted at Toronto with the 180th Infantry Battalion (The Sportsmen).

At first, the 180th Battalion trained in the city and later at the newly opened Camp Borden, roughly fifty miles (eighty kilometres) north of the city. During this time, the men learned the rudimentary skills of soldiering. On November 21, 1916, the battalion landed in England, where it was soon broken up to provide fresh men for units that were already fighting at the front. In early April 1917, Deward was placed in a large draft of former 180th Battalion men that went to the 19th Canadian Infantry Battalion, which at the time was making final preparations for the great attack on Vimy Ridge. Deward arrived at the battalion after the assaulting parties had left for the trenches and so he could only sit and watch the operation from a camp several miles behind the lines. He did not wait long, however, for his baptism of fire. In May, while relieving several other Canadian battalions in the front lines, the 19th Battalion was caught up in the German counterattack at Fresnoy and was severely mauled. Deward also saw his share of heavy fighting at Hill 70, Passchendaele, Amiens, and through the Hindenburg Line. He knew his share, too, of the tedium that came with routine army life: the work parties, route marches, inspections, guard duty, and so on. Deward also came face to face with perhaps the cruellest side of war when, in March 1918, he was assigned to the firing squad that executed one of his own company mates for desertion. All of this he recorded in a series of pocket-sized diaries that he carried with him.

On October 11, 1918, the 19th Battalion was engaged in heavy fighting near the French village of Iwuy. While running for the cover of a railway embankment, Deward was struck in the right thigh by a machine gun bullet, which first passed through the butt of his rifle. While the shattered bullet did not break any bones nor damage any nerve tissue, the wound was serious enough to warrant his evacuation to England, where he spent the remainder of the war convalescing.

Deward returned to Canada in 1919, and before the end of that year, he and Lucy were married. Perhaps having seen enough coffins while in France and Belgium to last several lifetimes, Deward did not return to National Casket but instead went to work for the John B. Smith Company, a wood moulding mill located on Strachan Avenue, Toronto, close to the training grounds where he had spent his early months in the army. Deward and Lucy eventually settled down on Milverton Boulevard, in the east end of Toronto, and in 1920 they began to raise a family. Sadly, their first child, a daughter, died in infancy. In 1923, however, Lucy gave birth to a healthy son, George, who survived childhood, a world war, and twenty-five years with the Metropolitan Toronto Police Service.

After the war, Deward was a changed man. Although he kept in touch with many of his wartime friends through the annual

Warrior's Day parade at the Canadian National Exhibition and through his involvement in the 19th Battalion Association, the man about town who is hinted at by the diary entries made while on leave in England and Scotland now much preferred the company of his family and the quiet of his own home.

In 1942, Deward watched his son, George, go off to war, taking up the fight that many veterans of the earlier conflict regarded as a betrayal of their sufferings and those of their dead friends. Knowing as he did what lay ahead for George, we are only left to wonder at what Deward felt, but never spoke, as he said goodbye to his only child.

Deward retired from the workaday world in the early 1960s after more than forty years on the job with the John B. Smith Company. He would not, however, enjoy his retirement for long. In 1963, doctors discovered an inoperable tumour in Lucy's brain. After her death, Deward moved out of the family home on Milverton Boulevard and took up quarters in a small apartment building nearby.

Deward died in 1967 from prostate cancer and today lies beside Lucy in the Resthaven Memorial Gardens cemetery, in Toronto's east end.

During the winter of 1926, Deward gathered together his collection of pocket diaries and transcribed them into a single, hardbound notebook. There is no hint or suggestion that he ever planned to publish his notebook. Indeed, he tells us quite clearly that he wrote it for himself alone (perhaps as a catharsis for his nerves, which he confides were in a bad state after the war), with no expectation that anyone without a firsthand experience of war could really understand what he was writing about. When Deward finished transcribing the diary, he placed the notebook on a shelf and left it there, promising George that someday it would be his.

Today, only one of Deward's original diaries exists, a green, cloth-covered booklet, The Canadian Pocket Diary, 1918, published by Brown Brothers, Manufacturing Stationers. On the second page is a place for the owner's name and address — "Cpl. D. Barnes, 19th

Canadians, #862690" — and other personal information, which is left blank. Further down on the page there is room to write the name and address of someone to contact in case of accident or illness — "Lucy Field, 1382A Queen E., Toronto." Further down still there is space to record the diarist's clothing sizes: Size of my shoes — "13"; hosiery — "4"; collar — "18"; cuffs — "5"; hat — "9"; shirt — "11"; gloves — "7"; underwear — "MYOB [Mind Your Own Business]."

The diary pages within are lined and divided in two, top and bottom, permitting two entries per page. Deward wrote the entries in pencil, and over the years the thin, grey lines have begun to fade and smudge. In light of the conditions under which the entries were written and the limited space on the page in which to create them, the smudges may well date to the time the entries were actually written.

If the surviving 1918 diary is typical, Deward transcribed some of the entries from the pocket diaries word for word, but paraphrased others. In many of the paraphrased entries, Deward left out a particular layer of detail, which he may have considered too tedious to write about again. For example, the original 1918 diary contains information about the letters he wrote on an almost daily basis: who he wrote to, who wrote to him, the letter numbers, and so on. Because these details are important for us to understand the full scope of Deward's wartime experience, I have restored them.

Because Deward never intended his diary to be published, the prose was laid down in a very terse, shorthand style that omits many articles, prepositions, conjunctions, and so on. Where these are lacking to such a degree as to compromise the text's readability, I have added them silently. Occasionally, too, Deward would leave sentences either incomplete or without sufficient information for someone not familiar with the history of the First World War to understand what he was trying to say. Where this occurs, I have added text to furnish sufficient detail for the reader to understand Deward's intent and enclosed it with square brackets. Wherever possible, however, I have left Deward's idiosyncratic syntax and expressions intact (for example, "shelled heavy" or "the ships signalled meaningly"). These occurrences are not indicated by [sic], as is sometimes the case in other edited diaries.

My main contribution is to put many of Deward's comments and observations into some sort of broader context by supplying an annotative text. Wherever practicable, I have placed this at the end of a diary entry so as not to intrude on it. In some cases, however, where the entry is sufficiently long, I have placed the note in the middle of the passage to keep it close to the statements that it expands upon. In all cases, the diary text is indented to distinguish it from the annotative test. You will also find a small grey rectangle near the left margin to indicated where diary entries begin.

Deward used punctuation sparingly, so almost all of the punctuation that you read is mine. I also standardize capitalization, spellings, and the names of French towns. In the case of Belgian cities, I use the historical French names for cities and towns instead of the Flemish names used today, for example, Ypres instead of Ieper. I have also standardized the spellings of personal names, rationalized against the National Archives of Canada's online database of Canadian Expeditionary Force personnel.

Finally, the diary format of Deward's 1926 notebook is not consistent. Some passages begin with a date, while others begin with "Next Day." Often a number of "next day" passages appear consecutively, and the reader quickly loses track of what day and in which month the action is now taking place. I have presented the text using a consistent diary format by working from known dates and checking Deward's description of his whereabouts and activities against the 19th Battalion's *War Diary*.

In a general sense, Deward's diary is a fairly common artifact of the First World War. Many such volumes have appeared in print over the years. As early as 1922, the Reverend Canon Frederick Scott, senior chaplain to the First Canadian Division, published *The Great War as I Saw It*, an arch-Victorian recollection of his travels with the division from 1914 to 1918. In 1927, the year after Deward compiled his pocket diaries into a single volume, James Pedley's *Only This*, perhaps the best of the early Canadian war narratives, first appeared in print. Pedley served as an officer with the 4th Battalion, and his memoirs provide us with a detailed description of everyday life at the front as well as a frank view of the politics and wrangling that took place within a battalion family. Over the intervening decades other works have emerged. In 1968, Will Bird published *Ghosts Have Warm Hands*, which records with great warmth and sensitivity his journey, both physical and metaphysical, with the 42nd Battalion. The hard-bitten *Journal of Private Fraser*, a 31st Battalion man, came to light as late as 1985, and most recently *The War Diary of Clare Gass* sheds light on the much neglected story of Canada's First World War nursing sisters.

No two people, of course, experienced the war in just the same way. Each of these personal narratives (and there are many others) gives a voice to the author's own unique experience, filtered through their perceptions and enlightened by their wit: that of a Church of England priest from Montreal, a law student from Toronto, a bank clerk from Calgary, a fledgling journalist, and a graduate nurse from Nova Scotia. In this particular sense, then, the First World War diary of Deward Barnes is entirely unique. But it is more than that:

> We took our positions, five kneeling and five standing behind; the sergeant on one side, and the officer on the other to give orders. If we did not kill him, the officer would have to. As soon as the curtain dropped (the prisoner was tied in a chair five paces away from us, a black cap over his head and a big round disc over his heart) we got the order to fire. One blank and nine live rounds. It went off as one. I did not have the blank.

That is the voice of Deward Barnes, an unwilling but dutiful member of a firing squad.

> The prisoner did not feel it. His body moved when we fired, then the curtain went up. That was the eas-

iest way for an execution I had heard of. The firing squad only saw him for a few minutes. We went back to the Battalion Orderly Room and got a big tumbler of rum each, and went to our billets, ate, and went to bed. We had the rest of the day off. It was a job I never wanted.

"I did not have the blank" and "It was a job I never wanted" is all we learn of Deward's feelings about the execution. We do not hear the grandiloquence of Canon Scott, nor the hard-boiled realism of Pedley. But the timing of these comments, after a string of details all the more harrowing for their brevity, tells us more than many of the more polished narratives are capable of. What we hear is something as impossible to recover now as it was common in the years 1914 to 1918: the voice of the Canadian soldier, Everyman in khaki, the men who today lie in the tens of thousands in the fields of Flanders and Picardy.

These men are lost to us because, generally, what they chose to record runs as follows: "Rain. Cleaned ammunition. Paraded with gun from 10:00 a.m. to 12:00 noon. Wrote Lucy no. 42 and Martha. Out at night. Played cards, received letter from Nora." That is Deward's diary entry for March 14, 1918 — the day following the Lodge execution. It is like many others in the pages that are to follow, entries that, in most cases, would consign Deward's diary to the archives rather than your bookshelf. But, oddly enough, they are just the details that give Deward's account the ring of truth, and that set off his revelations — of close fighting, of bitterness, and of soldierly pride — with all the force of which language is capable: not, "I felt sick with remorse over shooting one of my own," but "I did not have the blank." Like any trained infantryman, Deward could tell the kick of a live round from a blank one, and it is that kick he bequeaths to us, and with which the following pages abound.

Bruce Cane
March 2004

My Diary of the Great War
February 26/16 to March 7/19
1916–1919

Written in the winter of 1926
Corporal D. Barnes No. 862690

Confide yeah! in Providence
For Providence is kind
And bear ye all life's changes
With a calm and tranquil mind
Tho' pressed and hemmed on every side
Have faith and you'll win through
For every blade of grass has
Its own drop of dew.

Handwritten note at the front of Deward's 1918 pocket diary

My nerves were always good untill I had my last leave from France Sept 1918 maybe on account lasting so long the thought of what was in front of us. I haven started to get my nerves I have never got... since I came here I have always had to work... the... years experience, but could have do it, so I class myself as a war wreck, which people will never under- stand

CHAPTER 1

The Liederkranz Club to Camp Borden, February 26 to July 1, 1916

"... those boots were tough after wearing fine ones all my life."

I enlisted on February 26, 1916, with the 180th (Sportsmen) Battalion, under Lieutenant Colonel Greer. I later served with the 3rd Canadian Reserve Battalion at West Sandling Camp, England; and with the 2nd Canadian Entrenching and 19th Infantry battalions in France.

Lt. Col. Richard Haliburton Greer was a prominent Toronto crown attorney and a veteran militia officer.

It isn't clear why Deward chose to enlist with the 180th Battalion, of all the battalions then recruiting in Toronto. He might simply have joined up with a friend who, for reasons of his own, had chosen the 180th.

I fought in the battles of Arleux and Fresnoy (May 1917), Hill 70 (August 1917), Passchendaele (November 1917), the Second Battle of the Somme (March–April 1918), Amiens (August 1918), Arras (August 1918), Cambrai and Naves (October 1918) [and I have been to, but did not fight at] Vimy Ridge, Denain, Monchy Le Preux, Douai, the Canal du Nord, the Drocourt-Quéant Line, and Bourlon Wood. I went over-the-top 14 times.

Our battalion, the 180th (Sportsmen), was stationed in the old Liederkranz clubhouse (a German club before the war) on Richmond Street in Toronto. We slept at home then, that was while the battalion was recruiting.

In 1914, the Liederkranz Club was the "premiere German institution in Toronto" (a *liederkranz* is a choral society, usually of male voices).[1] In August of that year, it became the stage for a near-riot when a crowd of hooligans descended upon the building and demanded the club's executive haul down the Imperial German flag and replace it with a British one. When this demand was refused, the rabble themselves tore down the flag. Were it not for the involvement of Toronto police, the mob most likely would have stormed the building. It is not known just when the clubhouse was turned over to the army, but it may well have been expropriated under the War Measures Act (enacted on August 22, 1914), which gave the government extraordinary powers, including the right to seize, control, and dispose of property through orders in council.

Finally, when it was nearly up to strength (twelve hundred men) and it was nearing summer we were put in the Manufacturers' Building, Exhibition grounds. That meant sleeping on boards for the first time. We went there May 16, 1916. Those boards were hard and those boots were tough after wearing fine ones all my life. I did not keep a diary until I was leaving Toronto. But, while at the Exhibition, we had drilling every day and fatigues and had plenty of guard duty. It seemed funny at night while on guard to halt an officer with the challenge, "Who goes there?" when you knew he wasn't going to kill anyone; only getting back late from a good time. The Sportsmen were as fine a bunch of men that ever got together, although a very small percentage went to France as fighting men. A good many men, I believe, were in it for recruiting purposes but they clung together.

One morning we were put on the parade grounds without any breakfast and when we found out it was to drill we would

Courtesy Barnes family collection

Deward's family. A young Deward with his mother and his sisters, Norah and Beatrice.

Courtesy John Boyd/National Archives of Canada PA-177256

Recruits charging with bayonets, Exhibition Camp, January 1916. This photo was actually taken in the north ditch at the west end of Fort York, to the east of Exhibition Camp, where a mock-up of a trench parapet has been constructed. These must be very new recruits indeed. Notice that none of them are wearing belts or have been issued with equipment other than their uniforms. Notice too, they are going "over the top" carrying bayonet-fighting practice batons instead of rifles. A locomotive passing through the railway cutting to the north of the fort provides a suitably smoky middle ground, while the buildings in the background are the Toronto Municipal Abattoir, on the left, and National Casket, the coffin factory in which Deward was employed at the time the photo was taken, on the right.

not move. The battalion sergeant-major gave us an order and not a man moved. Finally, Colonel Greer came and did the same, but still no one moved. We wanted our breakfast. He had to dismiss us and get a meal ready. If we had done that in France they would have called the Imperial troops out.

Imperial troops were soldiers from Great Britain. During the First World War, Canada was a self-governing dominion of the British Empire, and Canadian citizenship did not yet exist. Therefore, when Canadian troops took the field in France and Flanders, they did so as British soldiers. To draw a distinction, therefore, Canadians often used the term "Imperial troops" when referring to soldiers from the British Isles.

We had some marches, they were hard too at that time. If it rained, we always had the day off. During my whole army experience, which was short and sweet, I never fell out of a march or lagged.

I am writing my own diary to myself, which is true and not exaggerated. It is impossible to give people the least idea of what war is if they were never through one.

The 180th Battalion began recruiting on January 26, 1916. The battalion accepted all qualified volunteers, but actively sought recruits from Toronto's athletic community. To raise their visibility with the sporting set, the 180th Battalion chose "Sportsmen" as their secondary title. The use of secondary titles was common practice among newly authorized units, because it helped them to focus their recruiting efforts on a specific group, or segment, of the population. Some units, such as the 208th Battalion, "The Toronto Irish," targeted certain ethnic groups, while others appealed to men of a particular moral stamp. The 201st Battalion, "Toronto Light Infantry," for example, only recruited teetotallers.[2] The 216th Battalion, "Bantams," accepted men who did not meet the minimum required height of 5 feet 3 inches, or 160 centimetres (the 216th accepted men as short as 5 feet 1 inches, or 156 centimetres).[3] This sort of "niche marketing" was an important recruiting tool for units eager to fill their ranks at a time when general recruiting efforts were at their peak (there were as many as nine infantry battalions actively recruiting in Toronto during February 1916).[4]

The Sportsmen's recruiting drives usually took place in large concert halls and always featured athletic competitions, military drills, and concerts given by men already serving with the battalion. This tactic was effective, especially at the Valentine's Day 1916 rally, where 283 "stalwart specimens of Canadian manhood" came forward to enlist.[5] One of the battalion's star recruits was the world champion long distance runner, Tom Longboat, from Brantford, Ontario, who offered himself for service on April 17, 1916.[6]

The large number of army units in Toronto during the winter of 1916 created an acute shortage of barrack accommodations. For Deward and the men of the 180th Battalion, it meant they would continue living at home and go to the Liederkranz Club each day for training. For their trouble, the men received an extra sixty-cents-a-day subsistence allowance in lieu of army food and accommodation.[7] For fourteen weeks Deward and the other recruits in the Sportsmen underwent the transformation from citizens to citizen-soldiers under the watchful eyes of their drill instructors. They were taught foot and arms drill, bayonet fighting, and the basics of musketry (shooting), while in the classroom they attended lectures on military discipline, bombing (grenade handling and throwing), and trench warfare.

With the arrival of warmer weather, many of the units that had been in barracks over the winter began migrating to various training camps in the outlying areas, easing the shortage of military housing in the city. This allowed the 180th Battalion to mobilize on May 16 and move into the barracks at Exhibition Camp. The camp was located on the grounds of the annual Canadian National Exhibition, on the lakeshore in Toronto's west end. Then, as now, the grounds consisted of several large, permanent exhibition halls, surrounded by open spaces for the midway and other outdoor attractions. This made it an ideal spot to house and train large bodies of soldiers. The buildings provided reasonably comfortable barrack accommodations and the open ground allowed plenty of room for physical training, marching, drilling, and even for digging practice trenches.

A detailed account of the daily routine at Exhibition Camp is left to us by David Corrigall, who spent the winter of 1914 to 1915 there as a junior officer with the 20th Battalion. Later, Deward would become well acquainted with the 20th Battalion, which served alongside his own 19th Battalion in the 4th Canadian Infantry Brigade. Corrigall wrote:

> The arrangements for the men ... were of a more primitive nature. Throughout the building large wooden frames about fourteen feet [four metres] long and eight feet [two metres] wide provided accommodation for eight men, four above and four below. A paliasse, a pillow and two blankets were provided for every man. At the foot of each berth hung the equipment. The rifles stood in racks fixed to the frames. Necessaries [toiletries] were kept in haversacks and clothing in the kit bag and pack. Everything was arranged in accordance with a set scheme ...
>
> A regular routine of barrack life soon set in ... In the early mornings, some time before dawn, trumpets and bugles sounded "Reveille," orders were shouted by the NCOs [Non-Commissioned Officers] and everyone awoke from peaceful slumbers to dress for the half-hour "wake-up" run around the grounds. From the Arts Building emerged all the junior officers to lead their platoons during this morning exercise. Their first duty was to hear rolls called, see the sick and listen to complaints; then to "fall in" their men under the supervising eyes of the Field Officer of the Week, the Captain of the Day and the Adjutant ... Then we all moved out into the grounds, where the electric lamps glowed dim and bleary through a grey, cold mist. "Run" for five min-

utes — "walk" — "knees up" — "breathe" — off again. Warmed up and panting, back to the "barracks" and dismissed. So the day began.

Then washing and shaving amidst a medley of whistling, singing, chatter, and laughter, polishing buttons, making up cots and laying out of equipment … Sick parade, then "fall in" for breakfast, and we marched by companies from the Horticultural Building to the Restaurant Building for the first meal of the day. There the Sergeant-Cook and cook's helpers had breakfast ready and mess orderlies were waiting to serve. The Mess was always clean and few complaints were ever heard, except about the lack of variety and continued appearance of "Mulligan" and prunes.

After breakfast we dressed for the first parade of the day. "Fall in" at 8:45 a.m. on company parade areas. "Duties" were first detailed and marched off. Then "Markers" sounded. They took up position under the R.S.M. on the battalion parade ground; then the "Assembly" call, when companies marched on their markers.

After the usual preliminaries of reporting "all present" or otherwise, a three-hour drill period started, interspersed with brief rest intervals. The first hour was usually devoted to physical training …

After physical drill came close order drill. As day followed day the training gradually developed from squad to platoon drill, from platoon drill to company drill, and from company drill to battalion drill. It was difficult to keep the routine from becoming monotonous …[8]

Although Corrigall and the 20th Battalion spent six months in Exhibition Camp before moving on, the Sportsmen's stay lasted only seven weeks. As noted by Deward, on July 2, the 180th Battalion packed up their kit bags and moved by train to Camp Borden, a newly opened training facility north of Toronto.

The conditions at Camp Borden were unavoidably more primitive than those back in Toronto. In the early summer of 1916, Borden had only just been carved from the scrubby pines of the Angus Plain, an ancient, sandy lake bed. We can only imagine what the Sportsmen thought when they saw their new home glide into view, as their train banged and swayed its way over the switch points and onto one of the camp's newly laid sidings. To some, it might have seemed the train had taken them further than was possible in a two-and-a-half-hour trip, as a frontier town of rough-sawn shanties, dirt roads, and tents rolled into sight.

Courtesy Canada Dept. of National Defence/National Archives of Canada
PA-004851 — detail

View of Camp Borden, 1916. This detail from a larger panoramic view of Camp Borden, which looks more like a shanty town, illustrates the relatively primitive conditions in the newly opened facility. As primitive as it was, Deward would later remark, "they made one of the finest camps in Canada of it." He also comments, "later on [in the war] I had often wished that we were still there."

When the 180th Battalion disembarked from the troop train, Borden was already the bustling home of a dozen or so infantry battalions from all over Ontario. Among those units already in camp was a Highland unit from Toronto, the 134th Battalion, which had just transferred to Borden from Niagara-on-the-Lake. Their historian, Kim Beattie, tells us a little bit about the conditions they encountered at Borden:

> They shortly moved to Camp Borden, in Simcoe County, and at once experienced all the discomforts of an unfinished camp. There was dirt, dust, and loneliness. That was another thing to dislike; the Camp's remoteness to Toronto. However, they made themselves at home and carried on.[9]

The camp did provide some basic amenities to help relieve the loneliness referred to by Beattie. The YMCA operated a canteen, where soldiers could purchase cigarettes, soft refreshments, and other small personal comforts. And there was a large wooden shed known to everybody as "The Strand" that was used as a theatre for staging both movies and concert parties.

While these Spartan facilities helped to stave off loneliness for a while, there was little that anyone could do about the dirt and dust. It was a nuisance to everyone, regardless of rank, as Deward soon found out for himself.

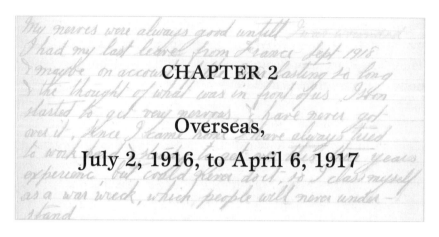

CHAPTER 2

Overseas,
July 2, 1916, to April 6, 1917

"Vimy ridge is seven kilometres away, can hear the guns plainly."

July 2, 1916: We were taken to Camp Borden fifty miles [eighty kilometres] north of Toronto. We thought then that it was a terrible place — nothing but sand — but later on I had often wished that we were still there. They made one of the finest camps in Canada of it. We had more duty there and it was our first start at real soldiering. We had a pass for home every two weeks if we happened to be off guard [duty] and that seemed like a long time to wait, but we were lucky and did not know it.

July 11, 1916: The camp was inspected by Maj.-Gen. Sir Sam Hughes and we had a march past. It was a terrible, hot day. When we arrived we were hot and dirty and they didn't allow us any water. The idea was to get us used to little water. We started our march past in column, no one was in step and carried their rifles any old way. When we all got the command to eyes right, we booed General Hughes and said, "Take us out of this rotten hole." That march past was a failure, but there was nothing done about it.

As part of the opening ceremonies for Camp Borden on July 11 1916, the entire garrison — by then some thirty thousand troops

— took part in a review for Major General the Honourable Sir Sam Hughes, Canada's energetic, though often erratic, Minister of Militia and Defence. Hughes arrived late, which forced the men to wait in the blistering sun for over two hours. While waiting, several of the men fainted and, tragically, one man died from the effects of heat stroke. Later, as the battalions began to march past the minister, thousands of trampling feet stirred the sandy ground, kicking up a dust cloud that engulfed the entire parade ground. In time, the cloud began to settle out on everything under it. Upon the command "Eyes Right!" the troops at the end of the parade were greeted by the sight of the normally immaculate Sir Sam caked in a thick layer of grime. Were it not for a pair of red-rimmed eyes blinking periodically beneath the brim of his pith helmet he might have been indistinguishable from the atmosphere. Later, as the minister mounted his special railway coach to accept the traditional three cheers from the troops, he was met by the chorus of jeers about which Deward writes. As historian Desmond Morton remarks, the incident "finally shattered the myth of a special rapport between Hughes and 'his boys.'"

Major General Sir Sam Hughes at the saluting base during the review of Canadian troops at Camp Borden, July 1916. In all, some thirty thousand troops passed the minister (at left) in review that day.

Courtesy British & Colonial Press/National Archives of Canada PA-066801

March past during review of Canadian troops by Major General Sir Sam Hughes, July 1916. This photo is taken from the spectator's perspective. In the background you can see thousands of troops formed-up in column for the march past. Notice, too, the rising dust cloud.

Later on, nearing our final leave, the men got restless again and one night went down to General Headquarters with stones and sticks. General Logie, I think it was, was hit with half a brick. These two incidents were done by the whole camp and not confined to one certain unit.

Major General William Logie was the commanding officer of Military District No. 2. In 1916, Canada was divided into ten military districts. The headquarters of each district was responsible to the Ministry of Militia and Defence for coordinating the military activities within its boundaries. Although District No. 2's headquarters were at Exhibition Camp in Toronto, it covered a vast tract of central Ontario from Niagara in the west to the eastern shores of lakes Simcoe and Scugog; and from Lake Ontario in the south to parts of the Algoma and Nipissing districts in the north.[10]

I found through experience that it did not do to keep men in large numbers together in one place too long, as they become restless. The army authorities knew it too. In England or France you were soon split up after anything like that. And in France, you were punished, if not individually, then the whole battalion suffered.

October 13, 1916: We started our final leave, which lasted four days. We mustered at 8.30 a.m. October 18 at Bayside Park, leaving again for Camp Borden.

Bayside Park in Toronto was a parcel of grassed-over land that in 1916 had only recently been reclaimed from Lake Ontario. The park — later known as Harbour Square — ran east from Bay Street and lay immediately south of the city's main railway corridor, which made it an ideal assembly point for troops awaiting trains.

Deward ready to depart. Here we see him ready to march, with his great-coat (top coat) rolled and slung over his shoulder, haversack suspended from his waist-belt, and swagger stick in hand. The photo was taken on October 17, 1916 — the final day of Deward's last home leave.

Courtesy Barnes family collection

Deward's fiancée,
Lucy Field.

Courtesy Barnes family collection

October 22, 1916: We left [Camp Borden] for St. John's, New Brunswick, arriving first at Union Station [in Toronto] at 5:45 p.m. bidding our last farewell to those who were there to meet us.

October 23, 1916: We are at Montreal at 4:30 a.m.; stayed there two hours.

We stopped at River De Lieu and at another station where there was a store. The boys bought half the store out and stole the other half, I think. At River De Lieu the Frenchmen sold water for whisky and got a good price for it.

Presumably, Deward means Rivière du Loup on the southeast shore of the St. Lawrence River, in the province of Québec.

October 24, 1916: We arrived at Moncton at 12:00 noon. Moncton is a lovely town; we had a march through it. We arrived at St. John at 5:00 p.m. We were welcomed by the mayor. In St. John we were stationed in a building on the Exhibition grounds near the barracks. St. John is a lovely city and everyone was used swell by the people. There was always some place to go, either church parties or house parties; you were always welcomed. We were at St. John nineteen days and did not have very much to do. Soldiers could not buy whisky but they got civilians to get it for them. I went to a few house parties and church festivals.

November 12, 1916: We left St. John for Halifax.

180th Battalion (Sportsmen) CEF. This photo of the 180th Battalion was taken during their stay in St. John, New Brunswick.

Courtesy National Archives of Canada PA-212978

> **November 13, 1916:** Arrived in Halifax at 7:00 a.m. We stayed
> on the train until 11:00 a.m. then marched through Halifax,
> which is an old-fashioned, dirty-looking place, I thought, and
> boarded the *Olympic*. I was lucky as I had a second-class berth, a
> room with four beds in it, two over each other. The 180th
> Battalion was one of the first to board and other units kept com-
> ing on board continually until next day.

In addition to Deward's 180th Battalion, the following units of
the Canadian Expeditionary Force (CEF) sailed in *Olympic* on
November 14, 1916: 147th Battalion, 158th Battalion (Duke of
Connaught's Own), 173rd Battalion, 194th Battalion (Edmonton
Highlanders), 222nd Battalion, a draft of signallers from Ottawa,
and a draft of aviators.[11]

The Royal Mail Steamer *Olympic* had a remarkable career. She
made her maiden voyage on June 14, 1911, and at a whopping forty-
six thousand tonnes was the first, and smallest, of three immense
liners ordered by the White Star Line. She was followed in 1912 by
Titanic, and in 1915 by *Britannic*. In October 1914, *Olympic* was
taken out of commercial service and converted to His Majesty's
Transport 2810 (*Olympic*). In 1915, *Olympic* was operating in the
eastern Mediterranean, ferrying troops to and from the Dardanelles.
In March 1916, she moved to the North Atlantic and began a series
of ten round trips between Liverpool and Halifax, carrying units
and equipment of the CEF to Britain; it was on one of these later
trips that Deward and the 180th Battalion sailed. By the time of the
Armistice, *Olympic* had ferried almost a quarter of a million soldiers
and steamed nearly 180,000 miles (290,000 kilometres) in war service. She was also the only allied merchant vessel to sink an enemy
warship, when she rammed the German submarine U-103 in the
English Channel in May 1918. *Olympic* spent the first seven months
of 1919 returning thousands of Canadians to Halifax, after which
she was handed back to White Star for refurbishment and return to
passenger service. She was much luckier than her two sister ships
(*Britannic* sank in 1916 after striking a mine; of *Titanic* no more
need be said). While she was in dry dock, workers discovered a large

dent below the water line: at some point during the war, a torpedo had struck *Olympic* but had failed to explode.

November 14, 1916: The *Olympic* left Halifax, with over five thousand on board, at 3:40. Some had to sleep on the floor and some on hammocks which were hung over the dining room tables after all the meals were over. The *Olympic*'s forty-seven thousand tons was the best and fastest at that time. We had to wear life belts when we went on deck, always. We had one pay on board and fire drill every morning. They had concerts every night just made up from the talent among the men. Bands played in the daytime. There were big dining rooms and it was surprising what you could eat. Of course, you had your certain time to eat and I did not miss a meal.

It was a lovely trip (calm) as far as ocean going went, but the boat always had a continuous rock from bow to stern day and night. I wasn't exactly sick but always had a funny feeling. A good many others were good and sick. A fellow came up to me and was telling me that he was never sea sick, and had been on the ocean before, and all the time he was getting whiter and finally he left me. I watched him — oh boy, he never got sick!

We passed two steamers on the trip, which took five days; very fast.

Depending on the weather, smaller and slower steamers might take seven or eight days to make the same trip.[12]

November 20, 1916: We saw land, the Irish Coast, at 6:00 a.m. and anchored off Liverpool at 10:00 a.m. We did not get off until next morning at 9:00 a.m.

November 21, 1916: All the boats, large and small, saluted meaningly. The first thing that struck me funny was the trains: small engines and small high freight cars — but those trains were fast. We left Liverpool and passed Rugby, the scenery was lovely. Arrived at London, Victoria Station at 5:00

p.m.; then to Shoreham-by-Sea, in Sussex, at 8:00 p.m. the same day (south of England).

By the end of 1916, an extensive network of Canadian facilities existed in southern and southeastern England to house and train the CEF. Camps such as Shorncliffe, Bramshott, Witley, and Seaford were mostly advanced infantry training and reinforcement centres. Other camps, like Bordon (not to be confused with Camp Borden, Ontario) and Bexhill, were used by the artillery and cavalry and as officer training establishments. Shoreham, the camp to which Deward was posted, was located on the southeast coast, near the seaside town of Brighton.[13]

England is a beautiful country all over. We did not do very much at Shoreham as it was only kind of a stop over place until they made room at a training camp. We did a few force marches and had a pay of £2/10 [two pounds, ten shillings or two and a half pounds — there were twenty shillings in a pound]. Shoreham Town and beach was nice, the sand was red and the cottages kept nice and white with red roofs. I did not approve of bar maids in the pubs.

As a private in the CEF, Deward earned a dollar a day, which was paid out in the local currency. In 1911, one pound sterling was reckoned to have the equivalent value of $4.86 in Canadian dollars.[14] If their relative values remained constant over the intervening six years, then £2/10 was the equivalent of about twelve days' pay. It is worth noting, however, that when Deward left Canada in November 1916, he chose to assign half of his pay to his mother.[15] Many soldiers did this to ensure their dependants received some form of income while they were away. The money was sent directly to the soldier's assignee. In addition to half of Deward's pay, his mother also received twenty dollars a month in the form of a separation allowance, which was paid to her by the Toronto and York County Patriotic Fund.[16] This fund was established by Toronto City Council in August 1914 to raise money for the dependants of men who were recruited into the army or naval services in Toronto.[17]

Deward was awarded an additional ten-cent-a-day field allowance starting in January 1917.[18] This was to compensate him for the increased cost of living he would experience in the field.

Canadians were better paid than their Imperial counterparts, and this occasionally led to resentment from Imperial troops when they discovered they were receiving less money for facing the same hardships and dangers as their Canadian cousins.[19]

December 2, 1916: I had my first leave in England from Shoreham, leaving at 1:45 p.m. I changed trains at Brighton, England's famous beach, and arrived at Victoria Station, London at 4:00 p.m. Nat Clyde asked Omer Rivett and myself to go to his sister's house in Glasgow and spend our leave. We got a motorbus from Victoria to Euston station, and as the train did not leave until 11:30 p.m. we went to Euston Theatre and then had supper (two shillings). We left Euston at 11:30 p.m. The train was crowded.

Nat Clyde was a thirty-year-old Glaswegian who was living in New Haven, Connecticut, when war broke out in 1914. Before immigrating to the United States, Clyde had served for several years in the 4th Volunteer Battalion, The Cameronians (Scottish Rifles). He put that training to good use in April 1916 when he went north to Canada and enlisted with the 180th Battalion. Omer Rivett — a barber from Waubaushine, Ontario — was working in Toronto when he enlisted in the 180th Battalion at twenty-six years of age on February 25, 1916, the day before Deward enlisted.[20]

December 3, 1916: We arrived at Carlisle at 6:15 a.m. and at Glasgow "Central Station" at 9:15 a.m. where I first met Dick Gaunt. We took a taxi to their house and were used like princes. Omer stayed there a couple of days and then went to Edinburgh, an hour's train ride. In Glasgow we went to shows, Hengler's Circus, Pavilion Theatre, and Empress Theatre. We saw West End Park, Clyde River and Park, Kelvin Grove Park and University, Kelson River, and the Glasgow Art Museum, where we spent half the day and did not see half of it. We went to see a football game going underground by rope railway under the Clyde River. There were thousands there.

The "rope railway" Deward refers to was the Glasgow District Subway. The trains ran in a circular tunnel beneath the city and were drawn forward by a moving cable that ran continuously between the rails at the rate of twelve miles per hour (twenty kilometres per hour). To make the train go, the operator activated a mechanism that seized the cable. To stop the train, the operator disengaged the seizing mechanism and applied the train's brakes. The trains were converted to run on electric motors in 1935.

December 9, 1916: Left Central Station at 11:20 p.m.; at Motherwell at 11:45 p.m. We had free eats and drinks and cigarettes given by the ladies of the town, although we had our lunch with us.

December 10, 1916: Left Motherwell at 12:10 a.m. arrived at Euston, London at 9:30 a.m. rode underground to Victoria Station, about half an hour's ride. Left Victoria 10:40 a.m. had free eats, and arrived at Brighton at noon and arrived at Shoreham at 12:15 p.m.

December 12, 1916: I was the stick guard man.

To be the "stick" man meant you were the best turned out soldier on morning parade. As a reward, you were usually exempt from all formal parades and extra duties for a twenty-four-hour period.

December 16 and 17, 1916: At the ranges on the 16th and 17th and finished on the 20th. The nearest town was Worthing and we had a route march through Port Slade.

During the Great War, the military discipline of shooting was referred to as "musketry." To stay sharp and gain confidence in himself and his weapon, a soldier needed frequent trips to the ranges for practice and instruction. A man who possessed a basic level of expertise could, for example, put five shots out of five into a twelve-inch (thirty-centimetre) bull's eye at one hundred yards (ninety-one metres) while lying prone (that is, on his stomach). He could put five out of five rounds on various pop-up targets (each exposed for only four seconds at a time) at 200 yards (182 metres) while kneeling. In thirty seconds or less — from a prone position — he could load his rifle with five rounds and hit a target at 300 yards (273 metres) with all five shots, and so on.[21]

December 28, 1916: Paid £1/10.

You will notice throughout Deward's diary that he receives different amounts of pay at different times. This is especially true while he is in France and Flanders. Due to the nature of active service, it was often difficult to pay the soldiers regularly; however, meticulous records were kept by the regimental paymaster, and when the situation allowed, all back pay was disbursed to the soldier as soon as possible.

January 6, 1917: We left Shoreham-by-Sea passing through Red Hill Junction, Henfield, Tonbridge, and Ashford and arrived at Sandling Junction, Kent at 1:00 a.m. It was pitch dark and we had an awful time finding our way. It was raining as well, the camp I think was an hour's walk away.

January 7, 1917: We had a medical exam and I passed A1 class.

A1 is a reference to Deward's fitness classification. The army used four major fitness classes to describe the level of duties the soldier was deemed capable of performing — A, B, D, and E (there was no Class C). The first three classes were divided into subclasses that gave the authorities further scope to declare a man's fitness level. For example, Deward was A1 — the highest fitness level. This meant he was both medically and physically fit, fully trained, and ready for service in France and Belgium. Prior to January 7, Deward was probably classed A2, which meant he was medically and physically fit but had not finished his training. If a soldier was rated B1, B2, or B3 he was temporarily unfit for service at the front (he might have been recuperating from disease, injury, or a wound) but was capable of performing manual labour to one degree or another. Soldiers undergoing a prolonged convalescence were classed D1, providing they would likely return to duty within six months. E, the lowest fitness class, indicated the soldier was unfit for service and unlikely to become so in the next six months — he was awaiting discharge.[22]

January 8, 1917: Inspected and our new address is 3rd Canadian Reserve Battalion.

On January 6, Deward was one of 823 men (36 officers and 787 other ranks) transferred by the 180th Battalion to the 3rd Canadian Reserve Battalion at West Sandling Camp, Kent.[23] This transfer depleted the 180th Battalion and marked the end of its life as an active unit. The majority of Canadian infantry battalions that landed in the United Kingdom were broken up — usually shortly after their arrival — and their members either sent to reinforce existing Canadian units in the field or assigned to a Canadian reserve battalion. The men sent to reserve battalions underwent continued training and awaited further assignment. The 3rd Canadian Reserve Battalion reinforced the 4th and 19th Canadian Infantry battalions and the 2nd and 4th Canadian Mounted Rifle Battalions.[24]

January 10, 1917: Route marched.

January 13, 1917: Paid £1. Some pay, with plenty of canteens to spend it!

January 14, 1917: I had a leave to Folkestone and saw the museum and had supper at the Soldier's Rest Room in the Town Hall. Folkestone is all hills and mostly narrow, winding streets. They have a great promenade above the sea there. The police wore a little electric light on top of their helmets, not many other lights around and they were shaded.

It isn't entirely clear what the lights on top of the police helmets were for, but they might have been to provide a warning for motorists of the presence of a police constable on point duty at night.[25]

January 18, 1917: We had our first day on the ranges here about ten miles [sixteen kilometres] away, going through Hythe and down a very steep hill and up it coming back, always in heavy marching order. The ranges were the best I had seen, all pebbles. It was on the channel beach the old forts were scattered. They were built when France tried to get over. On the way to the ranges we passed Saltwood Castle where Sir Walter Raleigh and Queen Elizabeth had lived, and they still had the pits off the courtyard (prisons). That march was the first time I had worn my Kitchener Boots — oh my but didn't I have blisters when we arrived home!

We had all discipline and hard training there, as it was our last camp in England. We were not allowed out of camp without a swagger stick and our pants turned over our puttees. Riding pants were not allowed. If you lost your stick, you had to use a nice straight tree limb. You were inspected to make sure you were dressed properly before you could get out of the camp.

We had to go on a run at 5:30 a.m. for half an hour. We then had to get into our hut to eat breakfast and get dressed for a parade, all in half an hour. Your boots had to be just so, only one pair of boots showing, your blankets folded a certain way and no parcels showing. Boots had to be dubbined. We paraded until 4:00 p.m. and no holidays. We had physical training, musketry, drilling, and three forced route ma. hes a week and a forced march at night every once in a while. We had Saturday

45

afternoons off but you could not get out until the hut floor was scrubbed with sand and the bed boards, about fifty beds in a hut, and the stove cleaned. You were lucky if you finished by five o'clock.

The old forts mentioned by Deward above are probably Martello towers. The nine-metre-high (thirty-foot) towers have a flat roof on which was mounted a cannon that could traverse a full 360 degrees. Between 1805 and 1808 dozens of these towers were built along the south coast of England as a defence against the anticipated invasion of Britain by Napoleon. Several Martello towers were also built in British North America during and after the War of 1812 to defend various harbours from attack by the United States.

Saltwood Castle was begun in the ninth century on what was probably the site of a Roman fort. By the twelfth century, Saltwood had become one of the strongest castles in the south of England. During the reign of Henry II, it belonged to Sir Ranulf de Broc, who was involved in the conspiracy to murder Saint Thomas Beckett. In the sixteenth century, the castle was seriously damaged by an earthquake and fell into ruin until William Deed restored it as a residence in 1884.

Canadian soldiers often referred to British Army boots as "Kitchener Boots," after Field Marshall Earl Kitchener, the British War Minister from 1914 to 1916. The boots issued to Canadian soldiers (two pair per man) were of inferior construction and quickly fell apart under trench conditions. Consequently, several weeks before leaving for France, Canadians were issued with a pair of Kitchener boots, which gave them a chance to break them in — just as Deward did — before they arrived at the front.[26]

The swagger stick Deward refers to was a short, straight cane, usually decorated in a military motif, which the off-duty rank and file had to carry while in the public eye (officers had to carry a stick all the time).

Puttee is the Hindustani word for bandage. Like bandages, puttees were long strips of khaki cloth that soldiers wound around their legs from the boot top to within four inches (ten centimetres) of the knee. A cloth ribbon sewn to the end of each puttee kept it from unwinding. The soldier wound the ribbon around the top fold several times, then knotted it. Any loose ends left over after tying the knots were tucked behind the puttees' top edge. If rolled properly, the trousers would blouse over the top of the puttee by two inches (five centimetres) and cover the ribbon. Puttees kept dust, mud, and stones from getting into the wearer's boots. They also acted like support hose by binding the lower part of the leg, which would provide comfort on a long march.[27]

Riding pants, or breeches, were very popular with the other ranks when going out for an evening or while on leave. It was held that breeches cut a more dashing appearance than the regular issue trousers. Breeches, however, were part of an officer's uniform, and it was a punishable offence for non-commissioned ranks to be found wearing them. Even though they risked losing their passes or having their leave cancelled, many soldiers acquired a pair of breeches at the first opportunity.

By now, Deward had three pairs of boots: the two pair of Canadian boots with which he was originally issued and his pair of Kitchener boots. Apparently, for the morning barrack inspection, he had to hide the extra pair, hence his remark, "only one pair of boots showing" (the third pair, of course, were on his feet).

Dubbin is a waxy grease used to soften and waterproof leather. The army provided soldiers with dubbin to waterproof their boots.

January 25, 1917: I was warned that I was to go to France and was put into the draft company.

When Deward says he was "warned," he means that he was notified that something was about to take place. Deward uses the word "warned" in this way throughout the diary.

January 29, 1917: I went to Hythe, around High Street and State. I was put on a two-and-a-half day bombing course in trenches that were specially made up in the hills.

As part of their advanced training, the men were often sent on short refresher courses to keep current in various subjects. In this case, Deward was sent on a bombing, or grenade, course where, through lectures and hands-on experience, he would have gone over the safety and handling procedures for various types of grenades, reviewed the latest grenade tactics, and been reintroduced to various types of German grenades.[28]

January 31, 1917: I was away all day. I passed Hythe, Ashford, Sandgate, and Folkestone.

February 2, 1917: I went to Hythe and lost my money belt there. Tom Allen found it. I finished the trench bombing course.

Tom Allen was a friend of Deward's from the 180th Battalion. Allen was born in Shant Bridge, County Antrim, Ireland, and had immigrated to Toronto with his father prior to the war.[29]

February 7, 1917: I saw the paymaster.

February 11, 1917: I started on my last course on those same ranges ten miles [sixteen kilometres] away, which lasted every day for six days and ending on the February 17.

February 18, 1917: I was on the Hythe piquet.

A "piquet" is a type of sentry or guard duty.

February 23, 1917: We route marched passing Syminge and Westonhanger.

February 24, 1917: I was transferred into "C" Company.

February 25, 1917: I went to see Saltwood Castle, which was built in the year [A.D.] 833.

February 27, 1917: I did another piquet. I had my photo, an enlargement, taken at Hythe one trip. One day we had an inspection by the Duke of Connaught. The "unfits" for front-line service of the 180th were sent to the 123rd Battalion.

Courtesy Barnes family collection

Deward's photo taken on February 27, 1916.

The Duke of Connaught was Canada's Governor General from 1911 to 1916.

The "unfits" that Deward refers to were probably men who were classified A2 during the January 7 medical examination.

The 123rd Infantry Battalion was raised at Toronto in November 1915 and sailed for England the following August. At the end of February 1917, the unit was given the choice of being either broken up for reinforcements or converted into a pioneer battalion.[30] Pioneer battalions served alongside the Corps of Canadian Engineers in the building and maintenance of roads and light railways, the digging of trenches and the excavation of dugouts, and the construction of various implements such as duckboards and trench bridges. Pioneers were also frequently used as stretcher-bearers. To retain its identity, the 123rd Infantry Battalion chose to proceed to France as the 123rd Pioneer Battalion.

March 5, 1917: We left West Sandling for France. The bands were playing and the boys all watching. It made you think of home. We left at 8:40 a.m. and marched to Shorncliffe, arrived at 10:30 a.m. Stayed there all night. It was hard to get anything to eat; they were short of rations just then for extra men.

March 6, 1917: We left Shorncliffe at 7:30 a.m. for Folkestone. Boarded small boat and left at 10:00 a.m. Arrived at Boulogne at 12:00 noon. The trip across the Channel was terrible. I never thought I could get good and sick, but I sure was. I happened to be put away down at the bottom and it was awful; [vomit] six inches [fifteen centimetres] deep, first rushed to one side, then to the other. I had to go on deck, which had a canvas curtain all around and ropes on the boat to hang onto. I never saw such waves in my life. One minute you would see one of the destroyers that were escorting us and you wouldn't see it again for fifteen minutes. The boat just took one long slow dip one way and the other waves were huge.

On landing at Boulogne we marched over the River Liane. It's an old-fashioned city. We were taken up a hill to a tent resting camp. It was a cold night and stormy and just getting dark when we arrived there. You couldn't get anything or weren't allowed out. It took us quite a while to get a tent and blankets.

The purpose of the canvas curtain on deck is uncertain. It might have been a safety device along with the ropes to prevent the men from falling overboard, or it might have been used as a weather break to provide shelter for anyone on deck. Alternatively, it might have been to hide the presence of troops from the prying eye of a U-boat periscope. Despite the elaborate mine barrages laid by the Royal Navy to contain this underwater threat, submarines continued to pose a danger to cross-channel shipping throughout the war.

As we learn from the 1911 edition of the Encyclopedia Britannica, "Boulogne has for a long time been one of the most anglicized of French cities; and in the tourist season a continuous stream of English travellers reach the continent at this point."[31]

In the late winter of 1917, the stream of tourists was in flood. As early as August 14, 1914, Boulogne had become a main port of entry into France for British troops and supplies when the first units of the British Expeditionary Force landed there. In a short time, the ancient port town was transformed into a bustling British base, replete with rest camps, medical services, and supply dumps. By a strange quirk of history, the great bulk of the British facilities were situated on the Camp de Boulogne, which was built in 1804 as a staging area for Napoleon's projected invasion of Britain, the same invasion for which the Martello towers were built on the south coast of England.[32]

March 8, 1917: We left the resting camp 1:00 p.m. and marched to Boulogne Station through the city. They had some street cars; old-fashioned. Left the station by train at 5:40 p.m. They had given us one big, dried, ground meat sandwich, about four inches [ten centimetres] thick, before we left. The meat kept falling out, that's all we had and we were on the train twenty-four hours. My but they are slow trains.

March 9, 1917: We arrived at Rouen at 1:15 p.m. and at Le Havre at 5:40 p.m. We slept in tents there and were crowded twelve in a bell shaped tent. Le Havre is in the south of France and was very warm. Our drilling ground was about six miles [ten kilometres] away, all uphill, called the "Bull Ring." It was some going too. All parade stuff and discipline, and when you were about half a mile from there they have Imperial instructors spread from there on. Hold your heads up, watch your step, and so on; just bawling you out all the time. We drilled most every day there at the Canadian Base [Depot] at Harfleur, near Le Havre.

On our way to the Bull Ring, women and girls sold us beer while marching. We had to go through all kinds of training from Swiss movements to bayonet fighting (sticking dummies — hung up and in trenches), and jumping over high fences and down into trenches. We had lectures, etc. in everything. Gas drills, marching with our gas helmets on, and through dug-outs filled with tear gas. We went from [the base camp] to the lines. Almost every day so many had to go.

The officer in charge always gave them a good talking to, not to pick up souvenirs and of course we used to listen, and of course every draft got the same bull, although it was true. The worst part of that camp was that we had very little money, and getting our meals, which were in long huts. I have waited in line one and a half hours to get a breakfast and many a time you would have to go without any. I used to get up at 5:00 a.m. so as to get in line early; go in, get a meal, and then line up again and get another. You got your breakfast or meals at the door inside. Someone would say "something good today!" but by the time you got there, you would get rice or figs.

We had to do our own washing and they had drying tents, "heated," where you could dry your clothes. I had a Canadian suit of underwear stolen and had to pay $3.50 to the army. We were one of the last to be at the base as it was being turned over to the Imperials and the Canadians went to Étaples.

Although Le Havre is nearly 200 miles (320 kilometres) south of Boulogne, it sits on the Normandy coast of northwestern France and is not in the south of France as Deward relates. Deward might have been tricked into believing he had gone further south than he really had in the length of time that it took him to reach Le Havre, having spent nearly twenty-eight hours on the train. In the Edwardian era, the south of France was a fashionable resort destination for the rich and famous, and one wonders if Deward's "south of France" reference might be an ironic in-joke among soldiers. Sid Cane, for example — who also served in the 19th Battalion during 1917 — often referred to his convalescence in "the south of France," but his service record shows instead that he spent two months at Étaples, which is even closer to Boulogne than Le Havre.

The Canadian Base Depot at Le Havre was a clearing house for Canadian reinforcements. Almost all Canadian soldiers landing in France at that time were first sent to the Base Depot, where they were held until needed by their units at the front. While there, a soldier was issued with his helmet, gas mask, field dressing (a large bandage), and identity disks. The disks were either round or hexagonal leather-fibre tags bearing an imprint of the wearer's rank, name, service number, and unit.

The PH helmet, or "gas helmet," that Deward refers to was an early form of gas mask. The "helmet" was actually a flannel bag that you pulled over your head, then tucked under the collar of your coat. The bag was equipped with a pair of glass eyepieces for seeing and a rubber mouthpiece for exhaling. The flannel itself was impregnated with chemicals (phenate-hexamine — hence the name PH helmet) that neutralized the gas as you breathed in through your nose. Although the newer, more efficient small box respirators (SBRs) were available to Canadians from the end of November 1916, they continued to carry the older PH helmets as a backup, in case the SBR was damaged.[33] The SBR was a true gas mask. It covered the nose, mouth, and eyes with a face piece that was connected to a filter canister through a flexible hose.

Will Bird of the 42nd Battalion, who later became a novelist, travel writer, and journalist with *Maclean's* magazine, was at the

Base Depot only three months before Deward and had a similar
experience in the dining huts:

> At meal time we waded through the slime to the
> door of a long dirty hut. Inside the entrance, a trio
> of unwashed characters broke up loaves of bread
> and tossed a chunk to each man, the size of your
> chunk depending on your luck. Another pair
> poured each man a tin of cold, greasy tea and you
> received a piece of stringy meat in your mess tin
> top. You went to long tables and ate your food from
> your fingers. Everything was dirty. Presently an
> officer and sergeant entered the front of the hut
> and walked rapidly between the tables, not looking
> right or left. At the rear door they paused just long
> enough to shout: "Any complaints?" They van-
> ished before anyone could reply.[34]

The Bull Ring was a notorious training ground that almost
always gets a mention in soldiers' diaries. In its original concept,
it was a huge circular training area "where troops could be finally
tested in large batches for the line. A squad would cut in at some
point in the circle in the morning and by the time each soldier had
gone through ... he was to have had his equipment ... tested ...
and his memory refreshed."[35] Will Bird, however, found the reality considerably different, being nearly driven to desperation by the
mud and the "inane chatter" of the instructors.[36]

Desmond Morton recounts some of this:

> Foul mouthed, abusive NCOs, nick named "can-
> aries" for their yellow arm bands, cultivated the
> "offensive spirit." Apocryphal stories of German vil-
> lainy abounded. Lieutenant C.V. Williams learned
> that a group of Germans had pretended to be
> wounded, slaughtered the Canadian stretcher-bear-
> ers who came to help them, and turned machine

guns on the Canadians' backs: One of our Battalions was terribly cut to pieces by it, but as soon as our boys found out who it was they let out one whoop, made for them and bayoneted them right and left even as they lay on the ground.

More cynical soldiers suspected that make-believe ferocity kept the "canaries" in their "bomb-proof" jobs. The spirit of the bayonet reached a shrill crescendo. "Remember boys, every prisoner means a day's less rations for you" was canary talk. "Carry a rusty fork in your puttees ... and when you get close, jab him in the eye."[37]

In May 1917, the Canadian Base Depot was moved further north to Étaples, which is only fifteen miles (twenty-four kilometres) south of Boulogne.[38] Memoirs written later, by men who were sent to Étaples, also refer to the Bull Ring, which suggests that either the Bull Ring moved or that "Bull Ring" became a generic term for any training facility attached to the base camps.[39]

March 31, 1917: On a Sunday we left Harfleur Camp on a draft at 3:15 p.m. Marched to Le Havre, full pack. We had to go down 150 feet [46 metres] below to Le Havre. I never saw so many steps. We arrived at the station at 5:00 p.m. and had to wait there for the train. We were not allowed to smoke, so I was put on smoke piquet. Had supper and lunch, and the train left Le Havre at 9:15 p.m. We had plenty to eat and were on the train all night and all the next day. The train was slow and had too many in each car. We could not sleep. One fellow slept in the basket, or rack, where the parcels go and it all came down on top of us. We arrived at Saint Pol, France at 11:30 p.m.

St. Pol is about twenty miles (thirty kilometres) west of Arras. From now on, Deward will seldom stay long in one place.

April 1, 1917: At Barlin, 9:00 a.m.

April 2, 1917: Marched one mile [two and a half kilometres] to Hersin, a mining town, and were billeted in washhouses with stone floors. Each house had a washhouse behind their own place, a little brick place with a fireplace and electric light. It was a jake place. It snowed every day.

"Jake" was a slang expression for "fine" or "good."

Vimy ridge is seven kilometres [four miles] away, can hear the guns plainly.

Our new address is Wash House No. 1, Rue De MacMahon Street, 2nd Canadian Entrenching Battalion. On fatigues, occasionally making roads, working on some railroads — loading and unloading, and breaking stones at the cup yards and everything in general, just like a bunch of crooks. At night we used to climb up a slag heap, maybe seventy-five feet [twenty-three metres] high, and watch the shelling at Vimy. At that tine the cavalry men used to train their horses to get used to machine guns. A small machine gun was mounted on a horse. After training, a horse knew enough to keep his head to one side.

We went to Hersin, there was plenty of traffic, transports, etc.

Deward was posted from the Canadian Base Depot to the 2nd Entrenching Battalion. It was one of four battalions maintained by the Canadian Entrenching Group as a forward holding unit for reinforcements on their way to other units in the field. From here, Deward's next posting would be to his active, front-line battalion. While waiting to be sent to their units, the men worked on the types of duties mentioned above by Deward. The entrenching battalions were disbanded in May 1917 and replaced by the Canadian Corps Reinforcement Camp.[40]

April 5, 1917: I was warned to go to the trenches. Had inspection, gas school — to test respirators, and a three-minute bath.

The gas school Deward refers to was the 2nd Canadian Divisional Gas School, which was presided over by a Divisional Gas Officer (DGO). Among other duties, the DGO was responsible for regularly inspecting the men's gas helmets and respirators.[41]

April 6, 1917: Good Friday, we had four eggs, the first I had in the army.

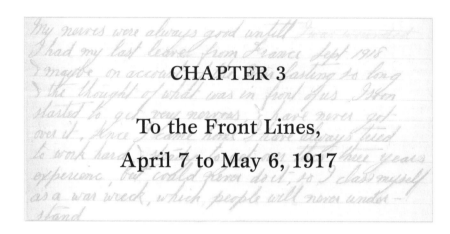

CHAPTER 3

To the Front Lines,
April 7 to May 6, 1917

"I always believed in digging a safe place."

April 7, 1917: We left Hersin at 10.30 a.m. and marched steady until 4:00 p.m. through muck and slush as it had been raining. We had heavy marching order (full pack). It was the hardest march I had ever had. I never forgot it. I had plenty of tougher marches later on, but I was hardened then. We went to McKenzie Camp in a wood near Mont-St. Eloi and slept in tents, and was kept awake that night by guns as they were getting ready for Vimy.

I am with the 19th Canadian Battalion now.

One fellow was so lousy that they made him sleep alone in a bivouac (he belonged to the 19th). He had hundreds of "cooties" outside his tunic; he never kept them down.

Bruoy is near here. I saw my first observation balloon brought down by the Germans.

Heavy marching order meant that Deward was carrying everything he owned, which would have weighed in at about seventy pounds (thirty-two kilograms).

During the week leading up to the assault on Vimy Ridge, the 19th Battalion used McKenzic Camp as a holding centre for reinforcements coming up from the Base Depot and for men who were designated left out of battle (LOB). When a battalion went into action, it always left behind a certain number of troops as a nucleus around which it could reform in the event of extreme casualties. At Vimy Ridge, the 19th Battalion designated one platoon from each company, or one quarter of the battalion's fighting strength, as LOB. McKenzie Camp was located in a wood three miles (five kilometres) northwest of Mont-St. Eloi and just a short distance from Canadian Corps Headquarters at Camblain-L'Abbé. There were four medium artillery batteries operating less than two miles (three kilometres) from the camp and many others in the vicinity, so for somebody new to the front, the noise must have seemed incessant.[42]

Unbeknownst to Deward at the time, he actually had been taken on strength by the 19th Battalion upon his arrival in France on March 6, but it took him a month of bouncing between base camps and reinforcement holding units until the 19th Battalion required him; he was one of ten other ranks to arrive at McKenzie Camp on April 7. During the month of April, the battalion received over 230 reinforcements, a high number that reflects the losses they suffered during the attack on Vimy Ridge (in March 1917 they required only 100 reinforcements).[43]

The 19th Canadian Infantry Battalion mobilized at Exhibition Camp in Toronto in October 1914; its ranks were quickly filled by militiamen from Toronto, Hamilton, St. Catharines, and Brantford.[44] As part of the 4th Brigade, 2nd Canadian Division, the 19th Battalion sailed for England on board the troopship *Scandinavian* in May 1915 — an earlier 4th Brigade that went overseas in 1914 had been broken up for reinforcements in Britain. The 19th Battalion went to France in mid-September 1915 and earned its first battle honour at Mount Sorrel, Belgium, in June of the following year. The battalion also fought in the battles of the Somme during September and October 1916 before wintering in the Vimy Ridge sector north of Arras.

The 18th, 20th, and 21st Battalions completed the infantry element of the 4th Brigade, which along with the 5th and 6th Brigades made up the 2nd Canadian Division.

"Cooties" is a reference to lice. We will hear more of this from Deward later.

Both sides used observation balloons to help the artillery spot targets. The balloons, and their crews, made tempting targets for enemy fighters.

April 8, 1917: Easter Sunday, a grand day. We moved to huts and tents near Arras, which the Germans held. I stayed in a tent. The huts, etc. were shelled very often, that's why they had some tents as some of the huts had been destroyed. In a shell hole outside, a horse was sitting up (dead). It looked funny for he didn't seem dead.

The 19th Battalion had left for the trenches before we had arrived so none of our draft was in Vimy except Alex Armstrong, who went in as a trench policeman; but he found himself going over with the rest.

(Easter) Sunday was such a nice day and Easter Monday, April 9, when the Vimy scrap started; it was snowing, slushy, and cold.

Deward must have been misinformed about Arras being held by the Germans. Although the city was heavily damaged by long-range shelling, it remained in Allied hands throughout the war.

The trench police were not a permanently formed corps, but instead were made up of infantry soldiers assigned to act as such by their battalion for the duration of a given operation. They were "traffic cops" who regulated the flow of men and material up and down the trenches during the active phases of an assault. In addition, trench police collected stragglers and ensured prisoners made it into the cages that were set up to receive them. Each traffic control point in a trench was manned by an NCO and two to four "reliable" men. Only men who knew the local trench system should have been assigned to trench policing duties, so it is odd that a new man like Armstrong ended up as one on his first trip to the line. After the operation was over, the men returned to their regular duties. Trench police do not appear to have been related to the full-time regimental police, who conducted criminal investigations, supervised prisoner cages, and maintained general discipline, working under the direction and control of an assistant provost marshal.[45]

April 9, 1917: The 19th Battalion took the German Third Line trenches at 5:30 a.m. It took them forty-five minutes to reach their objective. The Canadians took three thousand prisoners that day. I saw the German prisoners as they were sent back and caged in. A good many could speak English. I first saw at close view that day three armed planes (allies).

There is some confusion on Deward's part here. The 19th Battalion left its jumping-off positions at 5:30 a.m. with the commencement of the artillery barrage. At 6:07 a.m. 19th Battalion Headquarters received a message from their advanced reporting centre indicating their men were on the Black Line objective (the German Third Line trenches that Deward refers to above). At 6:40 a.m. the 21st Battalion passed through the 19th Battalion's positions to commence their attack on the Red Line objective (the Turko Graben trench system), and at approximately 9:00 a.m. the four battalions of the 6th Brigade passed through on their way to attack Thélus and Farbus Wood on the final Blue and Brown objective lines. The 19th Battalion's trophy list for the day included five machine guns, five "fish tail" bomb carriers (fish tails were a type of large trench mortar — see the notes on trench mortars that accompany Deward's diary entry for July 17, 1917), and two light trench mortars.[46]

April 10, 1917: The 19th went over-the-top twice more. I was out of that. Vimy was an artillery victory. The guns swept everything. I did two hours fatigue that day and was put into "A" Company, No. 2 Platoon, in the Lewis gun section. Went down to Camblain-L'Abbé, a small town where Sarah Bernhardt had a big chateau and where fifty camps stayed on her grounds.

Again, there is some confusion here about the 19th Battalion's activity. On April 10, the 19th Battalion's only action was to relieve the 21st Battalion in the Red Line; there is no indication the 19th Battalion was involved in a fight. This should not be surprising since the Blue Line and Brown Line, both of which lay well beyond the Red Line, were taken, consolidated, and secured on the afternoon of April 9 by units of the 6th Brigade.[47]

In the weeks following the Vimy Ridge attack, the officer commanding "A" company was Maj. George Denison. Denison was a Toronto lawyer and, at forty-seven years of age, an experienced prewar militia officer. Denison obtained a commission in the CEF in 1915 and proceeded overseas with the rank of lieutenant colonel in command of the 2nd Canadian Divisional Cyclist Company. In May 1916, the various Canadian divisional cyclist companies were consolidated into a single Canadian Corps Cyclist Battalion, which left Lieutenant Colonel Denison without a command. To avoid being sent back to Canada as a redundant officer, he took a reduction in rank and was posted into the 19th Battalion. Denison's family was something of a military dynasty in nineteenth-century Toronto, producing a Royal Navy admiral, a major general in the permanent Canadian Army, several militia colonels, and at their own expense raising a troop of volunteer cavalry that still serves as a reserve regiment in the Canadian Army (today known as the Governor General's Horse Guards). Denison's father, Col. George Denison, was also a lawyer and a soldier; the current Denison Armoury in Toronto is named for him.[48]

Deward mentions above that he was assigned to the Lewis gun section of No. 2 Platoon, "A" Company. Each infantry battalion in the Canadian Corps was divided into four rifle companies of between 150 and 200 men (designated A through D or 1 through 4, at the battalion's whim). In addition, each battalion had a headquarters company that could number well over two hundred.[49] Each rifle company consisted of four platoons, and each platoon consisted of four sections. In 1917, those four sections were designated as follows (in no particular order): Lewis gunners (to operate the Lewis machine gun), riflemen, bombers, and rifle-grenadiers (men trained to use rifle-launched grenades). A section usually numbered between seven and nine men.[50] Each section was commanded by an NCO, each platoon by a lieutenant, and the company — usually — by either a captain or a major. A battalion was under the command of a lieutenant colonel.

In a speech delivered to the Empire Club in Toronto on January 31, 1918, Maj. Wilfrid Mavor, MC, of the 15th Battalion, explained how a company commander went about fitting reinforcements into their new platoons:

> What we do with these reinforcements is to … line the men up and have a look at them; tell them the Canadian Corps is the best corps in France; tell them that they come to the best division in France; that they come to the best brigade, the best battalion, and they are going to be in the best company, and if it is not the best company it is their fault. Then we look them up and down, and tell them that soldiering in France is not the same as soldiering in England … Then you get hold of your company clerk … and line up those men and start to take down the particulars for your company books. You get your clerk to do this, and you wander around and talk to those men, find out what they are like, and you order the company clerk to pay special attention to what their trades were before they joined the army, and what they have been doing since. Then you categorize those men under four different headings.
>
> … A baseball player is put in the bombing section; he may be able to throw bombs pretty well. If he has been some sort of a machinist at some time, he is placed in the machine gun or Lewis gun section, as he will be more adept in fixing stoppages and that sort of thing in the Lewis gun. Then you put the husky fellows … and fellows that are good shots in the rifle section. You put all the boobs in the rifle grenade section. The reason for that, I think, is that we do not yet know the full value of the rifle grenade …[51]

Before the war, Deward had worked as a machine hand, and true to Mavor's word he was placed in the Lewis gun section, whose job it was to serve and maintain the platoon's Lewis gun. Despite its hefty twenty-eight and a half pounds (thirteen kilograms), the Lewis gun was, by 1917 standards, considered light enough for a single man to carry. Unlike the heavier Vickers gun, the Lewis gun did not require a tripod for mounting, and because it was air cooled it did not need a supply of water to keep the barrel from overheating. While it was arguably the best of its class at the time, the Lewis gun did suffer from some design flaws. One of the most vexatious problems was the weapon's pan-shaped, carousel-style magazine, which was open on the bottom. The opening allowed dirt to get into the magazine and interfere with its rotation and the feeding of cartridges into the chamber, creating "stoppages," or jams. A considerable amount of time, therefore, was spent training Lewis gunners on how to deal with different types of stoppages under varying conditions.

In the words of one training manual, the role of the Lewis gun was to "kill the enemy above ground and to obtain superiority of fire. Its mobility and the small target it and its team present render it peculiarly suitable for working round an enemy's flank or for guarding one's own flank."[52]

The Lewis gun "team" or section consisted of nine men: an NCO, who was in command, and eight other ranks to service the weapon. The other ranks were each assigned a number that defined for them a specific role in the section. Number 1 aimed and fired the gun. Number 2 tended the magazine and assisted Number 1 with clearing stoppages. Numbers 3 through 8 provided rifle cover for Numbers 1 and 2 and served as ammunition carriers; each of these men was equipped with a set of specially designed panniers that could carry up to eight spare magazines. In addition to their assigned duties, everyone in the section was cross-trained on the other's duties, so if Numbers 1 or 2 became casualties, the rest of the section could keep the gun in action.

Courtesy City of Toronto Archives, Fonds 1244, Item 793B

Lt. Col. George Denison, 2nd Canadian Divisional Cyclist Company. In May 1916, the various Canadian Divisional Cyclist companies were consolidated into a single cyclist, and Denison found himself out of work. To avoid being sent back to Canada, he took a reduction in rank in the hope that he might be posted to a front-line unit. Later that year he was sent to the 19th Battalion and became the officer commanding "A" Company, the company to which Deward was assigned when he arrived at the battalion. Denison was killed during the fighting at Fresnoy on May 8, 1917.

April 11, 1917: Major Ellis of the 19th was wounded. All officers except one were killed in "A" Company. Major Ellis was
the youngest major in France, nineteen years old.

The snow was three inches [seven centimetres] deep.

Between April 9 and April 14, the 19th Battalion reported
only 2 officers killed in action and 7 others wounded (the battalion also reported 32 other ranks killed, 154 wounded, 27 missing,
and 15 sick). Since each company had at least six officers (a company commander, his second-in-command, and a commander for
each of the four platoons), it is unlikely that the officers of "A"
company suffered as badly as Deward reports. The inaccuracies
that have crept into Deward's diary over the past few entries probably result from the fact that he was not present with the battalion
during the actual fighting and that, faced with a lack of first-hand
knowledge, he was simply writing down what was commonly
believed by the men to be true, the product of "trench rumour."[53]

April 12, 1917: I went to see Marden and McFadden of the
123rd Battalion, near here.

Burt Marden and James McFadden were friends of Deward's
from the 180th Battalion. They were among the draft of men sent
by the 180th to the 123rd Battalion on February 27. Marden was
a piano-maker by profession. Born in Sussex, England, in 1895,
Marden and his family moved to Canada prior to the war and were
living in the village of Todmorden (now a part of east-end
Toronto) when Marden enlisted. McFadden was a twenty-two-
year-old Irishman from Cullybackey, Antrim. Like Marden's family, the McFaddens too immigrated to Canada before the war and
settled in east-end Toronto.

April 14, 1917: We left McKenzie camp for Mont-St. Eloi, a one
and three quarter hour march away, at 1:00 p.m. On our way we
passed a ruined house where a whole band had been killed the
day before by a shell (heavy). We arrived at the ruins [of the

church] at the top of Mont-St. Eloi. That day, the boys came out [of the line] and I met Doc Rutherford.

This is a curious entry. The band of the 10th Canadian Infantry Battalion was indeed wiped out by a single large-calibre, long-range shell that struck their billet at Mont-St. Eloi (it also caused considerable casualties among the battalion's headquarters company). The incident, however, took place on May 1, not April 13 as Deward relates.[54] One wonders if some time after the fact — perhaps as late as 1926 — Deward went back to his diary and began filling in blank spots and, although he remembered the incident accurately, was mistaken about the date.

It isn't clear either who Doc Rutherford was; Deward only mentions him once. He might have been Cecil Rutherford, with whom Deward served in the 180th Battalion and who was also posted to the 19th Battalion.[55]

April 16, 1917: We left for trenches at 8:30 p.m. arrived at 11:00 p.m.; to dug-outs in Elk trench near Neuville-St. Vaast. It was wet, raining, and cold; and we had rum.

The rum Deward had was by no means contraband. Rum was made available by the army to men on active service.

April 17, 1917: We were working on roads, repairing and filling in shell holes, in snow and rain. It was cold. We were at Territorial Dump. "Lousy," we got back to Elk Trench and tried to sleep in dug-outs, but it was so lousy we had to get out and sleep in a trench full of mud. I had two rubber sheets, put one under me and one over. The rats were running over us all night. They didn't bother us, only you could hear and feel them running over your rubber sheet. This was an old trench, French, where they had battled nearly all through from the start of the war. Had been lost and retaken a few times and men had been blown to pieces, etc., then never found; the reason for so many rats.

Few features of daily life at the front caused as much misery for the soldiers as the common body louse. The crowded, dirty living arrangements that all ranks had to endure provided ideal conditions for these parasites to flourish by the millions. Even the most fastidious of soldiers soon found themselves infested with lice; infestations were unavoidable. Arthur Empey, an American serving with the British Army in 1915 and 1916, recorded the reaction of newly arrived reinforcements who encountered an infestation for the first time:

> The greatest shock a recruit gets when he arrives at his battalion in France is to see the men engaged in a "cootie" hunt. With an air of contempt and disgust he avoids the company of the older men, until a couple of days later, in a torment of itching he also has to resort to a shirt hunt, or spend many a sleepless night of misery.[56]

The "shirt hunt" was a method of delousing infested clothing in which the "hunter" picked through the seams of his garment, seeking out the offending lice and their eggs — laid by the hundreds. Another delousing method involved passing the seams of a garment over an open candle flame — although as Empey points out this method was a double-edged sword, because if you were not careful you burned not only the lice, but your clothes as well.[57] Pressing the seams of infected clothes with hot irons, soaking them in creosote, and treating them with chemical powders were each also used to delouse a soldier's wardrobe. Because his environment was itself infested with lice, however, none of these treatments kept them down for very long. Two Canadian inventions that did, however, help to ease the plight of the men at the front were the Amyot Disinfecting Chamber and the Orr Hut, named for their respective inventors. Both of these appliances featured racks upon which infested clothing was hung then subjected to extreme heat, which killed the lice and destroyed their eggs. Amyot's system used live steam, while Orr's method used a dry heat. Both of these devices were in general use throughout the British-held sector.[58]

At first, lice were thought to be only a nuisance. In 1918, however, a British bacteriologist, David Bruce, traced the origins of trench fever to lice that were carrying the Rickettsia Quintana bug. The bug was harmless enough to the louse, but once it got into the human bloodstream it wreaked havoc. Trench fever symptoms were similar to both those of influenza and typhus. Although the infection was rarely fatal, the afflicted soldier required hospitalization and was debilitated for several weeks with nausea, fever, and a severe, cramping pain in the legs. The recovery period after the infection's active phase could be several months, during which time the soldier was usually confined to a convalescent facility.[59]

One of the more gruesome aspects of life at the front was the presence of unburied bodies and body parts. A direct hit by a high explosive shell on a group of huddled men could scatter their body parts over a wide area, and although attempts were made, for both sanitary and sentimental reasons, to collect them, not all of the parts were necessarily found or could be retrieved. Likewise, men who were killed in areas exposed to enemy fire, or in No-Man's Land — the strip of land between the opposing trench lines — often were left to rot, because it was too dangerous to try and recover them. The presence of this carrion was a contributing factor to the large number of rats remarked on by Deward.

April 18, 1917: We were shelled on fatigue and still raining and cold. Had rum at night.

April 19, 1917: We rested in morning, on fatigue at 12:30 p.m. To Thélus on roads.

April 20, 1917: On fatigues.

April 21, 1917: We left those trenches at 8:30 p.m. for Cammell Tunnel, with long narrow passages. In Petit Vimy on right of Lens, arriving about 12:00 midnight. Shelled on road going, and quite a number were killed and wounded. We were short of candles and as crummy as can be. Front line two thousand yards [eighteen hundred metres] away.

Vimy Ridge was honeycombed with caves and tunnels — or "subways," as they were often called. Some of the caverns were actually chalk quarries that had been excavated for building material long before the war. Others were more recent additions, leftovers from the subterranean war waged by the British Imperial forces in 1916, or from the Canadian attack of April 9, 1917.[60] During the months leading up to the Canadian attack, tunnelling gangs drove or extended no fewer than eleven subways for a total distance of four miles (six and a half kilometres), providing protection for the attacking troops before the battle and a quick means of evacuation for the wounded after the fighting began.[61] With the ridge now firmly in Canadian hands, the tunnels continued to provide shelter for the men from the natural elements and the enemy's harassing artillery fire.

"Crummy" was another expression for "lousy" and came from the similarity in appearance of large numbers of lice to bread crumbs.

April 22, 1917: We stayed in a cave; one man was shell-shocked.

April 23, 1917: The entrance was shelled heavily in the morning but I was deep down in the cave and well back, quite safe unless gas came. On gas-guard at night. Tear gas came over. Duty from 12:00 midnight to 2:00 a.m.

The Canadian Corps' Trench Standing Orders required units to post a gas-guard, or gas-sentry, over every gas alarm station and at each Headquarters Signal Office, Advanced Dressing Station, and dugout with ten or more men or any group of smaller dugouts. These orders also called for gas-guards to accompany all working parties.[62] The sole job of the gas-guard was to remain alert to the signs of an impending gas attack (the rushing sound of pressurized gas escaping from cylinders, an approaching gas cloud, or the explosion of gas shells in the vicinity) and to raise an alarm should he detect any. The alarms consisted of klaxon horns, bells, or anything else that came to hand with which he could make a loud noise.[63]

Tear gas was used extensively by both sides as a harassing agent. The advantage of tear gas was that even in small doses it forced the enemy put on his protective gear, reducing his effectiveness and ability to fight. Some other gases, such as "Blue Cross," for example, were generally more tolerable in lower concentrations without having to don respirators.[64]

April 24, 1917: In the cave all day, five killed, eleven wounded. A shell went through the dug-outs. Nellie Cowan (ex-policeman of city) just left it before; he says "Gee, I'm lucky!" Major Ellis died.

We are all cramped up for want of stretching out. The passages were only about three feet [one metre] wide and we all had to sit down with our backs to the wall and our knees up. That is the way we had to sleep.

Maj. A.W. Ellis died of wounds at one of the army hospitals in Boulogne on April 13. News of his death must only now have reached the battalion.[65]

April 25, 1917: One man was wounded. I was sent out with two others to get spies. I borrowed a pistol. He was near Cammell Tunnel or Observation Tunnel as it was called, sitting on the hillside drawing. He was a major. We placed him under arrest and he came without any trouble; even offered cigarettes to our Colonel's dug-out and soon proved that he was an artillery major drawing for some future event.

April 26, 1917: We worked and were shelled, three wounded and one of them died. We moved up to the front line but were kept in supports. We left Cammell Tunnel at 8:30 p.m. Had tea and coffee on the way down, arriving at Camp between Neuville-St. Vaast and Mont-St. Eloi at 1:00 a.m. — in tents. While there

71

we had more machine gun practice, lounged around near the 123rd Battalion's reserve [lines].

April 30, 1917: Had to go to a compulsory concert in the afternoon at la Targette, it was swell. McFadden and Marden came up to see me. Tom Allen had a piece of shrapnel in his eye and lost it: sent to hospital.

May 1, 1917: General inspection by the general. Aeroplane raid, bombed at 12:45 p.m. Two German planes came over; ran for trench. I hate bombs. Shells can't be heard until they hit you, but bombs, you hear them long before they hit the ground and you don't know where they are going. You can often see them dropping if you happen to be looking in the right direction. It's true.

The battalion was inspected by Brigadier Robert Rennie, general officer commanding the 4th Canadian Infantry Brigade.[66]

May 2, 1917: Fatigue in morning and moved to Elbe Trench. Reserves at 8:30 p.m. in same dug-outs. Rum at night and on gas guard from 11:00 p.m. to 12:00 midnight.

May 3, 1917: We rested. Fritzie Red Devil planes came over and fired all along trench. We opened up with machine gun and rifle fire, but he got away. Our planes were not in it with his then for speed. He could make rings around ours.

"Fritzie," "Boche," "Hun," and "Heiney" were all trench-slang terms for the Germans.

"Red Devil" was one of several wartime nicknames for Manfred von Richtofen, best remembered today as the Red Baron. During the spring of 1917, Richtofen was in command of Jagdstaffel, or Jasta, 11 (*Jasta* is a contraction of *Jagdstaffel*, meaning fighter squadron), which was stationed for a time at the German aerodrome near Douai, twelve miles (twenty kilometres) due east of the 19th Battalion's position at Neuville-St. Vaast.[67]

Although the aircraft of Richtofen's Jasta were recognizable from their dashes of red paint, the Red Devil himself was not present at this attack. On May 1, the day after his near-run encounter with Canadian ace Billy Bishop, Richtofen left for a six-week leave of absence. During his absence, Jasta 11 was under the command of his brother, Lothar.[68]

Deward's comments about British aircraft are especially pertinent considering he had just witnessed "Bloody April." This was a particularly trying month for the Royal Flying Corps (RFC), during which it lost 151 aircraft and over 300 aircrewmen, mostly in the area around Arras — including the Vimy Ridge sector. Although the RFC enjoyed a numerical advantage in aircraft over the German Army Air Service, their machines were at this time generally slower and less manoeuvrable than the newer generation of German fighters. During "Bloody April," the life expectancy of a newly arrived RFC pilot was just seventeen days.[69]

May 4, 1917: We slept with respirators on.

May 5, 1917: Moved at 8:30 a.m. to old front-line trench near Neuville-St. Vaast, arriving at 9:15 a.m. Very hot, made bivouac. C. Arnold, W. Bell, and I slept. Very cold and still crummy. Germans still retaliating.

Cecil Arnold and William Bell were two of Deward's section mates and ex-180th Battalion men. Arnold was originally from Leicestershire, England; a printer by trade, he was living with his family on Balliol Street in Toronto when he enlisted in 1916 at the age of twenty. Bell was born in September 1895 in Unionville, Ontario, and, like Deward, was a machinist turned Lewis gunner.

May 6, 1917: Sunday, Bell, Arnold and myself worked hard all day long making a surface dug-out in our trench; all sandbags and gathering sheet iron for roof, which was not shell-proof — but we made a nice, real comfortable dug-out with plenty of room. Never used it, for at 7:30 that same night we had to move farther up the line, arriving at 8:30 p.m. Many dozens of times I have worked hard to make a safe place in the trenches and then had to move to another post. But I always believed in digging a safe place. And another thing I believed in was sticking to the first place I picked out, even if it was a shallow shell hole. I stayed that night, I was on water party for two hours. Shelled hard all night. Liquid fire and gas. German plane came low scouting.

Deward's reference to liquid fire is a puzzling one. The term is usually used in connection with the discharge of a flamethrower. In this case, however, Deward associates the liquid fire with artillery shells. It could be a reference to some sort of incendiary shell the Germans were firing into the Canadian lines or it might be the nickname given by the troops to a particular type of gas.

The hard shelling that Deward mentioned was a warning of things to come.

My nerves were always good untill I had my last leave from France Sept 1918 maybe on account lasting so long the thought of what was in front of us. It then started to get very nervous I have never got over it. Since I came home I have always tried to work experience but could never do it, so I class myself as a war wreck, which people will never understand

CHAPTER 4

Baptism of Fire,
May 7 to August 14, 1917

We stuck, fear had left us. I was never so cool before.

May 7, 1917: The starting of the Fresnoy Battle was about the worst I was in. It was my first real scrap and was terrible. In reality, it was mostly an Imperial battle and our division, the 2nd Canadian Division, immediately on the left of the Imperials, were the only Canadians in it.

On May 3, the 1st and 2nd Canadian Divisions captured the town of Fresnoy, which lies about five miles (eight kilometres) east of Vimy Ridge. This operation was part of a broader British plan to keep the Germans busy on the Western Front while Russia and Italy prepared for offensives on their own fronts.

The loss of Fresnoy and its commanding views did not sit well with the Germans. On May 5, the 5th Bavarian Division received orders to mount a counterattack to recapture the town and its environs, which by then were occupied by units of the 95th Infantry Brigade, 5th British Division, which had relieved the 1st Canadian Division on the night of May 4; the 2nd Canadian Division, however, was still holding its part of the line to the northwest of the town. In preparation for their attack, the Germans fired over one hundred thousand artillery rounds — much of it gas — into this area, providing the intensity of shelling on which Deward comments below.

At 3:45 a.m. on May 8, the Bavarians attacked. Although the main thrust of the assault was against Fresnoy proper and its Imperial defenders, some of the attacking formations fell upon the 2nd Canadian Division's lines immediately north of the town. The attack caught the 19th Battalion just as it was completing its relief of the 28th and 29th battalions, and it was in the face of this determined counterattack that Deward underwent his baptism of fire.[70]

Shelled hard all day, might have been caught. Lucky.

Moved up to the front line six miles [ten kilometres] away. It was raining hard and the ground was very sticky as that part of the country is all clay. I carried 120 rounds of extra ammunition [for myself], two bombs, two [empty] sandbags and ground signals [for aircraft]. And being Number 6 on the Lewis gun I had to carry two ammunition pan carriers, 376 rounds, besides our own equipment of fighting order — 616 rounds of ammunition altogether. A terrible load that I was not used to at that time.

Deward's load was indeed terrible, in every sense: he lugged forward more than sixty pounds (twenty-seven kilograms) of ammunition and weaponry, bound to his body with belts and straps. The bombs, rifle, and Lewis gun ammunition accounted for fifty-one pounds (twenty-three kilograms) of this; his rifle and bayonet added another ten pounds (four and a half kilograms).[71] In addition to this deadly overload, Deward also had to contend with the weight of his "fighting order": his entrenching tool (a small digging implement), his respirator, a rubber ground sheet, his steel helmet, an unspecified number of ground signals (probably two), his eating utensils, his iron rations (only to be consumed in emergencies), a full water bottle (or possibly two), toiletries, and his clothes, which by this time would have been soaked through with rain water and caked with mud. Altogether, the weight of Deward's burden might well have reached 120 pounds (54 kilograms).[72] And as he trudged his way up through the trenches, bent double like an old beggar, the forward areas were awash in German gas, which meant Deward had to suck hard for each breath through his respirator.[73]

We stopped in an old trench about half way up to the line for a rest. We were being shelled pretty hard at that time and it was getting late, but our corporal assured us not to be afraid, that everything would turn out alright. Although we had lost a few until then, I remembered after, quite distinctly, that he was white and pretty nervous, but turned out to be a real man.

However, we had to go on. The Germans were shelling immediately in front of us. It was pitch dark and the rain never stopped and we kept right on ahead straight for it. The shells were breaking and lighting the place up. We were green and did not know but at that time the Germans timed their shelling. Shell for so long in one place and then change over to another spot. By the time you were near to that spot, he had changed his range.

We called on the guide for everything. We kept on going with our load and it was hard. Never having to go under those conditions before, I was excited.

The "guide" that Deward mentions was likely one of several men sent by either the 28th or 29th battalion to help the 19th Battalion companies find their allotted place in the front-line trenches. The guides were especially important on this trip, because it was the 19th Battalion's first time in this part of the line.[74]

We finally hit the communications trench leading to the front line. By that time all of our officers in "A" and "B" company were killed, we only had NCOs left. Many a poor fellow never got to the front-line trench; the first trip for some. We stopped in the communications trench and I was so all in and just about at the end of my rope, as I thought, when they stopped and leaned against the trench side to rest their backs. I was doing the same thing and let myself go against the bank. I bumped into McDonald of Hamilton and he says "what the Hell are you doing?" I never forgot that. He was an experienced man and a good one. We finally got placed into position in the front-line trench about 2:00 a.m.

Although most of the officers in "A" and "B" companies became casualties later on, the majority survived the trip into the trenches. In the confusion and excitement of his first trip up to the front line under fire, it might have seemed to Deward that the battalion was suffering much heavier casualties than it really was. Alternatively, in his exhaustion after the battle, Deward might have confused the end of the action with the beginning.

Deward's battalion was moving forward to take over a 1,200-yard (1.1-kilometre) stretch of front-line trench from the 28th and 29th Battalions. Part of their new line took a sharp jog to the right as it approached Fresnoy. This bend formed a small salient, or projection, into the German lines that would later prove troublesome, as it allowed the enemy to direct fire on the 19th Battalion from three directions. The 18th Battalion held the line on the 19th Battalion's left, and the 12th Battalion, the Gloucester Regiment (belonging to the 95th Imperial Brigade) was on their right.[75]

May 8, 1917: The shelling was terrible. It was real heavy now as we got the whiz-bangs. And he certainly could send them fast. His field shells were a little lighter than ours and he fired them faster. Always when he was going to make a drive in the morning he shelled all night long; where the British saved them up for zero hour and surprise. But Fritzie worried us. He never let up. He kept those whiz-bangs and heavies going fast from 2:00 a.m. until daybreak. His heavy guns gassed our artillery and our side never fired a gun, the only time during the whole war that our artillery was put out of action.

"Whiz-bang" was trench slang for German high-velocity field-artillery shells. There appears to be two schools of thought on how the term was coined. Both versions of the story agree that "whiz" imitates the sound of the shell in flight. One version, however, suggests that, because the shells travelled faster than the speed of sound, the soldiers heard the passing of the shell ... whiz ... before they heard the report of the gun that fired it ... bang! The other explanation concludes that "bang" was the detonation of the shell itself.

The defensive fire by the British artillery on May 8 was alto-gether insufficient to beat off the German attacks. Many of the nearby batteries were severely knocked about and badly gassed by the German bombardment, as Deward remarks above; rain and fog also prevented the gunners from seeing the infantry's SOS signal flares, which they put up at the start of the German attack.[76]

> The whiz-bangs sounded just as though they were just missing the tops of our trenches, and going over the hollow trench gave them a peculiar sharp sound, besides the whiz. It made you think of home. Our corporal told us not to be afraid, to look over, only don't move when a flare went up. The rain never stopped. The trenches were all caving in and puddles of mud and water. We were soaked through hours ago and thick with mud. We watched. We knew they were coming and fear had left me by that time. My eyes must have been half out of my head from excitement.

It was common for soldiers to mentally retreat to a place of familiarity and comfort, especially when they were under extreme stress. Will Bird, for example, encountered the young shepherd boy "counting sheep" during a bombardment at Passchendaele.[77] For Deward, thoughts of home appear to have been his mental sanctuary, a place where he could safely retreat, however tem-porarily, from the reality of shelling. We will see him do this from time to time throughout his story.

One of the survival tricks that veterans would pass on to reinforcements like Deward was to freeze if they were caught at night in the light of a flare. Because of the high angle from which the flare shed its light and the pale glow that it created, an observer could have a very difficult time telling the differ-ence between detail and shadow on the illuminated landscape. If you stood still, therefore, you had a much better chance of not being noticed. It was a feat that would surely have required nerves of steel.

Finally, about 4:00 a.m. or just about daybreak, one of the boys says, "There they are." I couldn't see them just then and finally I saw one within a stone's throw away and then dozens of them. The front line of the Germans had been skirmishing and in the distance there were four lines of Germans. You could not see between them.

The German attack fell upon "C" Company, which was holding down the right of the 19th Battalion's line.[78] However, Deward — who was in "A" Company and who should, therefore, have been at the opposite end of the 19th Battalion's line — is able to describe the fighting from the start. This suggests that Deward's Lewis gun section had been detached from its parent company and sent to lend extra support for "C" Company. This appears to have happened from time to time, as Deward records a similar experience later in the war.

Our corporal placed the gun on the parados, on a high place, and opened fire behind (they had already got behind us). We had lost some of our section, so I was the next man called. I had to lay in a pool of water. I fired the gun and it jammed. Ours was the only gun that fired at all (afterwards Lance-Corporal Cowan and I were recommended for the D.C.M. [Distinguished Conduct Medal] but owing to so many other recommends we did not get it).[79]

The "parados" was a mound of earth that ran along the back of the trench. It helped to protect the men from shells that burst behind them. The "parapet" was a similar mound of earth that ran along the front of the trench.

The Lewis gun was prone to jamming because of the magazine design (see the note accompanying Deward's diary entry for April 10, 1917).

Circumstances were working against the 19th Battalion from the very outset. They were still involved in the business of completing their relief of the 29th Battalion when the attack began —

three 29th Battalion Lewis gun sections even joined in with "C" Company to help repel the attack. The weather and light conditions made it even more difficult for the relieving companies to find their way in an already unfamiliar part of the line and prevented the artillery from providing adequate supporting fire. Furthermore, the ferocity of the German bombardment and attack on Fresnoy proper created gaps in the line to the 19th Battalion's right and allowed some of the enemy to work their way in behind the 19th Battalion's positions.[80]

Another officer ordered us to retire a little ways into a salient and, being [Lewis] gunners, we had to stay there to cover the rest of the battalion getting out back farther. We held that post and just in front of us were Germans with our steel helmets on. We opened fire but our rifles jammed; had to use your foot [to kick the bolt open and] force empty cases out. I only fired two or three shots. I saw two fall, they were right on us.

The officer that Deward mentions was likely Lieut. Harry Bridge, who was, at that point, in charge of "C" Company. The "salient" to which the remainder of Deward's section retired was probably a support trench that lay about one hundred yards (ninety-five metres) behind the front line. Some of its barbed wire entanglements were still intact, which made it defensible.[81]

The detail about German soldiers wearing British helmets is not noted in any official reports on the action at Fresnoy. A similar incident, however, was reported at the Second Battle of Ypres in 1915, where German troops wearing British uniforms advanced toward the Canadian lines. The ruse was detected, however, and the imposters were driven off by rifle fire.[82]

Deward's report of the rifles jamming is strange. While jamming was a problem often linked with the Canadian-made Model 1910 Ross Rifle (which was withdrawn from general service with the Canadian Corps in the summer of 1916), it was not something that was associated with the British Lee-Enfield rifle, with which the Canadians were then equipped. If Deward is recalling this inci-

81

dent clearly, it suggests the battalion might have been issued with a bad lot of ammunition. If the cartridge casings were too thin, they could expand when fired and become wedged in the rifle's chamber. This would prevent the men from easily opening the rifle's bolt to extract the fired casing. Other instances of poor quality ammunition were recorded and included loose-fitting bullets and substandard cordite (the propellant).[83] Other possibilities are that Deward confused jammed rifles with the Lewis gun jam from earlier in the day, or that he added this detail while compiling his pocket diaries in 1926 and confused this incident with stories he had heard of the Canadian Division at the Second Battle of Ypres, where the problem of Ross rifles jamming was well documented.

> The same officer came up to us (as he was helping the battalion to get out) and said, "Well boys, we are done, do your duty and fight to the finish." We stuck, fear had left us. I was never so cool before. I did not bayonet any, but some did. The Germans were behind us, some killed just as they were about to get into our trenches, some sitting on top of our trenches dead, but looked alive. They were the Bavarians, Germany's finest regiment and the finest men I had seen. None looked under 6 feet [180 centimetres], and big. The Bavarians were always fine, big men until the latter days of the war.
> We hung on.

With the 19th Battalion in danger of being cut off from the rest of the 4th Brigade, the remainder of "C" Company — not the entire battalion as Deward reports — had to withdraw to a new defensive line in the "Alberta Road," one of several sunken roads running roughly north to south in the rear of the 19th Battalion's position. (These roads existed long before the war and had their own, local names; on the British ordnance maps, however, they were branded with distinctly Canadian names. From east to west they were: Alberta Road, Winnipeg Road, Manitoba Road, Saskatchewan Road, and Vancouver Road.) To cover their withdrawal, Lieutenant Bridge left several outposts in the support trench, among them Deward and the survivors of his section. Shortly after he instructed Deward to "do your duty," Bridge was reported killed.[84]

It was around 1:00 p.m. when orders were sent to us from the rear to get back to the sunken road. It seemed miles back. We were the last to get out. It had been raining hard all the time, and the shells and the trenches caving in had buried men who had been wounded and killed. The trenches were full of dead Germans and our own men. In the front line you miss most of the shells but back farther it was terrible, hundreds of dead were lying on the part we saw alone. There were hands sticking out of the mud and just faces. Some looked peaceful and others out of shape. The sight was terrible. It was that sticky clay. Every time you would go to lift your foot it would stick, and then stick to the other. You would sink to the tops of your boots in mud, trying not to step on faces, etc. And nothing to eat, no sleep, excited and dead tired, and trying to get back as fast as you can. It was hell.

For a time, the Germans were held at bay by the combined effects of artillery and machine gun fire. With the 19th Battalion's right flank unsecured, however, the enemy continued to work his way around and behind their position in a bid to isolate them from the rest of the 4th Brigade. By 1:30 p.m. the 19th Battalion's position was untenable, and this was when Deward received the order to fall back from the Alberta Road to a second defensive line in Winnipeg Road.[85]

On our way back through the trenches to the sunken road were wounded men. We could not carry them back with us so they had to get out the best way they could. We passed an Indian of our battalion who was just wounded in the leg (a bad one though) and a corporal of our battalion wounded in the stomach. We finally got through the communication trench to the first sunken road, "Winnipeg Road," where the battalion was making a stand. They had the trench barricaded at the sunken road. We

83

had to jump over it. Lieutenant Harman was at that post and in charge of the whole battalion and all Canadians that were there. He was dressed in a private's uniform, all other officers had been killed or wounded. However, we had to take our post in the sunken road, which was a deep one and far from shell-proof (too wide). We had to dig steps to the top as quickly as possible to be ready for them and get our gun placed. A shell hit the bank thirty feet [nine metres] from me and buried and killed Ball and Atkinson [formerly] of the 180th Battalion. Shelling continued heavily all the time, it never stopped. The sunken road was a death trap but we had to hold it for the time being. My post was right beside the barricade only up high and I did not recognize the officer in private's uniform. I did not see the stars on his shoulder straps then. The 19th Battalion only had about 125 men left and one officer, Lieutenant Harman, out of 700 men or so. Harman was afterward awarded the Military Cross and made a major and never saw the trenches again as he was put in charge of a course training school.

It was common, and often sensible, for officers to wear an other-ranks coat when going into the front lines or into battle.[86] They were prized targets for snipers, who were always on the lookout for the lapelled jacket, shirt, and tie of the officer's uniform coat. The stars to which Deward refers were the officer's rank badge. Sometimes called "pips," they had four points and were really shaped more like diamonds. An officer with one pip was a second lieutenant, a full lieutenant wore two pips, and a captain wore three. Majors wore a single crown; lieutenant colonels wore a crown and a pip. Initially, pips and crowns were embroidered onto the cuff of the uniform coat, but by war's end officers were wearing dull metal pips on their shoulder straps — as Lieutenant Harman appears to have been wearing on his other-ranks coat.

As Deward notes, the battalion suffered severely from shellfire while holding their positions in Winnipeg Road. Their *War Diary* notes, "Our casualties were very heavy whilst in Winnipeg Road, due to the enemy being able to shell us from three directions (in

front and on both flanks) ... Our total casualties were 11 Officers
and 225 Other Ranks of which the majority were killed outright
with shrapnel."[87]

Among the dead was George Denison. Like many of the 19th
Battalion casualties, he was struck down by shrapnel and subse-
quently buried by one of the trenches that Deward saw collapsing.
Prior to his death, as a mark of esteem, Denison's men frequently
referred to him by his former rank, lieutenant colonel, and this
may have given rise to a rumour that circulated through the 2nd
Division alleging the commanding officer of the 19th Battalion, Lt.
Col. L.H. Millen, had been killed during the attack. Denison's
body was uncovered, and today he lies in Écoivres Military
Cemetery at nearby Mont-St. Eloi.[88]

While Lieutenant Harman's service record confirms that in
1918, as a major, he was made the officer commanding the 4th
Brigade Training Company at the Canadian Corps Reinforcement
Camp, there is no indication that he was awarded the Military
Cross, however deserved.[89]

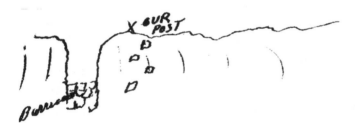

This is one of many sketches that Deward drew in the margins of his 1926
diary to help illustrate the action described in his text. It portrays the
barricade erected in the trench that ran through Winnipeg Road during the
action at Fresnoy on May 8, 1917. Notice the steps that he and his section
dug into the sunken road's steep bank so they could reach the top and set
up their Lewis gun.

Lieutenant Harman knew about this Indian and corporal, so he
detailed a corporal and six men to go after them. He detailed me
and I would not go. I told him I was a gunner and was not to
leave my post (that was before I noticed who he was) and that
was our training — which was all bosh. He sent me to get the

> Sergeant-Major, who was down a big dug-out. I got him and he
> told the Sergeant-Major that I was to go and lead the six men
> over the barricade and up to these wounded men. When I knew
> I had to go I was satisfied. I knew it was war and I never shirked
> once in any duty. It was about seven o'clock and he could see I
> was all in, but I had to go.

In this passage, Deward confesses quite candidly that he
refused an order to help bring in wounded men. Instead, he
offered up what even he admits was a nonsensical excuse — about
being a gunner trained not to leave his post — to someone who,
organizing the defences at Winnipeg Road, was clearly in authority. Until that point in the day, Deward had acquitted himself with
remarkable courage and composure in the face of a determined
assault, even preparing himself to "fight to the last" while covering the withdrawal of "C" Company from Alberta Road. But having survived the withdrawal and reached the relative safety of the
sunken road himself, he appears to have reached his limit. What
Deward was experiencing was not cowardice, nor was it shirking,
as he is afraid we will conclude. Rather, we are seeing a man on
the brink of physical and emotional exhaustion. Consider that he
had not slept in the previous thirty-six hours; he had marched
more than six miles (ten kilometres) in a gas cloud over broken,
soggy ground and under a ponderous load; he had fought in a desperate and confusing battle; experienced mass killing for the first
time; prepared himself for death several times over; and had seen
at least four of his closest comrades become casualties beside him
in a matter of hours (as evidenced by his move from Number 6 in
his Lewis gun section to Number 2). To Harman's credit, upon
hearing Deward's reply to his order, he sent Deward to fetch the
sergeant major (the most senior disciplinarian in the battalion),
allowing Deward time to compose himself and consider the serious consequences of refusing an order. Harman's plan succeeded,
and when Deward returned, with the sergeant major in tow, he
realized that, despite being "all in," he must go.

I was bayonet man and we did not know how far up the trench the Germans were. Places where the trench was torn away we had to get on our hands and knees and crawl past. I was leading for a while, sneaking around the corners and the corporal must have taken pity on me and he put someone else in front. We took turns then. The Indian was dead but the corporal was living and in terrible pain. We hadn't met any Germans, however. We got him back to the sunken road and Harman said I was to help take him back to a dressing station. He was in agony and at every little jolt he yelled. We started back at 8:00 p.m. hurrying past a certain place he shelled regular every five minutes to stop us getting out. I was so all in that I could only hold my end of the stretcher up a couple of yards and had to let it down, and kept that up all the time. The trenches were so narrow that when you came to a turn you had to raise the stretcher away above your head over the trench to get it around the corner.

Trench size varied, depending on where, when, and by whom it was constructed. These trenches appear unusually narrow and might have been recently dug and not yet widened.

We were making for Arleux, five miles [eight kilometres] away through trenches, as that was where the Advanced Dressing Station was. Only, it was on the Imperial front not far from the line — on the right of us. We would go a little ways and meet someone and ask him how far it was to the nearest dressing station (we did not know where it was then). "Oh, about a couple of hundred yards," they would say. And when we went about 700 or 800 yards [650 or 750 metres] someone would tell us it was about 3 miles [5 kilometres] away. We had no eats or water, we lost all that the first night.

We kept going and some way worked into the Imperial front line. The front line was never straight but at that part the trench was well made. The officer in charge stopped us, as they were going over-the-top on a raid. That was about 2:00 a.m. He did not make us go over with them, so left us with our wounded, you see. We were six hours getting this far, but we got correct directions from them. We stayed there until it was all over, they gave us some cigarettes before they went over. We put the stretcher on the firing step and stayed there two hours and then started again.

"The front line was never straight ..." as illustrated by Deward and his companions, who had been travelling toward the rear with their stretcher for almost six hours when they came upon the Imperial front line!

May 9, 1917: Finally got to the dressing station at 7:00 a.m. I never heard whether our wounded corporal lived or not.

It was a lovely day. We found a well and drank about two water bottles full and laid down in the grass beside it (the well) and went to sleep, the first sleep since Sunday night. We woke up, filled our water bottles, and left about noon for the sunken road again. We couldn't get any eats in Arleux, there was nothing there but the dressing station, but on our way back to the battalion we found surface dug-outs with the doorways built up with bully beef tins. I don't know how many we ate of those and then kept on going. Got back to the sunken road about 8:00 p.m. that night.

The battalion had by that time retired to the second sunken road, as they could not hold onto the first. I was reported missing for three days. We had something to eat as they had got rations by that time. The casualties were heavy. I dug in under shellfire in a funk hole and it did not take long. I am completely tired and done; worse than hell. Lost most of my equipment. We are in supports now as we have been relieved from the front line by full-strength battalions in the first sunken road.

Deward has survived his first battle, with many of his mates and most of his equipment (not to mention himself at one point) lost. Words fail him; he is "done." On May 9, the 19th Battalion was relieved in Winnipeg Road by the 18th Battalion and withdrew to Saskatchewan Road — which was actually the fourth of the sunken roads, not the second.[90]

May 10, 1917: We kept low all day so as not to let the Heiney planes see that the road was occupied. At night I was on water fatigue, water was scarce. We had to go back to Barlow and it took us two hours. No possible chance to write, but received letters. The rest of the night, four hours, I was on fatigue putting up barbed wire in No-Man's Land. Considered myself lucky to get back.

When not manning the front-line trenches or undergoing training, the men were kept busy by an endless number of chores, or fatigues. The work usually took the form of carrying parties — bringing supplies forward from the dumps and railheads in the rear areas — or engineering work — widening trenches, burying phone cables, repairing roads, and so on. This work was almost always done under the cover of darkness. One of the more dangerous fatigues was a wiring party. Wiring parties were anything but a party: stealing into No-Man's Land on a moonless night to erect or repair barbed wire entanglements. While away from the safety of the trenches, the men were in constant danger of being discovered by the enemy and being either shot or blown up. Consequently, great care was taken to be as silent as possible — difficult to do when you're trying to negotiate broken ground, in the dark, with a roll of barbed wire on your back or bundles of iron stakes under your arm. Usually, when a wiring party was at work, the battalion in the adjacent front lines would put out patrols to provide cover for the workers. As Deward remarks, however, most who went out on such work considered themselves lucky to get back.

May 11, 1917: Kept low all day. On burial detail all night, burying dead on our front-line trenches we had lost. Buried ten half-rotten; smell was awful — pulled one poor fellow's leg off. We had to dig them out of the trench or pull them out. We were supposed to dig a hole on top and bury them three feet [one metre] deep and put their rifle up for a mark, and get their identification discs; but it was pitch dark. The corporal would try to locate them and we would bury them by putting two or three in a shell hole and throwing dirt over them. It was too dangerous a place to waste time. I have failed terribly. I don't want that again.

The story of the Great War is often related by numbers: millions of men, thousands of shells, hundreds of miles of trenches, and so on. One of the saddest stories is told regarding the number of men who were reported missing and presumed dead. Roughly 49 percent of the 1,146,982 Great War soldiers commemorated by the Commonwealth War Graves Commission have no known grave.[91] The work of searching for the dead and burying them was often dangerous, as it was for Deward above, which meant the dead often went unburied — their bodies obliterated later by high explosives or merged with the earth upon which they lay. Even those in a marked grave were not safe, as many temporary battlefield burials (such as the ones Deward dug) were also destroyed by subsequent shellfire.

To provide identification in the event he was killed, each man was issued with a set of two disks prior to leaving the base depot for the front. Each disk had the same personal information stamped into it: rank, family name, initials, regimental number, some reference to the man's religious affiliation, and the unit to which the soldier belonged. The disks differed only in their colours or shapes — some sets had a red and a green disk, while other sets had a round and a hexagonal disk. The tags were made of either stamped leather or a dense, fibrous material and dangled from a cord around the soldiers' necks. Where a burial was possible, one disk was removed from the corpse and forwarded to the battalion paymaster for notification of next of kin and for record keeping. The other disk remained with the body.[92] It was usually the job of the unit's chaplain to make a record of the burials and then forward the details to the divisional burial officer.

Deward was clearly upset by this macabre duty and, presumably, felt defeated by his inability to bury the dead with the care and dignity he felt they deserved.

May 12, 1917: Kept low all day, on water party in afternoon to Farbus. Gas guard at night. Lucky if we get out at all. Shelled heavy all night, can't write yet. Water so scarce, it was always rationed out carefully and the days were terribly hot. Lucky to get anything at all. Read letters over in a funk hole, crummy and completely dead tired.

Germans put more shells over than ever around us, no sleep. Our battery put out of action, far worse than the Somme, hard fighting.

By making this reference to the Battle of the Somme, Deward is merely echoing the remarks of other, veteran members of the battalion. Having been at the front at this point for only four and a half weeks, Deward missed the tail end of the Somme fighting by six months.

May 13, 1917: Kept low all day. No water. My mouth and tongue blistered and parched, thirst is an awful thing. Hope we go out tonight. Relieved at 11:30 p.m.

Lasted from May 7, six days, mud head to feet, soaked through and lousy. Your clothes or equipment never off and never washed.

Very lucky to get out at all. Two Divisions of Germans had come over and they were retaliating for Vimy. It took them a month to get ready for it.

We left at 11.30 p.m.

This appears to be Deward's summary of the counterattack at Fresnoy.

May 14, 1917: Arrived at tents near Mont-St. Eloi at 3:30 a.m. The cooks had beans and mulligan heated up for us — and tea.

I ate two tins of mulligan. Slept and had breakfast at 10:00 a.m. dead tired and showed it. Must have lost 25 lbs. in six days. Marden and Mac came up to see me and I went back with them and had tea and brought back cake, tea, and candies as they had got four or five boxes between them.

"Mulligan" is a reference to Mulligan stew, a dish that was prepared from whatever was available at the time. Donald Fraser described a Mulligan that he prepared, "made from meat, crushed hardtack, rolled oats, and Oxo cubes, seasoned with salt and mustard."[93] When Deward says that he "ate two tins of Mulligan," the tin he refers to is his mess tin, a "combination tea-kettle and dinner set" that could be used both to heat food and to eat from.[94] The boxes that Marden and Mac shared with Deward were care packages sent from home. The contents of these packages often ended up in a Mulligan.

May 15, 1917: Up at 5:30 a.m. and on bath parade at 7:15 a.m. Machine gun inspection in the afternoon and [I] replaced all lost parts. Pay day and I received a box from Lucy, it was grand. I feel so lucky that I came out safe, the Canadians suffered heavy. Five days after, we left for the trenches again after being inspected by General Byng and having medals given out for deeds done at Vimy, on April 9.

Lucy Field was Deward's fiancé. They were married shortly after Deward returned to Canada and had two children: a daughter, who died in infancy, and a son, George, who is now a retired Toronto policeman.

Left rest camp for Mill Street trenches at 4:30 p.m. arriving at 8:00 p.m.

May 18, 1917: Couldn't sleep for lice but feeling good.

May 20, 1917: Feeling fine and had a dandy sleep at night.

May 21, 1917: On machine gun practice from 8:00 a.m. to 12:00 noon. Rain at night; miserable. Went to Zivy Cave, a German cave which is very steep with dandy tunnels and different places to get out. Running water in it and electric. Holds a couple of Battalions. Mill Street trenches near Pulpit Crater. We are in Divisional Reserves. Rain.

Deward would have reached Zivy Cave through Zivy Tunnel, one of the subways excavated in preparation for the attack on Vimy Ridge earlier that year. Zivy Cave itself predates the war and is one of the former chalk quarries that were converted into underground accommodations for the troops.

May 22, 1917: On machine gun duty from 6:00 p.m. to 9:00 p.m. for planes. Dandy sleep but lousy and it is raining.

May 23, 1917: On gas guard from 1:00 a.m. to 2:00 a.m. On machine gun duty from 11:00 a.m. to 4:00 p.m. firing at planes. Dandy day. Shelled at night. Stretcher Bearer Jones killed. Woke up by Stretcher Bearer Smith, told to move. His wind was up. I never move from a good place. Aeroplane fight at night, he got away. We have them beat in the air now for the first time. Rats and lice. I prefer rats any time, you can't get rid of lice. They get you nearly crazy.

The situation for the RFC improved considerably in May. Better aircraft and new tactics to counter the mass formations employed by the enemy combined to create a new and growing confidence among the RFC pilots in their ability to deal with the German fighters.[95]
To have your "wind up" meant that you were nervous or frightened. To "put the wind up" someone meant to frighten them or make them nervous.

May 24, 1917: Good old day, fine and just right. On the [Lewis] gun from 6:00 a.m. to 11:00 a.m. Always Horseman and I. I am

93

Number 2 on the Gun. I was the mess orderly; went down to Zivy Cave for water. Very lonely, but I had plenty to eat. Stretcher Bearer Smith told me his life, he must have been lonely too; [he was originally] from Columbus and Detroit, his correct name is, Frederick Young. Slept damp tonight. Litchfield Crater on left of Pulpit Crater [is nearby], where forty-five men were killed, it's a lovely landmark for them; April 10, 1917, is when they were killed. On gun duty from 4:00 p.m. to 9:00 p.m. Scratched all night long.

Being the mess orderly meant it was Deward's turn to gather the daily food rations for his platoon from the distribution point some distance behind the front line.

Stretcher-bearer George Smith was born Frederick Weyman Young in Columbus, Ohio, in 1896. Young, who in civilian life was a trained nurse, crossed into Canada at Detroit, Michigan, in March 1916 to join the 99th Battalion, which was then recruiting in Windsor, Ontario. He was one of approximately forty-seven hundred American citizens who came north of the border to join the Canadian Expeditionary Force. It was contrary to prevailing United States law for American citizens to enlist in the armed forces of a belligerent nation, so he probably enlisted under an assumed name to protect himself from detection and possible prosecution.[96]

Litchfield Crater lies approximately one kilometre east of Neuville-St. Vaast and is now a Commonwealth War Graves Commission cemetery. It is one of two mine craters that were used by the Canadian Corps Burial Officer for the interment of remains found on the surrounding battlefield in 1917. Nearby Zivy Crater is the other. Litchfield Crater now contains the remains of fifty-eight men from several nations, most of whom were killed on either April 9 or 10, 1917. Four of the men buried there belong to the 19th Battalion.[97]

May 26, 1917: Gun duty from 6:00 a.m. to 11:00 a.m. Nothing else to do. Left Mont-St. Eloi for front line at 9:00 p.m. arriving at the front line at 12:00 midnight.

May 27, 1917: Very quiet, not a shell coming. On duty from 12.15 a.m. to 2.15 a.m. Shelled for half an hour at about 1:00 a.m. very close too. A shell burst just in front of us and scattered earth over us. Horseman left our post. Our position is forty yards [thirty-five metres] in front of [our] front line, not a healthy place, and a good thing it is quiet. You had to go over land to get to our post and only when it was dark.

It was a very serious offence to leave your post. The maximum penalty was death. That Horseman lost control of himself and left the shelter of his post in No-Man's Land after a nearby shell burst suggests he might have been in the early stages of shell shock — what we today know as post-traumatic stress disorder. Since Horseman remained with the battalion, it appears that he regained himself and the incident was not reported.

May 28, 1917: On duty from 12:00 midnight to 2:00 a.m. I slept the whole day as we had to keep low in day-time. Dead tired; equipment always on and not much rest with it. McDonald and I are in a funk hole, not a shell all day. Shelled front line at night but we missed it. We had to put our gas respirators on.

May 29, 1917: On duty from 1:00 a.m. to 4:00 a.m. Got our rations at break of day. Slept until 9:30 a.m. Shelled roads in front of us for about fifty yards [forty-five metres] away.

May 30, 1917: Duty from 1:00 a.m. to 4:00 a.m. Read and slept in day-time, water is scarce. Dangerous position, sap leads into German trench which is barricaded. We can only get to our front line behind us overland at night. Couldn't sleep for lice.

From his description, it sounds like Deward's Lewis gun section was occupying an isolated strong point in No-Man's Land. Where the landscape in No-Man's Land allowed (for example, if there was a large crater or a section of disused trench), a strong point might be established, and occasionally fought over, to give one side or the other a degree of dominance in that locale. Deward's outpost appears to be at the head of a deserted German sap (a trench leading into No-Man's Land from the front line) that was blocked off by the Germans when they abandoned it.

May 31, 1917: Left the front line at 12:00 midnight after a quiet trip. These quiet trips were nerve-wrackers at night. Moved to Vimy railway station near an artillery position near Farbus. We got lost and arrived there at 3:15 a.m. Had tea and it sure went good. Not a healthy place though. The Germans knew we used it as there were all deep dug-outs along the railway bridge. On fatigue to the front line from 11:15 p.m. to 3:15 a.m. Lousy as can be, couldn't sleep. Breakfast at 3.15 a.m. Not much sleep since being in the front line. On front-line digging fatigue, making new trench connecting with Imperials. Left railway bridge at 9:00 p.m., arriving back at 3:00 a.m.

June 1, 1917: When going back went through trench for 300 or 400 yards [275 or 375 metres], through mud and water up to our knees. Soaked, kept low all day. No chance to post mail at all. Going on Divisional rest. "Are you crummy? I'll say so!"

"Are you crummy? I'll say so!" is probably a play on the title of a popular song at the time, "Are We Downhearted? NO! NO! NO!"

June 2, 1917: Left Vimy railway at 12:30 a.m. arrived Paynesley Tunnel at 2:00 a.m. Shelled on the way. Left Paynesley at 9:30 a.m., arrived at camp tents near Mont-St. Eloi at 12:30 p.m. La Targette and Camblain-L'Abbé nearby.

June 3, 1917: Left tents at 6:00 a.m. after having been polished up and all equipment and clothes replaced. Marching to attention most of the way as we are going out for Divisional rest for two months. It is very hot and we had to wear our steel helmets until, finally, we refused to wear them and took them off when we arrived at Verdrel (a one horse burg), where we were to spend our rest in French huts. At 3:00 p.m. the whole company had to do pack drill for two hours without any rest. That's what we got for not obeying orders on the march. During the whole rest we only drilled in the mornings, mostly. Of course you had duty to do once in a while of different kinds. Our rations were bad, we did not see much bread and when we did it was twelve to fifteen men on a small loaf (a thin slice for a day). We mostly had hardtack. Of course there were canteens around and if you had any money and were lucky enough to get in line before the biscuits were gone you were all right.

The YMCA's were close by. The first day out we had fish for the first time in France. Some fish! No ice and they were rotten! I would not eat any.

Verdrel is near Hersin and Barlin. While on rest we had all kinds of sports in the afternoons.

It might come across like cruelty for the army to insist that Deward and his comrades wear their helmets on the march and in the heat, but it was for their own protection. That day, the entire 4th Canadian Infantry Brigade was on the move, going into divisional reserve for rest and training, and as bitter experience had proved, large formations of troops on the move often attracted the unwanted attention of the enemy's artillery.[98] Much of the route they marched that day lay well within the range of the German long-range guns, which could wreak havoc with shrapnel bursts (the very thing helmets were meant to protect men from) on a column of marching men should they be detected.

When Deward mentions they spent their rest in "French huts," he means they were billeted in the town of Verdrel, as opposed to living under canvas in some camp.[99]

Pack drill was a form of punishment in which the men were required to practise their arms drill while wearing their heavy marching order, which we have already seen was a considerable burden.

Normally, Deward would have shared a loaf of bread each day with only two or three other men, but Donald Fraser noted, "when supplies are scarce it may run six to seven to one loaf and that loaf may be almost in crumbs."[100] We can only imagine the condition of a loaf given to feed fifteen! Hardtack (biscuits made from flour and water and baked until the consistency of sandstone) was a substitute for bread when supplies were scarce, but as Fraser also observed, "There are times when both bread and biscuits are scare. Rations, therefore, are up and down."[101]

As at Camp Borden, the YMCA operated canteens and huts in France and Belgium, just behind the lines. These huts, along with those operated by other charitable organizations such as the Salvation Army, were used extensively by the men to supplement their rations.[102]

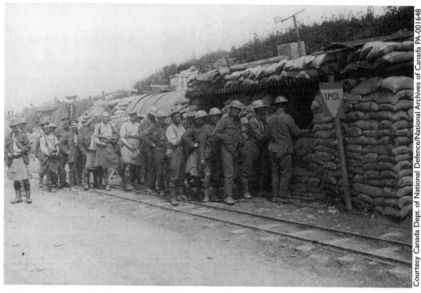

A Canadian YMCA hut in the Canadian area, August 1917. Huts like this one, dispensing coffee and other comforts to the men, were common throughout the war zone. Despite its sandbagged walls and roof, this hut is probably well to the rear of the fighting, since none of the men are wearing their respirator bags in the ready, or alert, positions. Note the narrow-gauge railway track running right in front of the hut's serving window.

June 7, 1917: We went to the ranges five miles [eight kilometres] away in Fresnicourt. The day before, I visited Gouy Servins and Petit Servins, all villages.

Deward's company spent the day at the ranges practising application shooting (how to compensate for atmospheric variables, such as crosswinds) and performing rapid fire exercises (firing twelve to fifteen shots a minute without any significant loss of accuracy).[103]

June 12, 1917: Gas guard from 2:45 a.m. to 5:00 a.m. We slept in long huts, three bunks over each other. Chicken wire for springs. It was dandy if you could miss the torn places.

June 16, 1917: Ball game between 18th and 19th Battalions. We lost sixteen to fourteen.

The training syllabus often included time for recreational sports.

June 18, 1917: Had compulsory brigade sports at Hersin about fourteen miles [twenty-three kilometres] away. We went in transport trucks; it was good; boxing and everything.

June 19, 1917: Inoculation in breast.

This was probably an inoculation against typhus.

June 20, 1917: Paraded sick, headache, and sore breast.

June 21, 1917: Bath parade to Gouy Servins.

John Becker of the 75th Battalion (which along with the 11th Canadian Infantry Brigade was also undergoing training in the Gouy Servins area) described his trip a week earlier to what probably was the same bath that Deward used:

> This particular bathhouse was a rough board building with a boiler fired by wood alongside. Inside we took off our clothes and threw underwear and socks in a heap at one end. The under-

wear was immediately grabbed by fatigue men
before it walked off under its own power. We
passed into another room and under long pipes
shooting streams of warm water. A sergeant-major
called "Soap on." We soaped for three minutes.
"Soap Off" — we had to immediately rinse ourselves as in another minute the water was shut off.
We passed on to the other end, wiped our louse
bitten hides, got clean towels, fumigated underwear, and resumed our clothes. The underwear
was what ever we were handed. Some of it had
been used for a long time … It was supposed to be
free from livestock [lice], but this didn't take into
account the babies that had laid their eggs in the
seams of my trousers and tunic, and an hour later
I was providing a dinner for those eggs and all
their brothers and sisters.[104]

June 24, 1917: Scrubbed and cleaned equipment with soap
and water all day and evening. From now on we start drilling
in afternoons.

July 1, 1917: Church parade to Hersin-Coupigny.

July 2, 1917: No parades. Saw the 29th Battalion go past;
McFadden, Cecil Martin, W. Clayton and dozens more, this is
their first time in a fighting unit.

These were all men with whom Deward served in the 180th
Battalion and who were later sent to the 123rd Battalion. They
were transferred into the 29th Battalion in late May.[105]

July 3, 1917: We left Verdrel; our rest is shot. We left at 3:00
p.m. arriving at Appleby Farm at 4:45 p.m. Billeted in farm-
house barns (stone floors) near Bully Grenay. Met McFadden,
he went into lines that night. Just before we arrived there a

man in the 22nd Battalion had been tied to a cross and shot. The cross was still there, had not been taken down yet (just because he was afraid and deserted).

The 19th Battalion's *War Diary* tells us their destination was Marqueffles Farm, not Appleby Farm, as Deward suggests above. Marqueffles Farm was a well-established camp and training area in the Lens sector, just north of Notre Dame de Lorette.[106]

On April 4, 1917, Gustav Comte deserted from the 22nd Battalion while moving into the front lines for the assault on Vimy Ridge. Two days later, another 22nd Battalion man, Joseph Lalancette, also went missing. They were discovered together five weeks later in Le Havre and arrested. Both men (each with previous convictions for being absent without leave) were found guilty of desertion by separate field general courts martial and sentenced to suffer death by shooting. The sentence was executed concurrently in the early hours of July 3. They lie buried next to each other in the communal cemetery-extension at the village of Aix-Noulette.[107]

The detail about the cross is puzzling. An eyewitness account of the Comte and Lalancette executions tells us that both men were seated in chairs when they were shot, which appears to have been the more common practice.[108] However they met their end, Deward clearly had some sympathy for them.

July 4, 1917: A man in our battalion was court-martialed and given two years hard labour.

July 5, 1917: Went to Bully Grenay for bath. We left farm at 7:00 a.m.

July 8, 1917: Arriving at Fosse 10 (Sains-en-Gohelle), between Bully and Hersin, near Petit Sains, downtown at night; lovely town.

Canadians on their way to pay Fritz a visit, July 1917. This photo of the 19th Battalion on the march was most likely taken on the afternoon of July 3, 1917, while on its the way to Marqueffles Farm. The battalion's *War Diary* notes only two occasions during July 1917 that the 19th Battalion moved en masse during daylight hours, and only once did the band march in front of the Headquarters Company — we can see two mounted figures to the rear of the band, presumably the lieutenant-colonel and his adjutant. The 19th Battalion was one of several units to have a pipe band even though they were not a kilted, or Highland, battalion. The tradition probably came from the 91st Regiment of Canadian Militia, a true Highland regiment (now the Argyll and Sutherland Highlanders of Canada), which supplied the 19th Battalion with many of its original officers and all four of its commanding officers.

In this context, the French word *fosse* refers to a mining pit. This area of northern France is dotted with coal mines. Considering the nature of small, provincial mining towns, you might suspect that when Deward says he went "downtown at night; lovely town" he is being more than just a little ironic.

July 9, 1917: We were paid fifteen francs. Bought eggs and chips and black coffee. We left Fosse 10 at 9:00 p.m.

Eggs and chips (that is, fried eggs and chunks of fried potato) were staples of *estaminet* fare — a kind of early twentieth-century

102

fast food. Strictly speaking, an *estaminet* is a regular bar or café, but those just behind the lines were more frequently rough-and-tumble establishments improvised by the proprietor in the front rooms of her home or in the outbuildings of a farm. These *estaminets* were another place that soldiers could go to complement their rations or to get a hot drink, like coffee or tea — or something stronger, like sweetened wine or watered-down beer.

As historian Jonathan Vance commented:

> The *estaminet* [was] the focal point of a soldier's life out of the trenches. In these rough cafés, the men could feast ... soothe their nerves ... flirt with barmaids, and sing bawdy songs. It was a setting that came to symbolize much that was good about the soldier's war. Indeed, if the symbols revered at unit reunions are any indication, the metaphor for the Great War was not mud, or barbed wire, or an endless row of headstones; it was the *estaminet*.[109]

July 10, 1917: Through Bully, Calonne and arrived at the front line at 1:00 a.m. Hard march, no sleep. Very quiet, but on duty night and day for two days. German outposts and snipers in houses one hundred yards [ninety metres] away. Kept low in daytime, we had to go overland to get there. No communications trench, we were in the front line.

The part of the line into which Deward was sent ran through the ruins of Lens, a large industrial town to the north of Vimy Ridge. This was a peculiar section of the line. In places the front-line trenches were little more than the connected cellars of destroyed houses. Donald Fraser, who was in Lens at the same time as Deward, described the area:

> The hostile line is difficult to figure out ... the trench system has broken down. We sleep in cellars and observe from the ruins of houses. Both sides,

103

therefore, are in precarious positions and may be said to hold their lines in little groups, disconnected for most and liable to surprise attacks. Troops skulk around the houses watching from corners and door entrances.[110]

A communication trench was any trench that linked one organized trench line to another (linking, for example, the front-line trench with the support line trench that ran parallel to it and some distance in the rear). They allowed men and material to pass between the two lines in relative safety.

July 11 and 12, 1917: Relieved at 1:00 a.m.

July 13, 1917: Arriving back at Maroc at 4:00 a.m. through Calonne and Bully. On our way out, two fellows were injured by accident. Bomb went off in pocket, pin must have been loose. [Lance Sergeant] Leonard of 19th and a 173rd fellow both died in afternoon. Had a bath half an hour's walk away. In the evening we were shelled and I changed my mind about sleeping on top of ground. Slept cold that night on brick arched cellar and the next night.

The "173rd fellow" would have been a reinforcement to the 19th Battalion who had joined up originally with the 173rd Battalion (from Hamilton, Ontario).

Deward must be mistaken about the death of Leonard, as his name appears in battalion orders later in August, confirming his promotion to the rank of sergeant on July 15.[111]

Considering the number of lethal weapons stored and transported in such close proximity to people, accidents like this must have been fairly common. Will Bird, for example, witnessed two similar incidents in a single twenty-four-hour period, one of which caused multiple fatalities.[112]

July 15, 1917: Real happy, received box from Lucy. It was swell.

Boxes from home were yet another way the men had of supplementing their diet and obtaining personal comforts. Sid Cane recorded the contents of one such box in his diary: "Received parcel Nov. 8, posted Sept. 19, containing smokes, cake, handkerchiefs, chocolate, gum, thin underwear, socks, tea, soap, health salts, Oxo, white precipitate powder, camphor, two lumps sugar."[113]

July 16, 1917: We left Maroc again for the front line with "B" Company. Only half the battalion going in and, as I am in "A" Company, our company was staying out, but they had to have all the [Lewis] gun sections go in, which meant an extra trip for me. Had to go overland; again no communications trench. Very quiet even though the Germans are one hundred yards [ninety metres] away. Rained all day.

July 17, 1917: Got exciting. Rain at night, no funk holes. We slept in the wet muddy trench, soaked through. Fish Tails and Rum Jars (trench mortars, I dreaded trench mortar shells), the first I had seen. Oh my! Fish Tails about 5 feet [150 centimetres] long and about 8 or 10 inches [20 or 25 centimetres] in diameter with fins on. The explosion is awful. In the daytime you could hear the gun pop (sounded like pulling a cork) and then hear the shell when it got to its height and began to come down. At night you could hear the pop and you would know what direction to look, and when it was going up you could see the fuse burning and could tell the direction it was going. If it was coming your way (watch out), run to the left as the shell had a tendency to go to its left, it seemed. They made you think of home. Came out of front line at 1:00 a.m.

At 190 pounds, the Aerial Torpedo was the largest of the German trench mortar bombs, and this is probably what Deward describes as a "Fish Tail." Both sides used trench mortars throughout the war, a type of light artillery used to lob high-explosive bombs from one front-line trench system into another. Because of their high trajectory and relatively low velocity, the mortar bombs were often easy to spot in the air. "Rum Jars," "Flying Pigs," and "Flying Sausages," nicknames suggesting their appearance in flight, were some of the different bombs that Deward might have encountered during a tour of the front line.

July 19, 1917: Arriving at supports in German dugout, under a sheet, at 3:30 a.m. Waited for water and received letters at 4:00 a.m. Some class Liévin town. Under shellfire. Rained day and night, slept good at night.

This area was occupied by the Germans until April 1917, when it was recaptured by Imperial troops, hence the German dugout in which Deward found himself under a sheet.

July 20, 1917: Left Fosse 3 Liévin at 11:30 p.m. arrived at the front line again at 12.30 a.m. I must have liked the front line it would seem, I had plenty of it. But they were quiet — you might say. Hot in daytime and cold at nights.

July 22, 1917: Left the front line at 12:30 a.m. and arrived at Fosse 10 at 4:30 a.m. Passed through Fosse 3 Liévin, Marble Arch, Calonne, and Bully. Passed hundreds of guns in the bushes and on the sides of roads. Getting ready and placed for Hill 70 Battle. Thousands of machine guns on that front. The next few days we practised over tapes, getting ready for Hill 70. Practising an advance over tapes proved a failure, the tapes were laid out as streets and buildings according to area maps and named before you got there. Each man was supposed to know what street or lane to go down when the real thing came (all bosh).

In preparation for the upcoming attack on Hill 70, the participating divisions of the Canadian Corps practised much as they had before the attack on Vimy Ridge. As Maj. David Corrigal of the 20th Battalion recorded:

We practiced the attack on a taped area at Marqueffles Farm, representing the trenches over which our advance was to be made. Some of the practices were carried out at dawn and were done first by companies, then by the battalion, and finally by the whole brigade. We rehearsed the plan repeatedly until every method had been tried and tested. We studied a large scale plaster model of the area, which was not only interesting but turned out to be most helpful.[114]

Judging from Deward's reaction to the training, the men in the trenches had less regard for the preparations than did their officers.

July 24, 1917: Went to church at Bouvigny Woods.

July 25, 1917: Went to ranges at Marqueffles farm, marched for half an hour with [gas] masks on. Given plenty of ranges and gas lectures.

The need for gas lectures was probably greater now than ever. Mustard gas was unleashed on the battlefield for the first time just twelve days before Deward wrote this entry, and its appearance brought a new level of misery to the troops. Unlike previous gasses, which dispersed fairly quickly, mustard gas was persistent. When the artillery shell that delivered the gas exploded, it spread an oily liquid that slowly evaporated, often taking days or even weeks to fully disperse. In the meantime, if a soldier came in contact with the liquid or its vapour, either directly or from exposure to contaminated clothing or equipment, he would fall victim to its insidious effects. As one Canadian historian notes:

Mustard gas was a slow acting agent that killed the nerve cells so that the victim would only start to feel the effects hours after being gassed. Eyes became inflamed and swollen, skin blistered, and

107

men vomited uncontrollably. Upon being taken to the [casualty] clearing stations, the gas cases became hoarse, coughed harshly, and went blind. On the second and third days the victims began to die. Not only did mustard gas kill, burn, and incapacitate, it also consigned the soldier to a permanent state of unease. With every puddle an imagined trap, with every patch of ground possibly containing a substance that burned and blinded men, it left the already exhausted soldiers with no rest, physically and mentally.[115]

July 26 and 27, 1917: Rain. Fosse 10 was the largest town we had been in, slept in houses across from mine. Used to see young girls, about twenty, carry two bags of coal on their backs. Girls worked in the mines.

The manpower demands of the French army meant that many French women had to assume non-traditional roles to ensure that the economy, and hence the war effort, continued to roll along.

August 4, 1917: We left Fosse 10 at 9:30 p.m. arriving at supports 150 yards [140 metres] behind front line in cellar (jake place); City of Saint Théodore.

Cité Saint Théodore is a suburb of Lens.

August 6, 1917: Shelled all day.

August 7, 1917: Gassed all day. All kinds of machine guns and always plenty of shelling but few casualties so far. French cellars built for war, arched brick roofs. You could see whole towns right down to the ground but half the cellars would be good and still standing. The whole country in fact was built for war, crooked sunken roads, etc.

August 8, 1917: The 18th Battalion made a raid on a 200-yard [180-metre] frontage back to the German supports. We were not called to the front line but left in supports. Saint Théodore at 2:00 a.m.

This raid also included platoons from the 20th and 21st Battalions. Although the raiders were able to gather information about the enemy's local defences, the intelligence came with a heavy price. Retaliatory artillery and machine gun fire enfiladed the raiders as they withdrew from the German lines and inflicted numerous casualties. The total bill for the raid was forty-nine men killed, wounded, or missing.[116]

August 10, 1917: The cellar we were in was big but dirty. Must have been a brewery or hotel. They had lousy chicken wire beds in it. We arrived back at Fosse 10 at 5:30 a.m. passing through Cité Saint Pierre, Bully Grenay.

August 11, 1917: Had photos taken, Bell, Patterson and I. I was pretty well worn out from those long hikes. Though on a dangerous front, it was pretty quiet. I did not like quiet times. It generally meant something.

We left Fosse 10 at 9:30 p.m. for reserves arriving at 2:00 a.m. We weren't to miss anything.

The Bell that Deward had his picture taken with was his section mate, William Bell. However, it isn't clear who Patterson was. On the photograph, someone has written "Patterson 99th Batt." The 99th Battalion had two Pattersons on its roll, Charles Patterson and Harvey Patterson (there was also a Martin Paterson, but we'll assume that Deward got the spelling right). Since Harvey Patterson was two centimetres [one inch] shorter than Deward, and the person in the photograph appears to be at least as tall as Deward, it may be that the third person in the picture is Charles Patterson.[117]

Deward, Bell (seated), and Patterson. This photograph was printed on a postcard so that it could be mailed home. Deward sent this to Lucy, and wrote: "Dear Lucy, After all, I'll send this but for heaven sake don't show it to anyone, ha ha some tough guys eh! [signed] Dewy XX." William Bell would be killed at Passchendaele later that November.

Courtesy Barnes family collection

My nerves were always good untill I... I had my last leave from France Sept 1918 maybe on accou... lasting so long the thought of what was in front of us. I then started to... my nerves I have never got over it, since I came home I have always tried to work hard to... for... years experience but could never do it, so I class myself as a war wreck, which people will never under-stand

CHAPTER 5

Hill 70 to Passchendaele,
August 15 to November 5, 1917

"I picked out the best place I could see, but a 21st fellow
was right behind it with half his body shot away."

August 15, 1917: [Hill 70 was] the greatest artillery fight I had ever seen. It was a beautiful sight of artillery duels (if you could take the horses out of it). The Germans, as well as us, always opened up immediately. Either side started day or night, machine guns were as thick as could be.

In early July, the Canadian Corps was ordered to mount a holding attack on the city of Lens. Originally, the operation's sole purpose was to engage a large number of enemy troops and thus prevent them from reinforcing their comrades further north at Ypres, where Haig was attempting a breakout to clear the Belgian coast of U-boat bases (known as the Third Battle of Ypres). However, Lt. Gen. Sir Arthur Currie, the newly appointed commander of the Canadian Corps, did not like the idea of attacking without a specific, tactical objective and was concerned that if the Canadian troops took Lens, they would be left in an exposed position on the low ground between the Sallaumines Hill to the south and Hill 70 to the north. In a conference with Gen. Sir Henry Horne, commander of the 1st Army (the formation with which the Canadian Corps was then serving), Currie is reported to have said, "If we [are] to fight at all, let us fight for something worth having."

Currie proposed taking Hill 70 from the Germans and winning dominance of the heights instead of being subjected to it. Haig accepted Currie's plan, and by August 15, all was ready for the first Canadian-conceived, Canadian-led, and Canadian-executed battle of the Great War.

Although many veterans became inured to the human suffering that they witnessed, most could never get used to the suffering of the draft horses, who, once at the front, had a life expectancy of only six days.[118] Perhaps this is what we are hearing in Deward's comment, "if you could take the horses out of it."

The Canadians had the famous British Lahore Battery behind them (never failed). However, our section was put into a house cellar and had to keep our fighting equipment on for a few minutes' notice. While we were waiting a shell landed just outside the door, blew our curtain down, and put the candles out.

The Lahore Battery to which Deward refers was actually the 4th Brigade, Royal Field Artillery. This brigade had been supporting the 3rd, and later the 4th, Canadian Division since early 1916. It began the war in support of the 3rd (Lahore) Division of the Indian Army, hence its name, but was transferred to the Canadians after the Lahores were sent to Palestine.

The 19th Battalion was assigned the role of support in the initial attacks at Hill 70, and this is why Deward and his mates were sheltering in a cellar, with their equipment on, waiting to move on very short notice.

The curtain blown down by the shell was probably a gas curtain. These were heavy pieces of fabric, usually treated with some sort of neutralizing agent and kept damp, that were hung over the entrances to cellars to prevent poison gas from infiltrating and collecting there. Gas curtains were supposed to hang over the entrance to any shelter that was below grade.

Advance started at 4:10 a.m. zero hour.

The Canadians [21st Battalion] reached their objective but lost the first trench later on. At 2:00 p.m. after a heavy loss they were out of munitions, we were suddenly called on to help and relieve them. They lost two-thirds of their men.

We started under very heavy shelling. I don't know how any of us got there. We started to keep to the trenches and just got nicely started when six men in front of me got blown up. I was the next and missed it. We all got out of the trench and went overland. Trusting to Providence, we had to go anyway. We ran all the way regardless of shells. It was terrible then, the way men got cut up. My Number 1 gunner was killed, the corporal grabbed the gun. There were dozens killed and wounded — your pals going down around you — but you had to go on.

After a hard run, and with our load of everything for an advance, we finally got to the line the 21st Battalion was holding, as they had lost the original objective. There were only half a dozen men holding the line [frontage] of a company. Weren't they glad to see us!

An anonymous 19th Battalion report on the action around Lens from August 15 to 17 suggests that "C" Company, 21st Battalion, which was defending the position Deward's platoon relieved, was "practically wiped out."[119]

We got orders (signs) to extend and go over-the-top on a bayonet charge to take back the original line. We did (all played out from the long excited run, we didn't get time to breathe). Yelling and shouting at them, they got frightened. Seeing reinforcements charging they scrambled back as fast as they could. Some jumped out of the trench so they could go faster. We killed a few with our rifles but did not have to bayonet any. We took the trench and the men dug in their positions as fast as possible.

It isn't clear what Deward means by "signs." He may be referring to a system of pre-arranged hand signals that could be used in place of vocal commands. The Germans evacuated the trench (marked "Chicory Trench" on the maps) so quickly that they left behind some wounded men of the 21st Battalion, whom they had taken prisoner.[120]

Our section was moved out over the glacis to a trench that ran directly into the Germans' new front line where he had [set up] a block. We had no way of communicating with our own front line. The German block was about 150 yards [140 metres] or so down the trench. We had one end and they had the other. We were an outpost. We dug in at 4:30 p.m.

The "glacis" was the area in front of the trench. Historically, it was a gentle slope of ground that led down from the top of a fortified wall and exposed attacking forces to fire from the defending garrison. In the Great War, this role — for all practical purposes — was served by No-Man's Land.

At this point, the officer commanding No. 2 Platoon, Lieut. James Bennett, had only 27 men to hold 275 metres (300 yards) of line. His first concern was to consolidate the position, and he did this by establishing a machine gun outpost (Deward's section) in front of his main trench to cover the approaches. Bennett also established a party of bombers forward of the main trench, as Deward notes below. Their position was even more precarious than realized, as there was a 180-metre (200-yard) gap in the line to their left, covered by only one trench mortar. Had the enemy counterattacked into the gap, No. 2 Platoon might well have been wiped out as well. Lieutenant Bennett showed a good tactical grasp of the situation immediately to his front and is credited with "making a little ... go a long way."[121]

It was hell! Heavy casualties and the trenches were all torn to pieces by shells. I picked out the best place I could see but a 21st fellow was right behind it with half his body shot away. It was the best spot, so I dug a hole (funk hole) in front of him and threw the dirt over him. Maybe he was never found. War is hell. I did not get his disc, hadn't time. The main thing is to dig in and get ready for an attack. We had to watch ourselves here. We put bombers on the side where Heiney had the block and then a [Lewis] gun post. No sleep that night, just watch; and on guard all next day. No eats. Only four men were left out of our section of eight, so we four men had to hold that post.

August 16, 1917: Just when it was getting dark we saw two men coming from No-Man's Land. I halted them but they kept coming until they got too close. I halted again but [they did not] stop, and as it was too dark to recognize them, I threw a Mills bomb at them. It dropped in the mud at their feet and did not go off (lucky). When they got real close they told us who they were, they had gone too far ahead and lay in a hole all day until it was dark enough. One was slightly wounded and needed help. We directed them out.

Sat sleeping in funk hole, during my time off, and was wakened up suddenly, half-buried up. A shell had hit on the parapet over my head and blew it in.

Deward might well have been half-buried by one of his own shells, some of which were dropping short of the mark. Lieut. Andrew Borrowman, an accountant from Calgary and the officer commanding No. 4 Platoon, was killed the same day by one of those shortfalls.

On August 16, an incident occurred on Deward's front that he does not record but that he must have witnessed and to which he is probably alluding when he says on August 17, "We weren't thinking of souvenirs." The incident reveals the strain that the men were under and was recorded by another eyewitness:

> One of our men (who from his actions appeared to be unhinged) jumped out of the trench, chased a German overland, caught him square in the back with a bomb and killed him. Instead of returning immediately as he could have done in comparative safety, he proceeded deliberately to search the body for souvenirs, and while doing so was sniped in the

115

shoulder and leg. Two men attempted to get him in. One was wounded and the other killed. Pte. Brennan, who had previously done splendid work, then crawled out with the same object, but was instantly shot through the head. The cause of all this now began to wriggle about in an attempt to get in and was immediately riddled with m.g. [machine gun] bullets. A costly souvenir hunt.[122]

August 17, 1917: No eats. Almost every hour there would be an artillery fight. It was wonderful to look at. We missed most of the shells there; they were in front of us and behind. About 10:00 a.m. an artillery officer found his way here. There was some wire in front of the German trench we were guarding and he wanted to get closer to it, to see what it was like. We told him we must be lost from the company as we had seen no one and had had no eats. He promised to report this and have some bread sent up to us from his quarters. He asked for volunteers to go up to the trench with him (we had only gone up a short distance the first day we were there and only saw a few German dead up as far as a traverse). Corporal Abrahams and myself volunteered. On the way up we went around this traverse using both ways. It was full of German dead. We were not sure how far up the Germans had the block. We kept on going; there were dead all the way up (our artillery must have hit that mark alright). We were getting pretty well up the trench, going along carefully. We weren't thinking of souvenirs — knew we could not go much farther.

George Abrahams was a native of Argyle, Ontario, and a nineteen-year-old student when he enlisted with the 123rd Battalion at Toronto in late 1915. He was later wounded at Passchendaele.[123]

The officer says, "We will just go a little bit farther and that will do me." Just then a German plane came over, we did not hear it before. It flew very low, the two men were as plain as could be.

We crouched into the side of the trench and were afraid to fire. We were too near the Germans. We came back to our post. He took Abrahams' and my name and said we would get a strong recommend [for a decoration]. We heard when we got out that he had been killed taking too much risk.

No eats. That made our third day without anything to eat, not a bite. The shelling kept up at intervals and during this day he made fourteen tries to come over in battle formation from City Saint Auguste direction, which was at a right angle in front of us making towards our front. He never got more than halfway over; the artillery would cut them up every time. That was in daylight. We still had our four men.

Another of Deward's marginal sketches. This one shows the trench and traverse that Deward, George Abrahams, and an artillery officer reconnoitred on August 17, 1917, during the fighting at Hill 70.

Deward's statement about being without food for three days is confirmed by a 19th Battalion report on the attack at Hill 70. This might have been one of the three occasions on which Deward dipped into his iron rations.

While creating his plans for the attack on Hill 70, Currie was well attuned to the likelihood of swift and determined German counterattacks and "planned to turn this German sensitivity towards the loss of Hill 70 to his own advantage."[124] As soon as the crest of the hill was achieved, previously devised arrangements for defence were quickly put into place. These included the use of ground-based observers equipped with telephones and aerial reconnaissance using wireless radio (for the first time ever in battle) to help register the heavy artillery on counterattacking forces as they were forming up. As each counterattack began to mass, it was destroyed by a tornado of artillery fire. The General Staff at

Canadian Corps headquarters had even anticipated how long it would take reinforcements to reach the German front lines and from what directions they would come. These units were subsequently met by, and destroyed with, equally ferocious barrages in the rear areas while they were moving toward the front lines. By these means, no fewer than twenty-one German counterattacks were broken up between August 15 and 18.[125]

At night it was always wonderful to look at, with the flares and breaking of shells. I never saw so much all the time I was in France.

August 18, 1917: At 2:00 a.m. we were relieved, thank goodness, by fresh troops. An officer was with that section of [Lewis] gunners (6th Brigade) who had relieved us. He had been drinking and was smoking a cigar. We told him to watch that cigar and gave him all we knew about our front. On our way out we had to go through gas and shellfire, wearing respirators. I couldn't stand the full mask over my face, just used the mouthpiece.

It was no wonder that Deward hated wearing the device. Inside the respirator's mask, there was a nose clip that pinched off the wearer's nostrils and a rubber mouthpiece that he clenched between his teeth and through which he sucked in his breath (the mouthpiece was connected by a rubber hose to a filter canister). By peeling back the rubberized mask and using just the mouthpiece, Deward was demonstrating bad gas discipline and was exposing himself to a severe injury and possibly death had he been inundated with the new mustard gas, which was in wide use at Hill 70.[126] As with the unexploding Mills bomb earlier, he was lucky.

It was pitch dark and as we always go in Indian file, our sergeant was in the rear. He had been drinking and was swearing and stumbling, and was going to kill the man in front if he didn't wait for him. You couldn't see your hand in front of you and between stumbling and falling and hurrying and wearing that mask we were glad to get out. When you go in file, if the first man just goes at an easy gait the last man will almost have to run.

In "Indian file" means in single file.

We went to Cité Saint Pierre and stayed there until night. Just after we were relieved the Germans came over on the 6th Brigade in Indian file, but were forced back. We went three days without anything to eat. We moved back to an old front-line winter trench, arriving at 12:00 a.m. Miracle to get through it all, only seven left in No. 2 Platoon out of twenty-eight, dead all over. Tough game.

On their way out of the line, "A" Company was caught by two separate hostile barrages and became widely scattered as they sought shelter. Lieutenant Bennett reached Cité St. Pierre later that evening along with five other men (Deward presumably among them); the rest of the battered company straggled in the following day. This had been a "tough game" indeed, but in the words of one 19th Battalion officer, "The men of Lieut. Bennett's devoted little party 'played up splendidly' throughout, holding on — under Lieut. Bennett's own inspiring example — uncomplainingly and with the greatest fortitude."

For their roles in the action at Hill 70, Bennett was awarded the Military Cross, and Deward's section leader, Corporal Cowan, who "did great execution with his machine gun," was awarded the Military Medal.[127]

Currie recorded in his diary that Hill 70 was "altogether the hardest battle in which the Corps has participated."[128] And it was a victory. As a holding attack, the Canadian plan succeeded brilliantly. Five German divisions were engaged and severely mauled. The Germans not only had to replace these losses but, faced with the real possibility of a continued offensive on the Lens front, could not detach troops for service further north in Belgium. Hill 70 remained in British hands for the remainder of the war.

August 19, 1917: Ration party at 1:00 a.m. Slept cold.

August 20, 1917: Rested. Advance by 6th Brigade on Assiniboia Trench. Nothing for us to do during the day. 6th Brigade got cut up and, short of ammunition, used bayonets all day — lost trench.

While Deward's account of the 6th Brigade attack is essentially correct, the brigade's objective was Cinnabar Trench, not Assiniboia Trench as reported.

August 21, 1917: At 9:00 p.m. moved farther up to reserves but were not called. While we were at Cité Saint Théodore from August 4 to 10, we were in a dandy cellar and had not much to do and plenty to eat. All we did was mostly in ration parties. We used to have all kinds of different ways to cook things, the whole of our section was together; we had a fire in the cellar and made our own tea, etc. But the worst thing was going after our own water. We generally took turns, two at a time; we had to go quite a way through trenches. Sure enough we always got shelled, too close to make it a pleasure. We generally went after it at about 5:00 a.m. but no matter what time we went, he always shelled where the water was. When he got through shelling we would always make a run for the water and get away. Believe me, we were nearly caught more than once.

August 22, 1917: 6th Brigade took back [Cinnabar] trench. A terrible trip. Left reserves at 11:45 p.m. from Cité Saint Pierre and arrived at Bouvigny Huts at 2:30 a.m.

August 24, 1917: Passed through Aix-Noulette, Marqueffles Farm. Had breakfast at 3:00 a.m. Left at 5:00 p.m. for Villers-au-Bois, one-hour march; feeling good. Villers-au-Bois was where we spent most of our rests in between trips around this part of the line; drilling, etc.

August 28, 1917: I left for a course at the Divisional School. Left Villers at 2:30 p.m. arriving by bus at Lières at 5:00 p.m. for a ten-day course. We got real parade soldiering here, everything was done quickly and you had to be spic and span. I hated it.

Soldiers often went on training courses to help them acquire new skills or brush up on old ones. Although Deward doesn't mention specifically what course he attended, advanced training was given in musketry, anti-gas procedures, trench warfare, machine gunnery, Lewis gunnery, signalling, and so on. Training offered the man a break from the battalion routine and some respite from the anxiety of the front lines, but judging by Deward's reaction, those discomforts might have been preferable to the horrors of "parade soldiering."

September 2, 1917: I paraded sick from trench cancer, running sores all up one leg. The doctor used to pull scabs off and put ointment over them. I had them for about three months. I was the Orderly Corporal one day.

From his description of the symptoms and the treatment he received, it's likely that Deward's "trench cancer" was a case of impetigo, a highly contagious bacterial skin infection that was a fairly common condition among the troops at the front.

September 8, 1917: Left school, Lières, at 10:00 a.m. arriving at Villers-au-Bois at 12:30 p.m. I didn't miss a trip [to the front lines], the battalion was out [of the line for rest and training].

September 14, 1917: Left Villers-au-Bois 12:30 p.m. for Paynesley Tunnel. We had machine gun practice, [firing] from one side of a crater to the other. We hit a dud shell, which exploded and wounded two. W. Mills hit in stomach. Left Paynesley Tunnel 8:30 p.m.

September 17, 1917: Arriving at the railway right of Lens at 10:30 p.m. Heiney's sunken road.

September 18, 1917: Working party at night.

September 19, 1917: Fatigue at night.

On September 18 and 19, about 250 men from the 19th Battalion, including Deward, spent the night digging, then widening a new front-line trench.[129]

September 20, 1917: Left Heiney Road at 9:30 p.m. Passed Neuville-St. Vaast, Mont-St. Eloi, arriving at Camblain- L'Abbé at 2:30 a.m.

September 21, 1917: Over tapes.

Although the 19th Battalion's *War Diary* also mentions training over tapes, it does not say specifically what the training was for or what form it took.[130]

September 25, 1917: Moved to Neuville-St. Vaast.

September 26, 1917: We do mostly work from now on.

From September 25 to 30, various working parties from the 19th Battalion built trenches and buried signal wires for buzzers and telephones.[131]

October 2, 1917: Not feeling good. Left Neuville-St. Vaast at 7:30 p.m. and arrived at close supports in Canada Trench; air duty all day.

Deward's service record does not reveal that he received any medical attention on this date, so whatever ailed him must not have been serious.

October 3, 1917: Working party at night, digging a jumping-off trench.

A "jumping-off trench" could be either a sap or a shallow trench in advance of, and parallel to, the front-line trenches. They were used by patrols or trench raiders to gain a foothold in No-Man's Land without alerting the enemy to their presence.

October 4, 1917: Warned for patrol, took a rifle, bomb, soft cap, and no equipment. [The patrol, however, was] cancelled.

The "soft cap" Deward mentions was probably some form of knitted hat, either the "cap comforter" or a balaclava. The cap comforter was a knitted tube that you could wear either pulled down past your chin and around your neck to keep your throat warm or rolled into a toque. In mid-1917 the balaclava replaced the cap comforter as an official issue. Raiders preferred to leave their helmets behind and don these shapeless types of headwear because, at night, they showed a far less distinct silhouette against the skyline.[132]

October 5, 1917: Moved from Canada Trench to front line for three days (quiet).

October 8, 1917: Left front line to [the Vimy] Ridge through the worst rainstorm I was ever in. Covered with mud, couldn't keep my feet, pitch dark, the clay soil was slippery. Sometimes you would step on the side of a shell hole and go skating. We lost track of time but it was a hard march. Moved back to Balloons, Neuville-St. Vaast. Then moved to Villers-au-Bois.

The "balloons" at Neuville-St. Vaast were almost certainly observation balloons. See Deward's diary entry and the accompanying note for April 7, 1917.

October 10, 1917: We left Villers again.

October 15, 1917: At 9:00 a.m. marched twenty kilometres [twelve miles] to Duval arriving at 5:00 p.m. Had supper at 8:00 p.m.

October 20, 1917: On guard. The first day I had not smoked a cigarette.

Smoking was, perhaps, the soldier's greatest pastime — in the trenches and out of them. One Canadian soldier observed:

> To him [the soldier] the cigarette is the panacea for all ills. I have seen men die with a cigarette between their lips — the last favour they had requested on earth. If the soldier is in pain, he smokes for comfort; when he receives good news, he smokes for joy; if the news is bad, he smokes for consolation; if he is well — he smokes; when he is ill — he smokes. But good news or bad, sick or well, he always smokes.[133]

Smoking also had a practical application in the detection of phosgene gas poisoning — the "tobacco reaction." Sometimes the soldier's first indication of exposure to phosgene gas was the strange taste or smell it gave to tobacco smoke.[134]

October 24, 1917: Left Duval at 12:00 midnight, marching ten kilometres [six miles] to the station near Saint Pol. Train left at 4:00 a.m.

October 25, 1917: On our way to Belgium. Arrived at Hazebrouck about 5:00 p.m. Thirteen hours on the train. Slept in tents about twenty minutes from town.

While the Canadian Corps was recuperating from the operations at Hill 70, Haig's plan to free the Belgian coast had ground to a virtual halt in the face of dual opposition: the determined

German defenders and the terrain, which had become a swamp under the heavy autumn rains. With winter approaching, it appeared that Haig would now have to content himself with winning just the high ground a few kilometres east of Ypres. To accomplish this, he turned to the now rested Canadian Corps. In response, the Canadians started moving north to Belgium in mid-October and began their preparations for the capture of a pulverized town called Passchendaele — and, eventually, the barely perceptible ridge atop which it sat.

The Canadian plan, drafted by Currie, was to capture the objective in three bounds, each separated by a brief pause of a day or two to bring forward the artillery and relieve exhausted attacking troops with fresh ones. The first bound was scheduled to start at 5:40 a.m., October 26.

October 26, 1917: Left Caestre Station at 3:00 a.m. took the train to Ypres and arrived at 1:00 p.m. Marched through Ypres (Belgium) to Sacrifice Billets (bivouacs), just in front of Ypres. Went past "Hell's Corner," then to the right and through a swamp, to our bivouacs. Rain. On fatigue working on plank road.

"Hell's Corner" is probably a reference to Hellfire Corner, a well-known and very dangerous landmark in the Ypres Salient. The corner was at an intersection on a stretch of the Menin Road between the town of Ypres and the village of Hooge, to the east. The corner was plainly visible to German batteries occupying slightly higher ground still further to the east, which meant they could observe all traffic movement on the road by day and shell it at will — hence the name. As a result, most traffic risked the Menin Road by night.

A bivouac was a type of lean-to shelter made from two rubber ground sheets joined together and slung between a pair of rifles stuck in the ground by the bayonet. It was big enough to shelter two soldiers.[135]

Because of the especially muddy terrain in the Ypres Salient during the autumn of 1917, Currie ordered that many of the roads in the Canadian-held areas be paved with wood planks, much like the corduroy roads of the early-nineteenth-century Canadian frontier.[136] This gave the soldiers and pack mules a solid footing on their way to the front. These plank roads proved so successful that they were eventually adopted throughout the British-held sector.[137]

In front of the Belgian city of Ypres, the front line took a large bulge to the east and created a salient into German occupied territory. Because the salient was surrounded on three sides by the enemy (to the north, east, and south), it was exposed to fire from three different directions. Little wonder the British Army suffered some of its heaviest sustained casualty rates in this part of the line.

The opening bound of the Canadian attack, which was carried out by the 3rd and 4th Canadian Divisions, did not achieve all of its objectives. By the time the fighting ended, however, the forward battalions were on higher, firmer ground and well situated for the next bound, which would take place on October 30.

October 27, 1917: On fatigue from 3:00 a.m. to 10:30 a.m. on a narrow gauge railway, putting new track down. Rain.

The relative ease with which narrow-gauge railways could be built enabled the Canadian Corps to use them extensively to bridge the transportation gap between the standard, or broad gauge, railheads (where supplies were unloaded) and the front lines (where the material was needed). Operating on two-foot (sixty-centimetre) wide tracks, these miniature trains carried altogether an average fifteen hundred tonnes of ammunition, construction supplies, food, fuel, artillery, and men up to the front lines every day.[138] On their return from the front, they also helped to evacuate the wounded and hauled away materials salvaged from the battlefield. In many cases, the tracks were prefabricated on steel sleepers and came in two different lengths — eight and sixteen feet (two and five metres) — so that most of the construction work could be done by gangs of semi-skilled labourers, such as Deward and his comrades in the 19th Battalion.[139]

Along with the plank roads, narrow-gauge railways were an integral part of Currie's overall plan to move supplies across the mud (which was so deep in some places that the tracks subsided, sinking the locomotives up to their boilers).[140]

October 28, 1917: On fatigue from 9:30 a.m. to 5:00 p.m. working on roads. Bombed by Heincy planes. Rain. We used to have long marches, we only did an hour's work or so. It took so long to get up the line, we came home soaking wet every day and our blankets were soaked when we got back.

The land around the Ypres Salient is at or just below sea level. Centuries of carefully built and tended drainage ditches were obliterated in the months and years of fighting before Deward arrived. As a result, the incessant autumn rains of 1917 had flooded and all but drowned most of the ground.

October 29, 1917: On fatigue from 3:30 a.m. to 10:30 am. Left bivouacs at 2:00 p.m. for Rest Camp Vlamertinge, arrived at 3:00 p.m. near Poperinge, Dickebusch, and Ypres. We did mostly anti-aircraft work (duty) all day and night until we left; four hours on and four hours off. We had plenty of German planes to fire at. Water was scarce, [so we] used to wash in puddles outside our huts (not fit water). We never had a wash while in the front lines or supports at any time.

The Germans enjoyed air superiority over the Ypres Salient during the autumn of 1917, and their aircraft proved a constant nuisance. A veteran of the 19th Battalion recalled that one day an enemy airplane flew low enough that "you could see the buttons on his uniform we were so close, and he leaned over the side of the plane and he waved at us, and we waved at him."[141]

Supplying the men with sufficient chlorinated drinking water appears to have been an ongoing problem in the forward areas of the Ypres Salient. To prevent the spread of dysentery, the adjutant of the 19th Battalion issued an order in mid-November authorizing the use of bisulphate of soda tablets to sterilize water when supplies of chlorinated water failed. The men were further cautioned, however, that when the bisulphate tablets were dissolved in water, they had a corrosive effect on their enamelled water bottles (one wonders what effect it had on the men). The order also stressed the dangers of using water that had collected in shell holes, which apparently the adjutant also considered "not fit."[142]

The second phase of the Canadian attempt on Passchendaele took place the following day, on October 30. This time, the 3rd and 4th Divisions achieved a greater measure of success by moving the front line to within striking distance of the final objective.

November 2, 1917: We left Vlamertinge at 10:00 a.m. Took the train to Ypres (a ten-minute ride). Marched to tents behind the lines. Our platoon carrying wounded, remainder of company to the front line, going over.

Deward's platoon was left behind to act as an evacuation party — stretcher-bearers. This was in accordance with a 4th Canadian Infantry Brigade order issued just two days previously that required each battalion to leave behind one hundred men for this purpose when moving into the front lines. This was probably in recognition of the difficulties the local terrain imposed on removing the wounded for medical attention.[143]

On the evening of November 2, while the remainder of the 19th Battalion was moving forward to relieve the 78th Battalion in the front lines, one of the men from "A" Company, Harold Lodge, fell out from the march. His captain warned him to return to his platoon, which he did. Later that evening, however, Lodge was reported missing and remained so until he was discovered — out of uniform — and arrested seven weeks later in Boulogne.[144] Although Deward was not acquainted with Lodge at the time, the incident would have ghastly repercussions for them both in the coming months.

November 5, 1917: The battalion came out of lines after three days and left for rest camp [at Potijze, then Brandhoek]. We stayed here.

CHAPTER 6

Execution,
November 6, 1917, to March 30, 1918

*"As soon as the curtain dropped ... we got the order to fire. One blank
and nine live rounds. It went off as one. I did not have the blank."*

November 6, 1917: Breakfast at 2:00 a.m. Left tents at 3:00 a.m.
took our packs to White Chapel, then got the stretchers, etc. at
the dressing station. Arrived when the barrage opened up, about
4:00 a.m.

The Canadians went over-the-top and took Passchendaele
Ridge and town. The Imperial and Australian forces had tried
before us and failed.

The third phase of the Canadian attack kicked off with the
usual dawn barrage. This time, however, it was fresh men, from
the 1st and 2nd Divisions, who pressed their shoulders tightly into
the creeping line of exploding shells. By 9:00 am, Currie's plan had
succeeded, and the village of Passchendaele, so long coveted by the
British forces, was firmly in Canadian hands. It was a feat of arms
of which Deward was justifiably proud.

Heavy shelling and casualties. We carried out eight [wounded]
that day and came back to tents at 11:30 p.m. We had a long way
to carry each one under shellfire, four to a stretcher and each
one kept an end on a shoulder. We could not keep to [the trench]
mats, but had to go [a roundabout] way, sometimes a quarter of

a mile out of our way. One fellow could slip in a little hole or sink in mud and let that end down. Some of the wounded were great, others moaned or yelled at each jar; it could not be helped. Often the four of us went through a big shell hole, water near the thighs. But we worked hard and did our best. It was rain and mud.

A "trench mat" is another term for duckboard, or a portable wooden path. The paths were laid by the thousands to create trails over the deep mud.

Courtesy Canada Dept. of National Defence/ National Archives of Canada PA-002107

Wounded Canadians on way to aid-post, Battle of Passchendaele, November 1917. These are the same conditions over which Deward had to struggle as a stretcher-bearer at Passchendaele. This photo shows well the devastated nature of the ground and the generally flat terrain. A large shell hole has filled with water in the foreground, illustrating the dangers from drowning that awaited the unwary.

Passchendaele was a terrible place; rain all the time, mud, and quicksand. Roads had to be built on brush. Thousands of yards of trench mats to walk on, everything in the open. I never saw so many guns and disabled tanks. Packhorses would get into the mud and have to be [dug out].

Another veteran of the 19th Battalion, Ed Youngman, remembered an incident at Passchendaele in which the unfortunate animal was not so lucky:

> The poor thing kept sinking down and down, inch by inch, and we were frantic. And finally the transport officer of the 18th Battalion decided there was only one thing to do, and when [the mule's] head was just above the mud the officer pulled his revolver out of his holster, and I will never forget the look in that poor brute's great brown eyes when he looked at the officer, and the officer shot him and then cried like a kid.[145]

> Men had to be [dug out] that got off the mats in different places. There were few trenches. What there were, were half full of water. All you could do was sit up to your waist in water and sleep that way if you could. I never saw so many men drop from over exertion, big fellows some of them were, too.

Deward is in no way exaggerating the depth of the water in which the men had to endure their posts. A few days later, on November 10, the 19th Battalion *War Diary* records that the water in some of the front-line trenches and occupied shell holes was up to the men's thighs. Even after eighty-seven years, the diary itself bears silent witness to the deluge. Many of the ink lines that form the hand-written text are fuzzy and blurred, from being either penned on damp paper or smudged by drops of water.[146]

> Carrying the wounded out, most all we carried had parts of their faces shot away, some nearly all their face, as well as dozens of dead laying all around. The wounded were carried out in relays, those at the front would bring them so far and as we were in the second relay we took them so far. An advance YMCA was here in a [captured] pillbox and we got cigarettes, coffee, candies every time, and rum. "Help yourself." Believe me

it went good. Hundreds could get wounded and die in the mud, stuck with slight wounds. It is always a sickening sight to see them half-buried. But the mud saved many from getting hit by shells. The overhead shells were bad but once the pieces hit the mud they stayed.

Pillboxes were small, reinforced concrete huts, usually housing machine guns, that the Germans built in this area as an answer to the problem of flooded trenches. Hundreds of them were constructed, and many of them remain today, pressed into use as tool or goat sheds by the farmers on whose land they sit.

The inconstant, waiting mud of Passchendaele could deal death or salvation. To the unlucky, or the unconscious, it turned a hard face and offered a slow, suffocating death by drowning, but to the fortunate it exposed a soft underbelly that swallowed shells whole and let them burst deep inside, where the blast and deadly splinters were safely contained. As one Passchendaele veteran remembered:

> The only reason we stayed alive was that the shell would land alongside and it would go straight into the ground; unless you were actually in the blast coming up from it, you were all right. You got damned dirty. There'd be a spout of mud and it'd dirty you up a bit but it was not very lethal. You got to be contemptuous of it.[147]

November 7, 1917: I was recommended for good work.

Deward means that someone in authority felt he should receive official recognition for his work through either having his name mentioned in dispatches or being awarded a decoration. Deward's service record indicates the recommendation was not acted upon.

November 8, 1917: The battalion went up to the front line for four days, while we kept on carrying the wounded. Men killed on mats, thousands of men in the open.

November 10, 1917: I left Brigade Headquarters with a ration party (eight of us) carrying rations to the front line in sandbags. Raining hard. Each of us got a big glass full of rum before we left at 1:30 p.m. Going up to two thousand yards [eighteen hundred metres] behind the front line leaving rations in a pillbox, we never left the mats and they were shelling them all the time. Dead were all over. Soaked through, we did not get back until 8:00 p.m. Steady walking, so you can guess the length of the mats. Seven of the eight were gassed. Six went down the line and one later on. I never got a bit of it, good thing my smeller is poor, I'm a lucky devil.

Deward's poor "smeller" was caused by chronic catarrh, an excess of mucous in the nose and mouth. The condition can be caused by a particularly bad cold, a bout of influenza, hay fever, or some other respiratory infection.

November 10 saw an end to the Third Battle of Ypres with a fourth bound, which was not part of Currie's original plan, to capture "Vindictive Crossroads," an intersection on the crest of Passchendaele Ridge. This position was carried by the 20th Battalion and two other battalions belonging to the 2nd Canadian Infantry Brigade.

November 11, 1917: The boys came out of the front line at 11:30 a.m., after losing half a battalion. Those of us who were left at the tents were waiting for them. We kept lots of sandbags about, three feet [one metre] high around the tent. That's the best you could do for protection. It was funny, for as long as you had a tent over you, you felt safe when shelling was going on or bombing planes came over. When the boys came back from the line some gave out and fell as soon as they saw us, they could go no further. And nearly every one had to be carried. I never saw such feet, water-soaked and swollen. A terrible lot were sent down the line and some were alright after a good rest. New reinforcements were always coming to the battalion. W.J. Bell killed November 11. Sent into the line covered with boils. It was a crime for the Medical Officer [to have allowed it].

The men with water-soaked and swollen feet were suffering from trench foot, an inflammation of the soft tissues with symptoms similar to frostbite. Men such as those in the front lines at Passchendaele, whose feet were wet and cold for extended periods, were especially susceptible to this condition. If left untreated, a serious case could result in the loss of toes, or worse. For Art Cane, a 19th Battalion man who contracted trench foot at Passchendaele, it meant six months of convalescing in England before he was again fit for service at the front.[148]

W.J. Bell was one of the men with whom Deward had his picture taken on August 11. We don't have to read too carefully between the lines to recognize that Deward holds the battalion's Medical Officer responsible for Bell's death. Bell is buried in Tyne Cot Cemetery on the forward slope of Passchendaele Ridge.

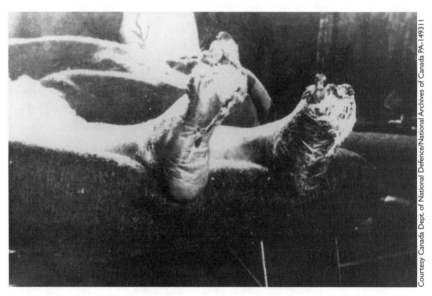

Courtesy Canada Dept. of National Defence/National Archives of Canada PA-149311

Case of trench foot suffered by an unidentified soldier, 1917. This photo shows the terrible disfigurement that a severe case of trench foot could cause. Note the loss of toes on the left foot. It is possible this case was contracted at Passchendaele.

While working on roads in Belgium, the roads were crowded with men and transports. At different times every day, German planes came over in battle formation (V) and bombed. They went very high, you couldn't hear their engines, but they seldom hit the roads. It seemed to be more dangerous off the roads.

The packhorses suffered. Just a few trips and there was nothing but skin and bones left. I was getting some black coffee at an advance place, where you could only get coffee, no milk or sugar, while the men with the packhorses were getting some too. The horses lay down and went to sleep amongst us men. Big men dropped from exhaustion and I kept on. All I was, was skin and bones. It was a terrible place as everyone knows.

November 13, 1917: We left the Ypres front at 10:00 a.m. [and headed] to [the] train [that lay] past Poperinge, arriving there at 1:30 p.m. Got W.J. Bell's belongings. Left with [Lewis gun] limbers (transport).

Although he doesn't say so, Deward probably collected Bell's belongings so that he could personally forward them to his family. Unless he had been with Bell when he died, this small act of devotion might have been the only meaningful way for Deward to put his dead friend to rest.

The Lewis gun limbers were carts specially fitted to transport the guns and their accoutrements while the battalion was on the march.

November 14, 1917: I walked from Belgium to look after guns. The battalion took the train. We left at 8:30 a.m. and passed through Poperinge, had dinner at Caestre, arriving at Hondeghem about 5:00 p.m. I slept in a barn and got forty-eight hours rations.

November 15, 1917: Left Hondeghem at 8:00 a.m. passed through Hazebrouke and Saint Venant — arrived at Robecq at 2:00 p.m. Twenty-two kilometres, nearly fifteen miles.

November 16, 1917: Left Robecq at 8:00 a.m. arriving at Auchel at 1:00 p.m. fifteen kilometres [nine miles] Quite a big town, paid twenty-five francs here and went to the French movies at night.

November 17, 1917: We left Auchel at 10:00 a.m. on trucks, passed through Houdain, arriving at Villers-au-Bois at 2:00 p.m.

November 19, 1917: Sent Christmas cards, cleaned ammunition.

Even with the horrible memories of Passchendaele still fresh in their minds, ahead, incongruously, lay the festivities of the Christmas season. And with it came the business of sending out Christmas greetings and the problems of censorship that this posed. To help ease the burden on the censor and to remind the men of their duty regarding written communication, the 19th Battalion issued the following order:

> There is no objection to the following being written on Field Service Post Cards, "A Merry Christmas and a Happy New Year." Attention is called to Censorship Orders, para 11, by which it is forbidden to send Christmas or New Year Cards, photographs, etc., to enemy or neutral countries.[149]

The Field Service Post Card was a printed form on which, normally, a soldier was only allowed to write the address of the person to whom he was sending the card, a date, and a signature. Beyond that, he could only communicate by circling the prepared statement that applied to his situation or by striking out those statements that did not. The Field Service Post Card did not replace letters home but merely provided the soldier with a fast and convenient way of keeping in touch with his family or friends under conditions that otherwise were not conducive to letter writing.

November 20, 1917: Cleaned ammunition, etc.

For the most part, cleaning ammunition was more than busy work, especially after the conditions experienced at Passchendaele. Ammunition caked in dry mud or coated with grit would not feed properly into the machine guns and could lead to stoppages or premature wear of the automatic loading mechanisms. This wasn't always the case, however, as on at least one occasion, with an imminent general inspection by the Corps Commander looming, the men were ordered to go one step further and actually polish their ammunition, with "every round to be made bright."[150]

Courtesy Canada Dept. of National Defence/National Archives of Canada PA-001421

Canadians polishing souvenirs (bullets) for Fritz, July 1917. This photo gives us an interesting look inside a well-revetted trench. From its depth and state of good repair it may well be a support or reserve trench in a quiet sector. The men sitting on the firing step are polishing ammunition. The man standing in the trench appears to be wearing British 1914 pattern leather equipment, which likely marks him as a member of the Canadian Machine Gun Corps, the only Canadian formation known to be issued with this equipment on a regular basis. Notice the myriad telephone cables running over the ground or behind the revetments.

November 21, 1917: Left for a fatigue up the line, digging new trenches. You are supposed to dig so much and then you were through. But if you did your bit first you had to keep on and work hard, you had to leave in time to get back far enough before daylight. We left at 3:30 p.m. Took the narrow gauge railway, arriving at Canada Dump. Walked to Canada Trench, arriving at

> 8:00 p.m. Left at 11:00 p.m. took train at Dump (electric, and it went quite close to the front line). Passed Zivy Cave and Petit Vimy, back at 6:00 a.m. quite a long ride.

The narrow-gauge railways operated several types of locomotives. Conventional steam engines worked in the rear areas where their smoke was less likely to draw the enemy's attention. Smokeless, petrol-powered engines of various sizes worked closer to the front lines. Although there were no purely electric locomotives, there were hybrid petrol-electric locomotives in which a petrol-driven generator created the electricity necessary to drive the locomotive's engine. This is probably what Deward refers to above.[151]

November 22, 1917: We were drilled (tough), same fatigue for the next three nights. One fellow got a pick in the bum and was sent down the line.

During this brief period of respite from front-line duty, the 19th Battalion supplied working parties almost every night to help repair trenches and tunnels and to carry supplies up to other units in the front lines.[152]

Considering the large numbers of men working in close quarters in the dark, it's a wonder more accidents like the one Deward mentions above didn't happen. James Pedley, an officer who supervised many such fatigues, was concerned for the safety of his men and remarked on one such occasion:

> Swarms of men were engaged in clearing away debris from a tunnel which was being pushed through under the road. A constant drum fire of obscenity filled the area. Fortunately, the footing was good or there would have been a grist of accidents among these men ... As it was, one lay quietly on his back with a white bandage on his foot. I suppose he had dug his pick into it.[153]

November 29, 1917: Left Villers-au-Bois by trucks to Mont-St. Eloi and marched to the front line. Arrived at about 4:00 a.m. Our duty — six hours on and six hours off.

It's wintertime now and our front is extended. A [Lewis] gun post is always put next to a big gap in the trench, where it takes care of — covers — a hundred yards [ninety metres] or so of trench. We use passwords and have to guard both sides of the trench [on either side of the gap] and the front. A man is on the gun and there is one at each side [of the gap], guarding the trench. As well always, you had to patrol so far and challenge anyone. They [the Germans] put patrols on the glacis between gaps and along the front. Plenty of duty. Stand-to at 4:00 p.m. stand-down at 8:00 a.m. All men had to be on-duty at those hours.

During this tour of the front, the 19th Battalion's line was a series of unconnected posts instead of a continuous trench system. This is why Deward found such big gaps in the trenches. Less than a kilometre west of Fresnoy, this was where he had received his baptism of fire just six months previously.

The nights are long and cold and pitch dark. I spent hours and hours looking over-the-top and of course in the [daytime] you took particular notice of objects such as trees. At night you could look so long that you could swear you saw something move. Then we put someone else looking, to be sure.

Rats used to run along the parapet, right beside your face. They often gave you a start too, when they came suddenly. I dreaded those long nights, watching out for raids.

Deward's experiences of standing sentry by night would have been familiar to almost anyone who had done the same thing. The strain caused many a soldier to see things that weren't really there, particularly when the moon was high. As the historian of the 20th Battalion remembers, "When there was a moon, the weird shadows kept us continually 'seeing things.' During these queer nights angle iron posts could be seen forming fours, patrolling, advancing, et cetera. Imagination ruled the nights."[154]

November 30, 1917: No. 4 Platoon was next to us. They had all their green men in one bay. Whether or not they knew the seriousness of doing this I don't know. The Germans sneaked right up to the corner of their bay, our men didn't see them, and the Germans jumped into the trench. They took two men prisoners away with them, but one of them got away and ran back. They never fired a shot. The rest of our men in the post came running down the trench in fright along with a more experienced fellow, Bert Bangay. Lieutenant Bell came running up with the rest of us and he met Bangay first. He threatened to report him for cowardice but Bangay [told him that he] had been sick and that he reported sick before we came up the line but the Medical Officer made him come anyway; he thought [Bangay] was swinging the lead. Then Lieutenant [Bell] made [Bangay] go out and report again to the Medical Officer. This time Bangay was sent down the line. [Bangay] died before we left the front line, he had been dying all the time. We fired from our post but you couldn't see anything, you could only make a sweep with the gun so I don't know whether we got any or not. Our guns were always set up to crossfire.

Edward Albert Bangay was one of Deward's comrades in the 180th Battalion and had been a railway baggage man before he enlisted in 1916. He was twenty-three when he died, and he left behind a wife, Violet. Bangay is buried in the Étaples Military Cemetery, seventeen miles (twenty-seven kilometres) south of Boulogne.[155] William Douglas Bell was a law student and an original member of the 19th Battalion, having enlisted with them at Toronto in the autumn of 1914. Bell was commissioned from the ranks in June 1916.[156]

Deward clearly is still harbouring a bitter resentment toward the battalion's Medical Officer for the death of his friend W.J. Bell, which is evident in his rambling digression about Bangay, a thinly disguised diatribe directed at the battalion's M.O. "Swinging the lead" is a old seaman's phrase that arose before the advent of electronic depth sounding equipment. When approaching unfamiliar shallows a man would have to stand at the front of the ship with a lead weight, which was attached to a length of rope knotted at known intervals. The man would "swing the lead" overboard and count the number of knots that fed out through his hands to determine the depth of the water. This was considered a pretty cushy job and was often given to a hand who for one reason or another was not physically capable of going aloft or performing other, more physically demanding work. Over time, the phrase became synonymous with getting out of hard duty by feigning illness.

According to a 19th Battalion report on this raid, at 3:00 a.m. a large party of Germans had assembled in No-Man's Land, just in front of the battalion's position. Three of the Germans then slipped into the trench occupied by No. 4 Platoon and overcame two of the sentries. In the ensuing struggle one sentry was wounded and the other was carried off as a prisoner. The report goes on to say that fire was immediately opened up on No-Man's Land by adjoining posts, one of which must have been Deward's Lewis gun crew. Although Deward wasn't sure whether they hit anybody, daylight revealed at least one dead German in a shell hole in front of the raided post. It would be difficult to say for sure which of the posts fired the fatal shot because, as Deward points out, at night their guns were set up to crossfire. This meant they were sighted such that the fire from the two guns converged at a predetermined point — where attackers were most likely to come from — and created a killing zone that could inflict the maximum casualties even under poor lighting conditions.

The succinct prose of the official report gives the impression of calm and order, a notion that is shattered by Deward's description of panic and turmoil.

December 3, 1917: We came out of the front line to supports.

December 5, 1917: Vancouver Road, gas guar from 3:00 a.m. to 5:00 a.m.

December 6, 1917: Went up line to hold gap at 4:00 p.m.

December 7, 1917: [Returned] 7:00 a.m. to Hudson Communications Trench, near Ottawa and Canada Trenches. Voted for conscription.

Advanced polls for the 1917 general election were available to Canadian service personnel — including, for the first time, women — from December 1 until election day, December 17.

By voting for conscription, Deward had cast his vote in support of the ruling Union, or coalition, government, which formed in mid-October 1917. The coalition was made up of Conservatives and those Liberals who were unhappy with Wilfrid Laurier's negative stand on conscription, and it was led by Conservative Prime Minister Robert Borden. It strongly supported the Military Service Act, which was passed by the Conservative government at the end of August 1917. The act proclaimed that all male British subjects living in Canada between the ages of twenty and forty-five were liable for conscription to active, overseas service. The act was extremely controversial, receiving practically no support in Québec nor, at first, in Western Canada — where it was feared it would take sons and workers away from their farms. Borden, however, rammed several bills through Parliament before its dissolution in early October that manipulated the distribution of votes, resulting in a substantial victory for the Unionists.

When the overseas military votes were counted, over 90 percent of the soldiers on active service had voted to support conscription.

December 9, 1917: In support trenches.

December 10, 1917: Went up to gap between two [trench] lines that had not been connected. I was on-duty all day and night (the password was "Strand"). Captain Harstone, who was small — but was a real man — came up inquiring as to my position. [I told him,] "I am always in charge." I also told him that I thought there was a German [outpost] in a certain place. He said, "We'll go and see." It was about 2:00 a.m. we went with pistols (I hadn't carried a rifle for some time). But we didn't find a post. [So we went] back to Triumph Trench.

At 5 feet, 8 inches [173 centimetres], Capt. John Harstone was actually almost half an inch [1 centimetre] taller than Deward, so it isn't clear what Deward meant by "who was small — but was a real man." A native of Peterborough, Ontario the twenty-two-year-old Harstone was a law student before the war.[157]

As the Number 1 on the Lewis gun, Deward carried a revolver instead of a rifle.

The 19th Battalion was again occupying a stretch of the front line not far from where it had stood at Fresnoy the previous May. In fact, Deward's Lewis gun post was at the conjunction of Triumph Trench and the Alberta Road, from which he had helped to cover the withdrawal of "C" Company on May 8.[158]

December 11, 1917: Gas guard that night.

December 12, 1917: Went up to hold same post at night.

December 13, 1917: Left close supports at 12:00 midnight, through Hudson and C.P.R. trenches and arrived Neuville at 6:00 a.m.

December 14 to 16, 1917: We worked on roads digging for next few days.

December 17, 1917: I was warned that I had been recommended for an NCOs course, [which would last] one month. I had been Number 1 gunner from Hill 70 and was always in charge of my section from then on. Although I did not have stripes, I was used as a corporal.

In most cases, before a man could receive promotion, he had to attend a non-commissioned officer's training course that would teach him the duties and leadership skills of a junior NCO. If Deward had been fulfilling the role of a corporal since August, it suggests a severe shortage of trained NCOs in the battalion and points to the high casualty rates among NCOs while in action.

December 19, 1917: Left Neuville-St. Vaast at 8:00 a.m. and passed through Mont-St. Eloi, Villers-Au-Bois, Camblain-L'Abbé to Estrée Cauchy.

Estrée Cauchy was the site of rest billets and was known to the troops by the more familiar "Extra Cushy."

December 20, 1917: Left at 10:00 a.m. in trucks, to Westrehem. I did not get my course, but we stayed at Westrehem during Christmas. Slept in lofts for a while. Half the boards were off. Cold, so Corporal Book, Corporal Bacon, and myself paid an old French woman for a bed next door. We slept in a room with a French man, in a feather bed. It was jake. She was a jolly old woman (a granny). Corporal Bacon, a French-Canadian, could talk to her.

On December 20th, the 2nd Division was withdrawn from the line for a month's training, a move that must have cancelled Deward's trip to NCO school.

Roy Book was a farmer from Silverdale, Ontario. The 19th Battalion took him on strength in mid-June 1916 from the 98th Battalion, with which he had enlisted when he was twenty years of age. Book served with the 19th Battalion through the Somme fighting and at Vimy Ridge before he was hospitalized for several weeks in late April 1917 with a case of trench fever. He was raised to the rank of corporal in early September, during the round of promotions made necessary by the battalion's losses at Hill 70. Book contracted an infestation of scabies in early November and was again hospitalized for a short period, just long enough to miss most of the misery at Passchendaele.[159]

144

Louis Bacon was a twenty-four-year-old lumberman from Anticosti Island when he enlisted with the 37th Battalion at Camp Niagara in June 1915. He took his place with the 19th Battalion almost a year to the day later. Bacon had something of a chequered army career. In early December 1916 — only a few weeks after recovering from a shell wound to his head and face — he was sentenced to seven days Field Punishment Number One for "using obscene language to an NCO." In early August 1917, Bacon was again up on charges for contravening General Regulations and Orders No. 1599 (the nature of G.R.O. 1599 is not specified on the charge sheet), for which he received a further three days Field Punishment Number One. Two weeks later, however, Bacon volunteered as a stretcher-bearer for the operations at Hill 70, where he "worked incessantly among the wounded, dressing [their wounds] and carrying them to cover."[160] For his actions at Hill 70 he was awarded the Military Medal for bravery. At the beginning of December 1917, Bacon was promoted to corporal to replace the wounded George Abrahams.[161]

Field Punishment Number One included being tied, spread-eagle, with your back to a wagon wheel for up to two hours a day, reduced rations, and extra duty.[162] In some Canadian units, however, two hours of pack drill replaced being lashed to a wagon wheel.[163]

December 25, 1917: We had our Christmas dinner in a big tent with two long tables. All we had that looked like Christmas was a small piece of pudding. They had beer and soft drinks. I got drunk a couple of times on Champagne and Vin Rouge; I was found on a road one night and taken home.

Westrehem is a small town and the estaminets did good. That's all the life that was there. [There were also] French girls in the estaminets.

This is the second time that Deward has remarked on the presence of women in drinking establishments. Earlier, he commented that he did not approve of barmaids in pubs. Here, he is non-committal. After witnessing young women toiling under sacks of coal and labouring in the mines of Fosse 10, perhaps his views on a woman's place are starting to change.

January 1, 1918: Got up at 8:00 a.m. no parade. Finished letter to Lucy. The three of us made up and paid Granny to cook us a swell dinner as our rations were porridge — without salt or milk — but with a piece of bacon on top. You were lucky to get any grease (Gippo), however. We bought cabbage, potatoes, chicken, beef bullion, tea, and French bread, and Granny cooked it. Some New Year's dinner!

Received a letter from Lucy, no. 11. Received Christmas card from Ira. Wrote Lucy no. 5, Nora and Beatrice.

Ira was a friend that Deward had met during his leave in Glasgow the previous December. Nora and Beatrice were Deward's sisters. In the early part of the twentieth century, letter writing was still the dominant form of long-distance communication. People who corresponded regularly with each other might write letters several times a week, or more. To help the addressee spot when a letter was delivered out of sequence or whether it had gone missing altogether, writers would often number the correspondence. This is what Deward is referring to above when he says that he "received a letter from Lucy, no. 11" and "wrote Lucy no. 5."

January 2, 1918: I was instructor of [Lewis] gun class while here, which was held in the [YMCA] tent. It was cold and snow was on the ground. Got a few pills at 4:00 p.m. (cold).

Received from Lucy no. 10 and no. 12 letters. Received also from Nora and Beatrice. Wrote Lucy no. 6.

January 3, 1918: Instructing class. Armstrong and Brown on leave. Cleaning the magazine. Warned for leave at 10:00 p.m. reported to the orderly room.

While the other ranks could expect ten days' leave once a year, officers were entitled to the same amount of leave every three months. In theory, a soldier could also apply for special leave back to Canada to attend to urgent matters. In practice, however, only a few hundred of the nearly third of a million Canadian rank and file who went overseas were ever granted that privilege.[164]

January 4, 1918: Reported at M.O. [Medical Officer] and battalion Orderly room at 8:00 a.m. paid £20–25 francs, left Westrehem 9:00 a.m. walked to Lillers via Auchy-Au-Bois and Lières. Arrived 11:15 a.m. Had ride on truck the last half hour. Left Lillers on trucks, 1:00 p.m. Arrived at Boulogne at 9:00 p.m. We went into rest billets; dandy place — blankets, wash, bath, canteen, and everything. Slept with L.C. Bell.

Before he could depart on leave, a soldier needed a certificate declaring that he was free of scabies and venereal disease. This explains Deward's early trip to the M.O. The certificates also stated the man had been given a bath and was issued with clean underwear. Deward would have collected this certificate and his other leave papers from the Battalion's Orderly Room, the unit's main operations centre or head office. With his pass made out and pounds in his pocket for passage, he was free to begin his leave.[165]

Leonard Charles Bell was another of Deward's associates from the 180th Battalion. He was posted to the 19th Battalion at the same time as Deward and was also granted fourteen days' leave at the beginning of January. The twenty-eight-year-old native of Islington, Ontario, was a gardener by trade.

January 5, 1918: Up at 7:00 a.m. Bought [an embroidered] pillow top of Ypres for Lucy and one of Mont-St. Eloi for Bella. Had lunch. Very bad cold.

Left Boulogne at 1:00 p.m. arriving at Folkestone at 3:00 p.m. Trains were waiting. Arrived at London's Victoria Station at 5:30 p.m. Went to the Maple Leaf Club and cashed a cheque. Had a bath and bought new underwear.

Went underground to Euston Station, sent telegram to Bella and back to Maple Leaf Club. Bought riding pants and went back to bed, which was clean, with clean pyjamas. Left my money at the office.

Bella was another of the friends Deward had made during his trip to Glasgow the previous year.

The Maple Leaf Club was properly The King George and Queen Mary Maple Leaf Club. It operated to provide Canadian servicemen on leave with a safe and inexpensive base of operations in London. The club offered a wide range of services for free or at a nominal rate, including beds, meals, tickets to London shows and attractions, libraries, writing materials, equipment storage, safekeeping for valuables, cheque cashing, and so on.

The wearing of riding pants, or breeches, was a popular way for the men to "dress up" their uniform while on leave. Strictly, breeches were for officers only, and anyone from the ranks caught wearing them risked losing his pass.

January 6, 1918: Up at 8:30 a.m. cleaned and had breakfast. Went to the Wax Works on tram. Closed. Back to Victoria underground station and restaurant. Wrote Lucy no. 7, sent cards to Nora and Bea. Sent cushion top and [1917] diary home. Took the underground to Tottenham Court Road, YMCA, and the [Maple Leaf] Club.

Deward must have thought his diary worth saving to take the trouble of mailing it home for safekeeping. One wonders, too, if by waiting until he was on leave to mail the diary home, Deward was consciously trying to avoid the all-seeing eye of the censor.

January 7, 1918: Up at 8:00 a.m. to restaurant and breakfast. Bought boots and puttees. Went to Madame Tussaud's Wax Works. There were two policemen as you went in the door and they looked real, and all figures inside were likenesses of great men in their dress (life size). Kings and Queens and coronation robes and all. In the dungeon were famous murderers in parts of the Chamber of Horrors.

We saw "The Better 'Ole" and came out before it was over. Back to Maple Leaf Club, then went to Euston Station and left at 11:30 p.m. for Glasgow.

"The Better 'Ole" was the creation of cartoonist Bruce Bairnsfather, a serving officer with the Imperial Army. The series featured a character named Old Bill, a gruff, sardonic "old sweat" who typified the popular notion of a British front-line soldier. A stage play based on the cartoon series debuted in London in 1918. It was also performed in Toronto, where it ran for several years.[166] In addition to the play, the series also spawned several movie treatments, including a 1926 version that stared Syd Chaplin, the older half-brother of Charlie Chaplin. Apparently, Deward didn't like the show. He doesn't tell us why, but one wonders if, as a serving front-line soldier, he found the stage adaptation more trite than true.

January 8, 1918: Arrived at Central Station, passing through Carlisle at 10:30 a.m. and met Bella. Took the car, slept in afternoon. Went to a party at night, took Ira part way home. Had a dandy time in Glasgow. I was used like a prince for ten days.

January 9, 1918: Up at 12:00 noon. Wrote Lucy no. 8.

January 10, 1918: Up at 11:00 a.m. Wrote Lucy no. 9 at Dick's machine shop. Stayed in at night.

Dick Gaunt was another of Deward's Glasgow friends.

January 11, 1918: Up at 10:00 a.m. Wrote Lucy no. 10. Downtown, called at Baird's. Went to an evening picture show with Dick.

January 12, 1918: Up at 11:30 p.m. Called for Dick and had a motor ride, then dinner and motored around the city. Wrote Lucy no. 11. Party at Baird's and played whist. Hutchison family games. Left about 1:00 a.m. [for] Argyle Street.

January 13, 1918: Up at 8:15, went to baths (dandy baths!). Wrote Lucy no. 13. Church at night. Chips.

January 14, 1918: Up at 10:00 a.m. wrote Lucy no. 14. Downtown to Central Station, snowed all day. At Mrs. Gardener's (upstairs) in evening, "singing."

January 15, 1918: Up at 11:30 a.m. wrote Lucy no. 15, wrote Nat, wrote L.C. Bell in London. Stayed in at night.

January 16, 1918: Up at 12:00 noon. Wrote Lucy no. 16. Downtown. Party at Baird's (pantomime).

January 17, 1918: Up at 11:00 a.m. wrote Lucy no. 17. Downtown with Dick. Botanic Gardens. Called at Baird's. Left Glasgow at 10:00 p.m. feeling blue. Bella treated me A-1 and gave a box of sandwiches and cakes.

January 18, 1918: Arrived at Euston at 8:00 a.m. Took underground to Maple Leaf Club, Marble Arch. Had breakfast, then to the Tower of London, and Saint Paul's Cathedral. Show in afternoon. Sent Lucy £8. Show at night. Wrote Lucy no. 18. Had supper at the YMCA. [Feeling] punk. Met L.C. Bell.

Feeling "punk" meant feeling unwell.

January 19, 1918: Left Marble Arch at 5:30 a.m. took underground to Victoria and got kit [from Maple Leaf Club]. Left at 7:00 a.m. (never liked London, too big). Arrived at Folkestone at 9:30 a.m. Got the boat and arrived at Boulogne at 1:30 p.m. Up hill to rest camp. Wrote Lucy and posted a green envelope at the YMCA in Boulogne.

Green envelopes were issued to the men once a week. Unlike regular correspondence, green envelopes were not subjected to automatic censorship at the battalion level, but might be censored at a base in the rear area. On the outside of the envelope, the soldier had to sign a declaration, swearing that the contents of the envelope referred to nothing but private or family business.[167]

January 20, 1918: Got up at 2:00 a.m. Marched to train. Left at 7:00 a.m. arrived at Lillers 1:30 p.m. (wrong place). Waited for a draft of the 4th Brigade. Left Lillers for Chocques at 6:00 p.m. arrived at Saint Pol at 8:00 p.m. Went to rest camp in huts, wrote Lucy no. 19 and got a delay ticket. Went to bed at 9:00 p.m.

Through some foul-up, Deward either boarded the wrong train or was misdirected. The consequences of this were serious. If he overstayed his leave, Deward could be posted Away Without Leave (A.W.L.) and subjected to arrest and punishment. By obtaining a delay ticket from the Railway Transport Officer, however, Deward was able to validate his absence and avoid detention upon his return to the battalion.

January 21, 1918: Up at 8:00 a.m. washed and shaved. Took train to Mont-St. Eloi (the French trains are slow) and walked to Neuville-St. Vaast. Arrived at transport at 5:00 p.m. Received letters, nos. 4, 5, 6, 7, 8, 9, 14, 15, 16, 17, 18, 20, 21 from Mother, Daisy, Ada, Jessie, and Nora. Slept in the transport lines after reporting to the Battalion Orderly Room.

It isn't known whether Daisy, Ada, and Jessie were friends or relatives. Significantly, however, they are all women, which underlines the key role that women played in supporting the men at the front.

January 22, 1918: Wrote Bella. Wrote Lucy no. 19 (green envelope). Left transport, Neuville-St. Vaast at 4:00 p.m. and walked to the narrow gauge railway with the limbers. Passed Fosse 6 on way here. Reported to Company Orderly Room (headquarters). [We are on the] Avion front forty yards [thirty-five metres] from the enemy. Rain.

Dugouts. Writing a letter, August 1916. Soldiers often had to write where and when they could.

January 23, 1918: On wiring party putting wire up in No-Man's Land. Left at 3:00 a.m. Left front line for supports. Brigade Dump at 7:00 p.m. Arrived 8:00 p.m. at Brewery. Dandy big place, holds [an entire] company and a YMCA canteen. [We were in the] Red Line.

Received letters from Nora, Bert Marden, Corporal Abe; wrote Lucy no. 19.

The term "Red Line" most likely refers to the Brigade's close support lines and probably comes from the use of a red pen to indicate the position on maps. These lines were not related to the objectives in an attack as was, for example, the Red Line at Vimy Ridge.

Presumably "Corporal Abe" was George Abrahams.

January 24, 1918: Up at 4:00 p.m. for duty on support trench half an hour's walk away. Up until 1:00 a.m. Wrote Lucy no. 20, Nora and Beatrice. Received letter from Nora.

January 25, 1918: On-duty from 1:00 p.m. to 9:00 p.m. Cleaned gun. Received letter from Nora, received Lucy's box and a letter from Corporal Book.

Book's service record shows that he was on duty with the 19th Battalion during this period, so it isn't clear why Deward would have received a letter from him. One possibility is that Book wrote to Deward while he was on leave in London, but the letter missed him and was forwarded back to the continent only to catch up with Deward now.[168]

January 26, 1918: On-duty from 4:00 p.m. to 1:00 a.m. Long hours for duty. Wrote Lucy no. 21. On-duty at 9:00 p.m.

It was more usual for the soldiers to rotate through a period of four hours on duty and eight hours off duty.

January 27, 1918: On-duty until 5:00 a.m. Received a letter from Nora and Lucy's no. 13.

January 28, 1918: 21st Battalion raid. On-duty from 1:00 p.m. to 8:00 p.m. then relieved. Left Brewery at 8:30 p.m. to Neuville-St. Vaast. Walked and arrived at 11:00 p.m. Received letter from Nora.

January 29, 1918: Up at 8:00 p.m. Paid twenty francs. Wrote Bert, Abe, Ada, and Jessie. Received Lucy's letters, nos. 22, 24, 27. Nothing to do.

January 30, 1918: Change of underwear. No bath. Received letter from Lucy, no. 23. Wrote to Dorothy, Daisy, Lucy (no. 22), Mrs. Field. On fatigue to Brewery cleaning out muddy trench that had caved in (deep). Left at 4:30 p.m. back by 2:00 a.m.

Dorothy was one of Deward's sisters. Mrs. Field was Deward's future mother-in-law.

January 31, 1918: Up at 8:00 a.m. Clothing parade. To Givenchy or Fosse 6 near Souchez. That night on fatigue again to Red Line, 4:30 p.m. to 2:00 a.m.

A clothing parade was where the soldier's set of issued clothing was inspected, repairs made, and deficiencies made up from the quartermaster's stores.

February 1, 1918: Had to take Private Lodge, a deserter, to Mont-St. Eloi clink. He was handcuffed to Alex Armstrong with me on the other side and Sgt. Sam Newell behind. We had pistols and were ordered to shoot to kill if he attempted to get away. He had escaped twice before. Going along the road he could tell us every hole, etc., before we got to it. He had been over it before. It was pitch dark. We cut across an orchard at his suggestion, a shortcut. Believe me we watched him, not taking a chance at him suddenly snatching a pistol from our holster. He knew he was done this time. All roads were guarded and all vehicles and traffic stopped on roads to look for passes, etc. We got back and left Neuville-St. Vaast at 11:00 a.m.

Harold Lodge enlisted with the Canadian Engineers at Toronto in the spring of 1915. He served with the 4th Field Company in France as a driver from November 1915 until he transferred to the 19th Canadian Infantry Battalion in July 1916. That August, Lodge suffered a gunshot wound to his neck and spent a month recuperating in hospital. He returned to the battalion at the end of September 1916 and served without incident until November 2, 1917.[169] Sometime after lunch on November 2, while the battalion was moving forward from Potize to relieve the

78th Battalion in front of Passchendaele, Lodge deserted. His absence was not discovered until after 10:30 that evening, when the relief was complete and "A" Company had taken up its positions in battalion reserve. Lodge remained at large until December 12, when he was discovered at Boulogne in the uniform of the British Red Cross Society and arrested. Nine days later, Lodge escaped from custody. He eluded recapture until January 7, when he was again arrested at Boulogne (which was, according to James Pedley, a mecca for deserters seeking to escape the continent), this time as a stowaway on a ship bound for England.[170] On January 11, Lodge managed to escape once more, but was apprehended, yet again at Boulogne, just three days later.[171]

Alex Armstrong was another of the 180th Battalion cadre then serving with the 19th Battalion. The thirty-two-year-old Toronto grocer was a native of Ayrshire, Scotland.[172]

February 2, 1918: Left for Villers-au-Bois, arriving at 3:00 p.m. On street picket from 7:00 p.m. to 8:00 p.m. Drilling every day.

February 3, 1918: Church and bath, wrote Lucy (no. 24), Nora, Fred, started letter to Lucy no. 25. Played 500 with Gerry, Nick Carter, and Book.

"500" is a Euchre-like card game in which the first player or team to score five hundred points wins.

February 4, 1918: Ranges from 7:00 to 11:30 a.m. Cleaning gun in the afternoon. Wrote Lucy no. 25. Played cards at night — King Pedro.

"King Pedro" is the name of a card game that was widely popular in North America during the nineteenth century. The game is played with two pair of partners, who sit opposite one another. Twelve cards are dealt to each player, and the remaining four are placed face down on the table to form a kitty. After bidding for points, the players discard half their cards. The object of the game is then for each pair, or team, to take tricks that contain trump cards and thus score points.

February 5, 1918: Mess Orderly, off parade. Wrote Lucy no. 26. Wrote May. On guard (last relief).

February 6, 1918: On gun, shooting. Was warned for [Lewis gun] course, paid thirty francs.

At this time, the battalion was undergoing training while in divisional reserve. The training syllabus for February 6 called for Lewis gunners to practise for most of the afternoon, so Deward's shooting must have been at the ranges.[173]

The Lewis gun course was something over and above the training that he underwent with the battalion. This course was much more advanced (see Deward's daily descriptions below), and was likely run by the Canadian Corps' Lewis gun School.

February 7, 1918: I went to Neuville-St. Vaast for clothing, but got nothing. I left for Mont-St. Eloi, about a one-hour walk away. Got on train at 9:00 p.m. it did not leave until 1:30 a.m.

February 8, 1918: Arriving at Lillers 11:00 a.m. Marched to Lières arriving at 2:00 p.m. to bed at 7:00 p.m. A lot of machine gun [Lewis gun] courses here.

February 10, 1918: Bath. Orderly Corporal for supper. Wrote Lucy no. 27.

February 11, 1918: Ceremonial parade. [Lecture on] stripping gun and naming parts. Gas respirator inspection. At concert, "Y Emmas," it was good.

Earlier in the war, the job of arranging entertainment for Canadian troops at the front fell to the individual battalion chaplains, who spent as much time organizing concerts, movies, and sports as they did shepherding their flock. By 1917, however, the job had passed to the Canadian YMCA, which by the end of that year was running twenty-five concert halls and cinemas in France and Belgium. Performing on these stages were a variety of concert parties — performing troupes — from various units of the Canadian Corps.

The man most associated with entertaining the troops was Capt. Merton Plunkett of the YMCA. Plunkett made his fame as a singer and stand-up comedian in the tent city at Albert during the closing days of the Somme offensive and quickly became influential in shaping the Canadian Corps' policies on maintaining morale through the use of theatrical presentations in the forward areas. Plunkett formed a concert party of his own, the Y Emmas. The name comes from the phonetic alphabet of the day: "Emma" was the phonic for the letter M. The model for the Y Emmas was the Princess Patricia's Canadian Light Infantry Comedy Company. But instead of performing and soldiering, as the Patricias did, the Y Emmas were excused front-line duty and became full-time performers, which eventually became the practice for most concert parties. Plunkett went on to become an impresario of amateur soldier-talent and was associated with the formation of many concert parties through 1917 and 1918 — the most famous of these being the Dumbells, the 3rd Canadian Divisional concert party, which went on to have a successful show business career after the war. By war's end, there were no less than thirty Canadian concert parties operating in France.[174] The intensity of their performances is best summed up by the Reverend Canon Frederick Scott, senior chaplain to the 1st Canadian Division:

> Could any performer ask for a more sympathetic hearing? Not a joke was lost upon the men, not a gesture was unobserved; and when some song with a well-known chorus was started, through the murky atmosphere of cigarette smoke would rise a volume of harmony which would fairly shake the building ... Some of those men that were joining in the rollicking ragtime tune were dying

men. Some of the eyes kindling with laughter at the broad farce of the play, within a few hours would be gazing upon the mysteries behind the screen of mortal life.[175]

February 12, 1918: Ceremonial Parade. [Lewis gun] mechanism [lecture] and gun drill. Wrote Lucy no. 28.

February 13, 1918: [Lewis gun] mechanism [lecture] in morning, gun drill in afternoon, stripping [the gun] blindfolded. Wrote Lucy no. 29.

February 14, 1918: Stripping blindfolded the mechanism on a German Maxim. Wrote Lucy no. 30.

As early as March 1917, Canadian Lewis gunners were receiving specific training on how to operate captured enemy machine guns.[176]

February 15, 1918: Mechanism lectures and shooting "trial." Band concert at night.

February 16, 1918: Cold. Full pack ceremonial. [Practised clearing] stoppages, timed stripping without taking the cylinder off. Cleaned gun. Received no. 29, no. 30, no. 31, box no. 18, wrote Lucy no. 31.

By stripping the Lewis gun "without taking the cylinder off" Deward is most likely referring to the gas cylinder, which was used to direct some of the gas from the fired cartridge away from the muzzle and back to the firing mechanism, re-cocking the gun for the next round.

February 17, 1918: Church at YMCA tent. Walked to Lillers (quite a big place) and back, four kilometres [two miles] away. To bed early.

February 18, 1918: Firing on ranges, helping with the [Lewis gun] limbers. From 3:00 to 4:00 p.m. examination. Played cards.

February 19, 1918: Examinations, passed with highest marks, "excellent," everything in soldiering. On a wiring party in afternoon, wrote Lucy no. 32.

February 20, 1918: Gas lectures. Boys came out of line, very quiet trip. That was the only trip I had missed in the trenches. Received Lucy's no. 34 and from Nora. Wrote to Nora and Lucy no. 33.

February 21, 1918: Miniature warfare. Bath. Saw L.C. Bell at night.

Deward was a proud and proficient soldier, and by this time, some of his qualities were clearly being recognized. His reference to "miniature warfare," however, remains puzzling. A review of the 19th Battalion's *War Diary* for the end of February 1918 shows they were undergoing training while in divisional reserve. Specifically, February 21 was spent taking baths, getting paid, and attending various quartermaster's parades for new issues of clothing and equipment.[177]

February 22, 1918: Up at 4:30 a.m. we slept next to the chicken pen. We left Lières at 7:15 a.m. marched and passed through Ferfay to Pernes. Arrived at 9:15 a.m. took train. On the way here, Lieutenant Fletcher was in charge and took us all in and paid for drinks at Ferfay. At 4:00 p.m. arrived Mont-St. Eloi. At 9:30 p.m. marched to Villers-au-Bois arriving at 12:30 a.m. for the rest of the night.

February 23, 1918: We left at 8:00 a.m. for Chateau-de-la-Haie, Madam Sarah Bernhardt's estate. Arrived at 10:30 a.m. Saw football game in the afternoon. "A" Company won 3 to 2. To bed early.

Château-de-la-Haie was one of several properties owned by the French actress Sarah Bernhardt. Because of its proximity to the front lines, Madame Bernhardt had turned the property over to the military for use as a camp and training ground. John Becker of the 75th Battalion left us this brief glimpse of the camp:

> In the surrounding trees were groups of Nissen huts. These were constructed of galvanized iron sheets erected in a semi-circle from the ground overhead, [had] board floors, and usually had a stove in the centre. We slept on blankets on the floor about 40 to a hut. These huts at the Château were arranged in groups, the groups being called Niagara, Ottawa, Toronto, and Vancouver Camps.[178]

February 24, 1918: On ranges in the morning. Wrote Lucy no. 34, wrote Nora. Received nos. 35, 36, 37, 39; received from Nora.

February 25, 1918: Over to gas hut. Wrote Lucy no. 35, nothing to do.

The gas hut was a facility for ongoing training in the use of respirators. A soldier was considered sufficiently trained if he could don his gas mask and have it properly adjusted in less than six seconds, and this required frequent practice. As the instructors would often quip, "In the case of a gas attack, there are only two classes of soldiers, the quick, and the dead." With their masks in place, the soldiers were passed through a room full of chlorine gas. These exercises helped to assure the men that their protective equipment really worked, which would give them added confidence when wearing the device in battle.[179] Although gas training took place under controlled conditions, it was still extremely dangerous and accidents sent many a careless man to hospital.[180]

February 26, 1918: On parade. Lewis gun firing. Boots repaired. Wrote Lucy no. 36. Went to See Too's concert with Peters and Walker.

The See Too's was the 2nd Canadian Division's concert party. They took their name from the insignia of the 2nd Division, a capital letter C surrounding a Roman numeral two.

John "Jock" Peters was one of Deward's section mates. The twenty-three-year-old native of Coatbridge, Scotland, was working as a clerk in Hamilton, Ontario, when he joined the 120th Battalion in the middle of November 1915. He arrived in England in August 1916 to undergo his advanced training, and after a short stint in the 134th Battalion, he was posted to the 19th Battalion in France in late May 1917, about eight weeks after Deward had arrived at the battalion.

We don't know who Walker was.

February 27, 1918: I was put in charge of the Lewis gun section for this trip. We left the chateau at 3:00 p.m. arriving in the front lines at Lens at 8:00 p.m. We relieved the 22nd French Canadian Battalion, who had their wind up. Terrible place to get at through trenches, wire and jumping over things and pitch dark. Our post was the first street in Lens and the outpost was on the second street. The first street was call Rum Jar Alley. He (Fritz) used to send a terrible lot of shells from trench mortars (called Rum Jars). When off-duty we stayed in a cellar of a house by a pump and he knew the well was there. It was a bad place and we were shelled every so often. Received letters, nos. 32, 33, 40; received letter from Abe, received letter from Martha.

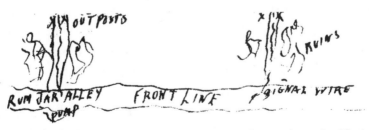

Sketch showing the post that Deward's section took over from the 22nd Battalion on the evening of February 27, 1918.

The 19th Battalion was now taking up positions not far from where they had fought at Hill 70.

February 28, 1918: Stood-down at 6:00 a.m. to eat. We always got tea in the winter trenches. It came up in gasoline cans and sometimes you thought you were drinking gas. We were rum jarred and thought for sure he would get our cellar. The dirt and dust came down as he knocked part of our house down. When we looked outside an iron bed was hanging over the wall. Cellars are always good [for protection]. Stood-to at 5:30 a.m. Lens and suburbs are thickly housed.

March 1, 1918: Stood-down at 6:00 a.m. Long nights. Stood-to at 5:30 p.m. Went out to our outpost that night with an officer and another private, three of us. It was about half a block from the front line, houses all in ruins. Had to go over brick and debris to get there. Outposts were in the cellars of each row. Keeping watch in front, you couldn't move in daytime. From each outpost to the front line we had a wire which gave signals to a man, who was on duty at these places all the time to signal back and forth. When we got to the post they told us that they were sure that a German outpost was in front about fifty yards [forty-five metres] away. So, the officer says we'll go see. We started from our outpost crawling on our hands and knees. Extended out, the three of us with pistols, and it was sure slow going. I thought we would never get there between crawling and stopping to listen, but when we got there, there was nothing. But we knew they were not far away. I wasn't anxious to venture any further and I guess the others weren't either. We were expecting everything to happen on that front at any minute. It was a dangerous place, snipers and outposts all over. We were always on edge and had little sleep over it.

One day we thought we heard the Germans tunnelling under us. You could hear them. It was reported and they sent men up from the Intelligence department to take soundings.

They could hear nothing. It would be a fine thing to get blown up. An exciting trip!

Tunnelling, or mining, had been a feature of the Western Front for some time and had its origins in medieval sieges. The practice involved digging a tunnel under the enemy's trench, filling the end with explosives, and blowing it up — along with the enemy trench above and anyone who was occupying it at the time. As a consequence, elaborate orders were put in place to deal with enemy mines. Often, there were warning signs that the enemy was mining a trench. The most usual was the sound of digging, which during quiet moments could actually be heard on the surface. More often than not, however, the noises attributed to mining activities turned out to emanate from other sources: construction work on another part of the trench line, sentries stamping their feet, rats on the parapet, loose beams or branches blown by the wind, running water, the beating sound of a man's own heart, a half-dead fly buzzing in the bottom of a hole (it was thought to be the sound of a drill working underground), or even actual mining — of their own side.[181] That such a variety of innocent noises could be attributed to mining indicates the anxiety that at any minute you could be blown sky high and crushed to death amid the falling debris.

Received letters from Nora, Ira, Bella, two from Beatrice.

March 2, 1918: Stood-down at 6:00 a.m. Corporal Bacon, Peters, Sergeant Hiley and I stood-to from 5:30 p.m. Artillery fight and trench mortars. It's a death trap here. Wire signals to outpost. We never fired a shot from here, it didn't do to make him sure we were there. He could shell us out of existence in five minutes. Tea at 11:30 p.m. every night. There was plenty of water and they made the tea farther back in a deep cellar when it was dark enough so [the Germans] couldn't see the smoke. We got rum every morning — to steady our nerves, I guess. Stood-down at 6:00 a.m.

Frank Hiley was another of the 180th Battalion men with whom Deward served in the 19th Battalion. Hiley was born in Staffordshire, England, but grew up in Wales before immigrating to Canada in his early twenties. The thirty-one-year-old carpenter by trade had over eleven years of combined experience in the Pembrokeshire Yeomanry and the Canadian militia when he enlisted in the CEF at the end of January 1916. Hiley and his wife made their home in the Balmy Beach district of Toronto.[182]

March 3, 1918: Went to sleep and wakened up at 1:00 p.m. shelling. Peters, Hiley, and I on a job. Stood-to at 5:30. The Germans were expected over. We had two bombs in each pocket. That morning an officer, Lieutenant Switzer, came around at stand-down and says "Why don't you fire the gun?" He just came in the line and does not know the front; had been drinking. I told him I would not fire the gun. He threatened to report me. I wasn't getting trapped for an officer, there was nothing to fire at. He was finally reverted and put in jail for cowardice later on. I wished he had reported it, but he didn't!

Albert Switzer was a Canadian living in Detroit, Michigan, when he enlisted with the 99th Battalion at Windsor, Ontario, in late February 1916. Like Hiley, Switzer was a carpenter. At one point in his military career, he must have been something of a rising star. He was posted to France with the 19th Battalion in the middle of September 1916 and, incredibly, only three months later was sent back to England to receive a commission — and this in spite of having spent fifty days of the intervening time in hospital recovering from venereal disease. At the end of May 1917, Switzer returned to the 19th Battalion with his commission. He was only with the battalion for five weeks before landing in hospital to receive further treatment for syphilis. Switzer was released in mid-September, but was back in hospital in early November, suffering from trench fever. Switzer returned to duty with the 19th Battalion at the end of January 1918 and remained there, except for a month-long posting to the 2nd Canadian Machine Gun Battalion during April and May, until the end of the war. In mid-April 1919, shortly after arriving back in England, he contracted influenza and died. Undoubtedly, Switzer was placed in a difficult position: promoted above the men with whom he had served only briefly and having little experience as a front-line soldier. Under the stress of this situation, he may well have lost his ability to relate to his men and may have become the target of jealous resentment and spiteful rumours. Had he turned to drink for solace, it could explain why he appeared intoxicated the night he encountered Deward (there is even evidence that Switzer stood a court martial for drunkenness in 1918 — not for cowardice as Deward suggests) and, possibly, why he took a posting away from the battalion for a month.[183] As we shall see later, however, Switzer had another reason for wanting to distance himself from the 19th Battalion. Today, Lieutenant Switzer lies in the Bramshott (St. Mary) Churchyard cemetery in Hampshire, England.

> One night, all the men on the outpost next to us ran away and left their post, every man of them. Sergeant Scott was too good to report it. They got frightened. We had four days in the front line and left at 8:00 p.m. for supports in Liévin.

We are left to wonder if the men who ran away were harrowed by the fear and wonder of spectres that could haunt the night watch. Panic can be infectious. Deward told us earlier he "could swear" he saw "things move" when standing night sentry. And James Pedley wrote:

> There were few men so lacking in imagination as not to see grotesque shapes in the darkness of No-Man's Land. By the uncertain gleam of the flares every tuft of grass was metamorphosed into a German trench helmet. I have had the same experience often — you see the man not ten yards away — you doubt whether or not it is a man — he turns his head, or moves an arm — for sure it is a man. Then another movement, and you smile, for it is only a

bush. We all saw, and were frightened at, such apparitions; but the most of us had enough nerve control to fight off the panic that they engendered.[184]

Quitting a front-line post was an extremely serious offence and offered a maximum penalty of death. That Sergeant Scott did not report the offenders speaks well for the calibre of senior NCOs in the battalion, who apparently felt comfortable enough with their grasp of the men that they could deal with the culprits on their own.

March 4, 1918: Arrived Liévin at 12:30 a.m. in a hotel cellar. It wasn't so far away but it was hard getting out of the line. That day, I cleaned the gun and was on fatigue. The Germans came over on the 21st Battalion who had relieved us, we just got out in time. They came over with our steel helmets on and full pack. They got through to the support trench, but were forced back. They were after prisoners. He sent gas over and we stood-to.

Liévin had a population of seventy thousand people and had streetcars. Received letter from Bert Marden. Wrote Lucy no. 37 and Nora.

Deward again mentions Germans wearing British steel helmets, and again there is no mention of this in any of the official reports on the action.[185] The fact that this is unsubstantiated here and previously leads one to wonder if this kind of trickery existed more as rumour than ruse.

March 5, 1918: Gas guard from 3:00 a.m. to 4:00 a.m. Went up to the 21st Battalion for Brailsford's kit. RAP by brickfield up Crocodile Communication Trench. Left Liévin "Mansion House" at 5:00 p.m. for new close supports — Crimson Trench. On fatigue at night to Crow's Corner, up past Cow Trench. Gas guard from 10.30 to 11:00 p.m.

An examination of [Harold] Brailsford's service record reveals no reason that Deward should have to go "up to the 21st

Battalion" for his kit. Brailsford may have been acting as one of the 19th Battalion's guides the previous night, during the relief by the 21st Battalion, and had left his kit behind. This, however, doesn't answer why Brailsford couldn't go for it himself.[186]

The "RAP" was the Regimental Aid Post, or first aid centre. This was usually the first place a casualty went for treatment and its location, therefore, was important information for all.

"Crow's Corner," or Crow Dump, was a ration dump where Deward and his carrying party must have reported at night to draw water and food.[187]

March 6, 1918: The 21st Battalion pulled a raid off at 2:00 a.m. Shaved and not washed. Airman brought Heiney plane down, one fell out, the other crushed to death. The 4th Brigade got credit for stopping the offensive, their "feelers," as they are called. The Germans who broke through the 21st Battalion's lines had full packs on, which meant they intended to stay. And ten thousand Germans stood-to behind them on the Lens front. If the "feelers" could have held on, the rest would have come. But we, the British, had too many men for them. No wonder we had been nervous on that front.

We used hundreds of Geophones. So did he. They were placed near us and then at night everything important could be heard.

Besides [gathering] information, sometimes you raided for prisoners, and sometimes just to kill all you can. Raids lasted from ten to twenty minutes, you had to bring your wounded back with you.

Left Crimson Trench 10:30 p.m. through Liévin. Wrote and sent Lucy a green envelope.

In just over two weeks' time, the Germans would launch their massive spring offensive, Operation Michael, also known as the *Kaiserschlacht*, or "Emperor's battle," which pushed the Allied lines back in some places as much as forty miles (sixty-five kilometres) — and very nearly won them the war. It is likely that the raid on the 4th

Brigade front on March 4 was a probe to test the local defences and the defensive posture of the garrison, in preparation for this offensive. The presence of large reserves waiting to exploit a successful raid, however, would seem to support Deward's suggestion that they were planning to stay. While it might be overstating the case to claim the 4th Brigade stopped a German offensive, it's worth noting that, although the Allied lines buckled heavily to the north and south during Operation Michael, the lines in the Canadian-held sector of Lens were largely bypassed and remained unchanged through the duration of the offensive.

Geophones were a stethoscope-like device used to hear sounds transmitted through the ground. Although they were very effective at detecting mining operations, it is unlikely they were as sensitive as Deward's claims would make them.

Trench raids were localized attacks, usually conducted at night. The size of the raid could vary from just a handful of soldiers to an entire company — or larger, depending on its objectives. As Deward mentions above, a raid could have one of several goals: reconnoitering the enemy's trenches, grabbing prisoners for interrogation, or inflicting as much mayhem on the enemy as possible. Raids were extremely dangerous undertakings that were frequently more popular with the General Staff than they were with the rank and file. Edmund Blunden, the noted British war poet, observed, "The word raid may be defined as the one in the whole vocabulary of the war which most instantly caused a sinking feeling in the stomach of ordinary mortals."[188] In writing of the trench raids that occurred during the winter of 1917 to 1918, the official Canadian historian Colonel G.W.L. Nicholson made the following summary: "These operations, each in itself of minor proportions, over the winter had taken a fairly substantial toll. Between 1 December 1917 and 21 March 1918 the Canadian Expeditionary Force suffered 3552 casualties, of which 684 were fatal."[189]

March 7, 1918: Got headache about 2:00 a.m. Arrived Chateau-de-la-Haie at 2:30 a.m. Had breakfast, slept till 10:30 a.m. had breakfast again. Cleaned up. Paid twenty-five francs. Kit inspection. Still had an awful headache, went to the M.O. Started another green envelope, no. 38. Went to bed early that night.

March 8, 1918: Mess orderly. Cleaned gun. Bath. Played checkers with Gerry Anning. Wrote Lucy no. 39. Wrote Bert Marden and Abe.

The twenty-four-year-old Anning was born at Toronto Junction, Ontario (now part of west-central Toronto), and gave farming as his occupation when he enlisted in the 123rd Battalion at the end of 1915. Anning arrived in England in mid-August 1916 and three months later was serving at the front with the 19th Battalion. In mid-March 1917, he received a slight gunshot wound to his hand and left leg, but remained on duty. Otherwise, Anning remained out of harm's way for the duration of the fighting. While overseas, he met and fell in love with a woman from Belfast, Ireland, whom he married in early 1919.[190]

March 9, 1918: The battalion paraded at 9:00 a.m. Cleaned Lewis gun. Off in the afternoon. Clothing parade. Received photos from Bella. Went to See Too concert with Peters. Time changed one hour ahead (daylight saving time).

Another term for daylight saving time that was common then was "Summer Time."

March 10, 1918: Up at 7:00 a.m. Church at 9:15 a.m. at See Too hut, games in the afternoon. Received letter from Rivett. Wrote Lucy green envelope.

March 11, 1918: Left Chateau de la Haie at 10:00 a.m. Marched through Gouy Servins, Bouvigny, Petit Sains, Fosse 10, and arrived Noeux-les-Mines at 2:30 p.m. Billeted in houses. Big town. Went out with Peters, wrote Lucy no. 40. We are Corps Reserves at one hour's notice.

Being in Corps Reserve meant the battalion had to maintain a certain state of readiness, capable of responding to a call for assistance at the front within an hour.

March 12, 1918: Kit inspection. Bath at 12:30 p.m. Wrote Bella, Rivett, and Ira. Received letters from Lucy, nos. 41, 42, 43, 44, 45, 46, 47, and from Mother and Beatrice.

Court martial of Private Lodge. Sentenced to be shot. As he had been in our company I was afraid I might be put on the firing party. I had done everything in war up until then but that I dreaded. I was warned to see the sergeant-major at 9:45 p.m. When I got there, I had to go upstairs in a room with others. There were twelve of us (two spare) and an NCO of course. I knew, or guessed, when I was first warned to see the sergeant-major [why he wanted me]. The sergeant-major called each one of us down separately and told us. I tried my best to get off but he said Captain Harstone had picked out the best shots in the company and it was my duty. We had to report again to the sergeant-major and captain for instructions. He told us that we would not handle the rifles, only fire them. The officer in charge would load them and afterwards examine them. We got back to our billet at midnight.

Lodge's court martial was actually held on February 23. Lodge was found guilty on one charge of desertion and on two charges of attempting to desert. Despite receiving a good character reference from Maj. H.C. Hatch, the officer commanding the 19th Battalion at the time, the court considered the deliberate and repeated nature of his offence serious enough to warrant the maximum penalty, and Lodge was duly sentenced to suffer death by shooting. His sentence was reviewed and upheld by Field Marshall Haig on March 10, 1918.[191]

The night before Lodge was executed, James Pedley, an officer with the 4th Battalion, in billets at nearby Bracquemont, spent the evening calling on friends and acquaintances in the 19th Battalion. Among those he visited was his good friend from the

University of Toronto Law School, Arthur Duncan (Duncan had also been one of Deward's officers in the 180th Battalion). Pedley later wrote:

> It was a notable night for the 19th. At dawn next day a deserter was to be shot ... While Arthur and I talked in the gathering night we knew that the sun had gone down for the last time on one poor tortured soul. It made us a bit solemn. As a matter of fact, the rumour afterwards circulated that the doomed man spent the night quite happily, playing poker with his guards, whereas the officer who was detailed to command the firing squad had a terrible night, threatening to become delirious more than once as the thought of his awful task seared him.[192]

March 13, 1918: Woke up at 4:00 a.m. I reported to the sergeant-major at 4:15 a.m. and then went to the Battalion Orderly Room at 4:30 a.m. to see Lieutenant Switzer. Two men were laid off, leaving only ten men and Sergeant Thatcher and Lieutenant Switzer. We went to the ranges where the execution took place. They had a curtain around, high enough that you could not see over, on a space of fifteen by fifteen yards [fourteen by fourteen metres] with a drop curtain in front of the firing squad. By this time the whole battalion was lined up outside so as they could hear the shots and would learn a lesson about deserting. Guards were placed all around, with fixed bayonets, during the night. The officer (Lieutenant Switzer) had loaded the rifles and left them laying on the ground at our position. We got into position and were warned to fire straight, or we may have [to suffer] the same fate. The prisoner was taken out of a car (we saw him get out, with a black cap over his head and guarded) and placed on the other side of the curtain. After a while the Provost Marshall told us that the prisoner would not have anything to do with communion or the Church and all he asked is for us to shoot straight and make a good job of it. We took our positions, five kneeling and five standing behind; the sergeant on one side, and the Officer on the other to give orders. If we did not kill him, the Officer would have to. As soon as the curtain dropped (the prisoner was tied in a chair five paces away from us, a black cap over his head and a big round disc over his heart) we got the order to fire. One blank and nine live rounds. It went off as one. I did not have the blank. The prisoner did not feel it. His body moved when we fired, then the curtain went up. That was the easiest way for an execution I had heard of. The firing squad only saw him for a few minutes. We went back to the Battalion Orderly Room and got a big tumbler of rum each, and went to our billets, ate, and went to bed. We had the rest of the day off. It was a job I never wanted.

Wrote Lucy no. 41 (green envelope) and Nora and Beatrice. Downtown with Peters at night. Played cards with Gerry Anning.

It was a cruel twist of fate that obliged Deward, a man sympathetic with those who had lost their nerve, to participate in the death of a deserter. Deward was a good soldier and worked hard to develop his skill at arms against the enemy, which makes the irony especially bitter when he learns those skills are why his superiors chose him for a job he "never wanted." Lodge too, after all, had been a good soldier. Not all men convicted of desertion, however, were sentenced to death, and most of the condemned had their sentences commuted to prison time. With a clean record and a good word from Major Hatch, Lodge might also have received a more lenient sentence, but his determination to escape duty limited the court's leeway in sentencing and denied him any chance of clemency.

As might be expected in any large, diverse group of people, attitudes in the CEF toward capital punishment varied considerably. Many believed it was necessary to maintain discipline. Capt. Agar Adamson of Princess Patricia's Canadian Light Infantry and Lieutenant Colonel Tremblay of the 22nd Battalion, for example, lobbied to have some of their own men shot as examples to the rest of their respective battalions. Other men were "angered" and "dumbfounded" that the army would drive a comrade beyond his endurance and then kill him when he broke.[193]

The Reverend Canon Frederick Scott ministered to William Alexander of the 10th Battalion the night before his execution in October 1917. Later, while reflecting on his wartime experience, Scott was moved to write the following, which would surely have resonated with Deward:

> I have seen many ghastly sights in the war, and hideous forms of death … but nothing ever brought home to me so deeply, and with such cutting force, the hideous nature of war and the iron hand of discipline, as did that lonely death on the misty hillside in the early morning. Even now, as I write this brief account of it, a dark nightmare seems to rise out of the past and almost makes me shrink from facing once again memories that were so painful.[194]

Harold Lodge was one of twenty-three Canadians executed during the Great War for either desertion or cowardice (two other Canadians were also executed for murder).

The purpose of having one rifle loaded with a blank round was to offer faint hope to the men of the firing party prior to the exe-

Deward's sketch of the Lodge execution site, showing the curtain wall that surrounded the prisoner and the firing party. Notice how the battalion was drawn up on either side of the screen to hear the shots ring out and "learn a lesson about deserting."

cution that they would not actually fire a shot into the prisoner. Naturally, when the order to fire was given, any doubt would be gone. Deward certainly could tell the difference between the feel of a live round and a blank one, as could any trained soldier.

March 14, 1918: Rain. Cleaned ammunition. Paraded with gun from 10:00 a.m. to 12:00 noon. Wrote Lucy no. 42 and Martha. Out at night. Played cards, received letter from Nora.

March 15, 1918: [Attended the] battalion parade with the Lewis gun from 10:30 to 12:00 noon at the school house. Games in afternoon. Received box no. 19. Alex Armstrong, Jock Peters, and I went for walk all around town.

March 16, 1918: The battalion paraded to the ranges from 10:30 a.m. to 3:30 p.m. Dinner at 3:35 p.m. Received letter from Bella, received nos. 48, 49, 50. Stayed in at night.

March 17, 1918: Up at 8:00 a.m. church at 9:00 a.m. Football 10:30 a.m. — "A" and "D" Coy's. "A" Coy won, 1 to 0. Wrote Nora and Lucy, no. 43. Out with Peters at night. Received letter from May.

March 18, 1918: Battalion parade with Lewis gun, 11:00 a.m. to 12:30 p.m. Sports, "A" & "D" Coy. 4 to 1, in favour of "D" Coy. Wrote May. Stayed in.

March 19, 1918: Rain. Lewis gun 10:30 a.m. to 12:15 p.m. Paid 20 francs. Wrote Bella. Went for a walk, Alex, Peters, and I.

March 20, 1918: Company inspections, then off all day. Played cards. Wrote Lucy no. 44. Went to French movie show. Peters, Gerry, George Morrison, Dick Davis, and I went.

March 21, 1918: Battalion parade. Went to ranges for attack practice. Baseball game, "A" Coy. Went for a walk with Peters.

The town was bombed and shelled at night. It was the beginning of the German offensive. They came over on the Arras front. Their officers were on horseback. They thought they were going to march right through. The first seven waves were cut down, they had seven men deep in each wave.

In the predawn of March 21, through the last, dying hours of winter, seventy-six German assault divisions assembled along a fifty-mile stretch of the British front between Arras and La Fère, ready to spring the Kaiserschlacht. The German high command was playing their last card; it was a gamble that, if it paid off, would win a decisive victory in the west before overwhelming numbers of American forces arrived in France. Bolstered by reinforcements from the Eastern Front, where a peace treaty with the Bolshevik revolutionaries had been signed earlier in the month, the German Stormtroops struck like lightning at the British Third and Fifth Armies, sending them reeling back in shock some forty miles (sixty-five kilometres), forcing a wide gap in the lines. The week of fighting that followed inflicted heavy losses in men and material on both sides. By April 5, the exhausted and bloodied Germans had lost their momentum, and the offensive began to falter. Stiffening British resistance and supply shortages eventually halted the advance short of Amiens and allowed the British to consolidate their positions.

The Germans were not beaten yet, however. On April 9, they launched another massive attack against the British, this time in Flanders, where they retook the Passchendaele Ridge and most of the territory won from them in the autumn of 1917. On May 27, this time against the French, the Germans made similar, large-scale gains in Champagne before they were fought to a standstill on the banks of the Marne River. In both these attacks, the action followed a pattern similar to that of the earlier one, with initial spectacular gains followed by overextended supply lines and a slow grinding down of forward impetus. There were two more offensives, one in June and another in July, but by early August, the best of the German Army was spent. The great gamble was lost.

During this period, the Canadian Corps — minus the 2nd Division — was not engaged by the enemy and continued to hold an increasingly longer stretch of the front line in the Vimy-Lens sector. On March 23, Deward and the 2nd Division were placed in General Headquarters Reserve and put at the disposal of Field Marshall Haig. They remained under British command until the beginning of July, when they were reunited with the rest of the Canadian Corps.[195]

March 22, 1918: Battalion inspection with Lewis gun. Off for afternoon. Played cards. Received letter from Abe. Wrote Lucy no. 45.

March 23, 1918: Battalion parade with Lewis gun. Off in the afternoon.

March 24: Had warfare at ranges for staff (smoke bombs) from 8:00 a.m. to 10:00 a.m. Went to the Paymaster. We were warned to move at 12:00 noon and left Noeux-les-Mines at 2:30 p.m. Marched to Gouy Servins to a chateau arriving at 6:00 p.m. Very hot day, ringing wet from sweating and heavy pack. Had tea and went to bed at 9:00 p.m.

March 25, 1918: Up at 5:00 a.m. Left Gouy Servins at 9:30 a.m. in trucks, arriving at 10:30 a.m. Billeted in huts on the right of Vimy. Tea at 3:00 p.m. Wrote Lucy no. 46 and Nora and Beatrice.

March 26, 1918: Spent the day digging trenches at Daylight Railway. Left at 7:30 a.m. and back at 1:00 p.m. Played cards. Received letters from Bella and Abe. Heiney plane brought down by machine gun.

"Daylight Railway" was probably the soldier's name for a local position.

March 27, 1918: Up at 4:30 a.m. stand-to. Germans expected. Played cards in the morning, then on fatigue to Daylight Railway again, cleaning a trench, and back at 6:00 p.m. Warned to pack and leave at 7:30 p.m. Left at 8:15 p.m. forced march about twenty-five miles [forty kilometres] — the longest forced march we had had getting from one front to another. We would march one hour, then rest for five minutes (wearing our heavy marching order) and this was kept up until we arrived at Bailleulment at 2:30 a.m. It was a tough march.

March 28, 1918: Slept in hay loft. Breakfast at 9:00 a.m. Goodman treated us to cake and coffee at French house. No mail allowed to be sent. No canteen or paper. We are on fifteen minutes notice "stand-to."

March 29, 1918: Good Friday. Very sick headache. Called out at 12:30 p.m. (had dinner in field) — Germans thought to have broken through. Cancelled. Was glad we did not go, too sick. Posted letter and field post card. Left Bailleulment at 10:45 p.m. to the last line of trenches, arriving at 4:00 a.m. Passed Wailly eight or nine miles [thirteen or fourteen kilometres] from the start. Good Friday.

March 30, 1918: Stood-to all morning, slept all day. Moved to supports at 7:30 p.m. Arrived at 9:00 p.m. dug funk hole and gun emplacement from then until 12:00 midnight. Slept cold. Rain and cold. We mostly have to sleep in the open from now on. Dig a hole and put your rubber sheet over it. The nights are chilly. Sometimes in a field, sometimes in a trench. Wherever they happen to stop. Kept out of towns mostly.

CHAPTER 7

Operation Michael and the Spring Offensive, March 31 to June 13, 1918

"I fired the gun point blank at them, they all went down."

March 31, 1918: Easter Sunday. Up at 6:00 a.m. lovely day. Received letter from Rivett, two from Nora, and sent field [post] cards to Lucy, Nora, and Bella. Feel fine, cleaned gun. Nothing to do. Rain. Fired four pans [of ammunition] at planes; nearly all [of us were] on fatigue. We left supports at 6:30 p.m. He brought seven [of our observation] balloons down.

April 1, 1918: "April Fools Day." Rain. Up at 6:00 a.m. nearly all on fatigue. Had roast meat, ho ho. Left supports for the front line. Had to stop on account of shelling. Arrived 12:30 a.m. Rain.

Deward's small aside, "ho ho," probably says a great deal about the poor quality of the rations they were receiving at the time. Most of Deward's "A" Company spent five hours in the dark widening and deepening a nearby, soggy trench.[196]

April 2, 1918: At 12:30 a.m. two hours on, five hours off. Heiney expected. Rum in the morning, four on a loaf. Shelters. A few dead lying around. Rain. Company dug trench in front, except for the Number 1 and Number 2 on the [Lewis] gun. 7:30 p.m. to bed.

April 3, 1918: On-duty at 5:00 a.m. Cleaned gun. Received Lucy's nos. 51, 52, 53, and 58. Received from Babe Chubb, Gertie Dodds, Bert Marden, Bea. Wrote Lucy no. 47.

April 4, 1918: Received Lucy's nos. 54, 57, 59, 60, 61. Received Frieda's letter. Rain all day. We are on the Arras front and at the nearest point of the line to Arras.

April 5, 1918: We moved to a new support trench. Stood-to at 5:00 a.m. Germans expected. Hostile shelling, heavy from 5:30 a.m. to 9:30 a.m. Germans started to come over but his advance party was cut up and he changed his mind.

Captain Harstone was sniped, wounded. This was a bad trench and it had been raining all day. You had to lie in the trench, in water and mud, for a rest. He sent gas shells over all night back farther. When he started that shelling from 5:30 a.m. to 9:30 a.m. he started to come. This usually happens on a rainy, mucky day. He didn't get any more than halfways over and we all opened fire.

I remember well a new man with us, a young fellow, Jim Latimer (who later on lost an eye). He had made a couple of trips but this was his worst. New men are not so afraid the first trip or two when it is quiet because they don't realize what damage can be done. Latimer used to laugh at the way some of the old timers and others would shake. This time poor Latimer was shaking like a leaf and as white as a ghost, the first time he had seen some of his pals killed.

We left this trench at 10:30 p.m. and went through Wailly. It rained all day and I was mud head to foot.

Captain Harstone received a gunshot wound to his chest that also perforated his abdomen. He was evacuated to the 6th Canadian Field Ambulance and eventually to England, where he underwent a prolonged convalescence. He returned to duty with the 19th Battalion on September 19, 1918.

On April 5, about 180 Germans attempted a daring daylight

raid on the 19th Battalion's trenches after a heavy preparatory bombardment by artillery and trench mortars. The enemy advanced in two parties; the larger, about 150 strong, attacked "C" Company on the battalion's left, while the other party attacked "B" Company on the right (Deward and the rest of "A" Company were in battalion support, to the rear of "B" Company). The larger party was driven off by rifle fire from "C" Company, but the smaller party established a brief toehold in "B" Company's trench before it too was driven off. The battalion suffered five casualties, all wounded. The Germans left one man dead in the trench and eight others in No-Man's Land.[197]

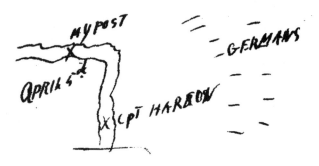

This sketch shows where Captain Harstone (Deward identifies him as Harson in the sketch) was wounded by a sniper and the direction from which the German raid came on April 5, 1918.

April 6, 1918: Arrived at Bailleulment at 7:00 a.m. It was a long hike. I marched along asleep part of the time. Tired out; ate, and slept until noon. Walked to Bellacourt during the day and went to next town to YMCA for biscuits. To bed early (tired).

Sleep was always in short supply for men at the front, and soldiers were only too ready to grab a nap where they could, even if it meant doing so on the march. One veteran of the Imperial forces remembered that being tired was almost a way of life:

> For most of his time the average private was tired ...
> If a company's trench strength was low and sentry-

posts abounded more than usual in its sector, a man might, for eight days running, get no more than one hour off-duty at any one time, day or night. If enemy guns were active many of these hours off guard duty might have to be spent on trench repair ... So most of the privates were tired the whole of the time; sometimes to the point of torment, sometimes much less, but always more or less tired.[198]

Today, we recognize the perils of sleep deprivation. Poor decision making, rigid thought patterns, trouble concentrating, impaired memory, and longer reaction times are all common among the sleep deprived. For a soldier at the front, any one of these effects could be fatal, especially if, while grabbing a much-needed catnap, he slept through a gas alarm. We are left to wonder how many fatal accidents or errors in judgment resulted from a simple lack of sleep.

April 7, 1918: Up at 7:00 a.m. Kit inspection. Got gun. Bath three towns away. Wrote Lucy no. 49. Wrote Nora, Beatrice, Hazel Chubb, Bella, Gertie Dodds. Received box no. 20. Fried eggs and enjoyed eats.

April 8, 1918: Cleaned gun and mud off coat. Wrote Frieda, Ada, and Jessie, Lucy no. 50. Received letter from Nora. Rain. Had lobsters and soup.

Since it's unlikely the rank and file were eating lobsters and soup, even while in reserve, this is probably another of Deward's ironic comments on the quality of the food the army was providing. See, too, Deward's diary entry for April 11, 1918.

April 9, 1918: Left Bailleulment for front line on right at 2:00 p.m. Passed Bellacourt and had supper in the field, then to the front line arriving at 10:00 p.m. Dandy trench with firing step. On-duty all night. Rain. Scots Guards [were posted] on our right.

April 10, 1918: Breakfast at 4:00 a.m. Off-duty at 6:00 a.m. Slept and changed socks in funk hole. On-duty all night long. Tea at 10:30 p.m. Artillery strafe that night. Received Letter nos. 62, 63, 64 from Lucy, and from Nora.

April 11, 1918: Breakfast at 4:00 a.m. off-duty at 6:30 a.m. Slept until 11:00 a.m. Had fried onions and coffee, some class for the front line. Tea at 10:00 p.m. Continued no. 51. Fritz expected; artillery strafe.

Between 6:30 p.m. April 11 and 6:00 a.m. April 12, the Germans dropped 206 shells of various calibres on the 19th Battalion's positions.[199]

April 12, 1918: Stand-to 4:00 a.m. Just at break of day we saw a German party near our line, they must have been wiring and stayed too late to finish it. I fired the gun point blank at them, they all went down. Slept from 7:00 a.m. to 12:30 p.m. Dinner and slept until six. Tea at midnight. We always had tea at night there, and tea and rum in the morning at stand-to time. On-duty every night from 5:00 p.m. to 6:00 a.m. A nervous front.

Germans were expected anytime. Nice weather now. We are near Boyelles.

Continued no. 51, wrote Lucy no. 52.

Sketch showing the location of the German wiring party that Deward discovered near the Canadian lines at daybreak on April 12, 1918. As Deward explains, "I fired the gun point blank at them, they all went down."

Deward indicates no remorse over killing the exposed wiring party. His action with the Lewis gun was in keeping with the policy of "offensive defence" that was maintained by the 4th Canadian Brigade on this "nervous front."[200] It had been less than a month since the opening attacks of the Kaiserschlacht and only three days since the opening of a new German offensive further north, in Belgium.

April 13, 1918: Breakfast at 4:00 a.m. stood-down at 6:00 a.m. Slept to 2:30 p.m. Made tea and soup. Stood-to at 5:00 p.m. Tea at ten. It was mostly gasoline. Nice weather in day, rain and cold every night. Wrote Lucy no. 53.

The men's drinking water was often brought forward in tins that had been previously used to transport gasoline. Regardless of how much the tins were rinsed, the water would always taste of gasoline, and apparently so did anything that was made with it.

April 14, 1918: Breakfast at 4:30 a.m. stand-down at 6:00 a.m. Made soup and bully, slept cold in day-time. Tea at 11:00 p.m. Continued Lucy's letter.

The front line was in front of Boisleux-St. Marc.

April 15, 1918: Breakfast at 4:00 a.m. stand-down at 6:00 a.m. slept to 3:00 p.m. Stand-to at 6:30 p.m. tea at 11:00 p.m. It was a nerve-wracking place, you were always looking for something to happen. I've seen some of the boys shaking here, they could not stop it. I was the most experienced man in the trenches by now. I was afraid but not shaking. I could sleep if I knew a good man was on guard but we knew they were coming sometime so you can guess the feeling we had.

One morning a dud shell hit the back of the trench behind Private Mudge in the next post to us. You could see the base of the shell. He comes down to see me and says that they are after him. He would not stay at that post but made another. Maybe they were after him, for later on [in the war] he lost both his legs.

Wrote Lucy no. 54.

We can start to get a sense of the effect that Hill 70, Passchendaele, and a year of front-line service had on the 19th Battalion when, one year to the day after Deward met up with them for the first time, he is one of the most experienced men left in the unit. See too the note on "wastage" that accompanies Deward's diary entry for April 17, 1918, below.

Even though the main German offensives were taking place further to the north, the prospect of a breakthrough on Deward's front was obviously starting to take its toll on his comrades. We see also the value of character among the men when Deward tells us that he could only get some sleep when he knew "a good man was on guard."

April 16, 1918: Breakfast at 4:00 a.m. stand-to from 4:30 a.m. to 5:30 a.m. now. Slept sound and was woken up at 8:50 a.m. and told that the Germans were in our trench. The [1st Battalion], the King's Liverpool Regiment were on our right now. Our platoon was the last of the Canadians, and then Liverpools. The Germans, about sixty of them, got over during the night and laid in holes and a little trench in front of them [the Liverpools]. They stayed there the rest of the night. At 8:50 a.m. which was their zero hour, the German guns opened up heavy and they jumped into the trench. The Liverpools held a corner of our line, which the Germans wanted to get into. If successful, the Germans would have had their way and driven us out, too. The Liverpools were all new men, mostly boys it seemed, (men were getting scarce at that time).

When the Germans shell and fire for a raid it's always along the whole trench except when the raid is on. The Liverpools got in a panic and some jumped out of the trench. A real panic, crying and frightened. No. 1 Platoon of the 19th Battalion was lying immediately behind them as a reinforcement for us. They jumped out and charged (it was getting on in the afternoon now). They bombed them out. Lieutenant Borthwick, who led [the counterattack], got killed. Sergeant Newell, Sergeant Thatcher and Stretcher Bearer Nichol later received the Military Medal [for their part in this charge]. We were relieved and left the front line at 11:00 p.m.

Lieut. G. Bruce Borthwick was a twenty-seven-year-old accountant from Toronto and one of the 19th Battalion acquaintances that James Pedley was visiting the night before the Lodge execution. For his work leading the counterattack that drove the German raiders from the Liverpool trenches, Borthwick was cited for "intrepid leadership of his platoon and [for setting an] inspiring example to his comrades." He was killed at the height of the action by the blast from an enemy grenade and today lies in the Bellacourt Military Cemetery.[201]

By supporting the King's Regiment against the German raid, the 19th Battalion repaid, however unintentionally, a hundred-year-old debt. In 1813, the Grenadier Company of the 1st Battalion, the King's Regiment (then designated the 8th Regiment of Foot), was decimated while defending the town of York, which would later become Toronto, against a superior force of invading United States troops. The Kingsmen fell mostly at the west end of York's military reserve, land that later in the nineteenth century would become the grounds of the Canadian National Exhibition, where the 19th Battalion first paraded and undertook their initial training in 1914.

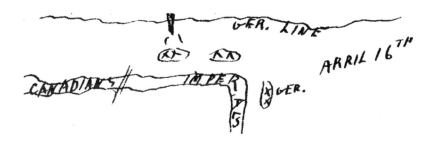

This sketch shows the situation on the morning of April 16, 1918, as the German raiding parties were waiting to spring upon a company of the 1st/King's Regiment, which was occupying the trenches to the right of the 19th Battalion's position.

April 17, 1918: Arrived at Bretencourt at 2:00 a.m. Got tea and bully beef; then to bed and slept in a big tent until 12:00 noon, shaved, etc. Paid twenty francs. At 3:00 p.m. met Cecil Arnold and over to YMCA, supper and wrote Lucy no. 55. The front line we just left was called Boiry [included Boisleux-St. Marc], right of Arras.

Bretencourt is a small place near Beaumetz [Beaumetz-les-Loges]. There was a butcher shop there so we had some steak, heaven knows what kind it was. We slept in a big marquee tent, it was a good place to be, only that one afternoon a shell hit square on our cookhouse and blew it up, men and all. In all these trips in the lines there were always some killed and wounded, no matter how quiet it was. We had to be reinforced every little while to keep up to strength.

By telling us "there were always some killed and wounded, no matter how quiet it was," Deward is describing "wastage." Wastage refers to the number of casualties a unit could expect to lose from all causes (for example, disease, accident, enemy action, and so on) in a month. In 1916, for example, an infantry battalion could expect 10 percent wastage, that is, one in ten men were likely to become casualties during any given month. Machine gunners also experienced 10 percent wastage, while cavalry and artillery experienced 5 percent and 3.5 percent wastage respectively. The Forestry Corps, with a wastage rate of 2 percent, was statistically one of the safer units in which to serve.[202]

A review of the 19th Battalion's *War Diary* for the month of April 1918 does not reveal a reference to the cookhouse incident, so this likely took place at another time and Deward is recalling it here.

April 18, 1918: Up at 7:00 a.m. Bath parade. Got new barrel for gun. Dinner of eggs. Next town is Bellacourt. Had pork chops and eggs at night. Finished Lucy's green letter. Wrote Nora, Beatrice, Willis, and J. Irvin. Beaumetz.

All of the parts on a Lewis gun were replaceable, including the barrel, which would begin to suffer from wear — affecting accuracy — after prolonged use.

April 19, 1918: Up at 7:00 a.m. Cleaned gun. Boot parade. Eggs for breakfast, eggs for dinner, and strawberries. Eggs for supper, and cherries. Wrote Lucy no. 56. Received letters, nos. 65, 66, 67, 68 [from Lucy] and [also] from Beatrice.

Boot parade was a routine feature of life out of the trenches. It was an opportunity for the platoon officer to inspect the men's footwear and to have the quartermaster replace boots that were showing signs of excessive wear. Note that Deward refers correctly to his noonday meal as "dinner" and his evening meal as "supper."

April 20, 1918: Bretencourt. Packs were turned in. Lewis gun inspection, played cards, and fried veal for dinner at 3:30 p.m. In the afternoon we had a lecture by Lieutenant Lewington on Maxim guns. Put our Lewis guns on limbers at 5:00 p.m. and left Bretencourt at 7:00 p.m. for the Purple Line. Passed Wailly and got the guns off their limbers, and then headed overland through Agny, arriving at 9:30 pm. On-duty from 10:00 p.m. to midnight. Cold.

During the Great War, the term "Maxim gun" was used somewhat generically in reference to a family of tripod-mounted, medium machine guns based on a design by American inventor Hiram Maxim. Maxim guns were used on both sides of No-Man's Land. Although the various models were similar in concept, they differed in details, and it was common for the respective armies to train their machine gunners to use captured weapons. Because of this, it's likely Deward was being trained on the use of the German variant, the Maschinengewehr 1908, or MG '08.

The term "Purple Line" most likely refers to the brigade's intermediate support lines; like the term "Red Line" mentioned earlier, its name probably comes from the use of a coloured pen to indicate the position on maps.

April 21, 1918: A nice day, but cold. On-duty from 6:00 a.m. to 8:00 a.m. Fired ten magazines at aeroplanes, Heiney plane brought down. On-duty from 2:00 p.m. to 4:00 p.m. and 9:00 p.m. to 10:00 p.m. Fellows got boxes, received letter from R.T. Wrote Lucy no. 57. We are at Telegraph Hill, four kilometres [two miles] from Arras.

It isn't clear here if Deward means that his Lewis gun brought down the aircraft. Unfortunately, the battalion's *War Diary* doesn't shed any light on the incident.

April 22, 1918: Stand-to from 4:00 a.m. to 5:00 a.m. Breakfast at 7:00 a.m. Stand-to from 8:00 p.m. to 9:00 p.m. on duty from 10:10 p.m. to 11:45 p.m. We are in supports now. Wrote Lucy no. 58, R.T., Beatrice. We had all we could eat.

April 23, 1918: Slept all morning, St. George's Day and Lucy's birthday. On-duty from 5:00 p.m. to 7:00 p.m. and 3:15 a.m. to 4:30 a.m. Stand-to 4:30 a.m. to 6:30 a.m. Slept all morning. Cleaned Lewis gun, twice. Wrote Mrs. Field and finished Lucy's letter. Heiney plane brought down by other plane.

April 24, 1918: Stand-to from 4:30 a.m. to 6:30 a.m. Slept all morning. Cleaned Lewis gun. No mail collections. Ready to move and left the Purple Line at 6:00 p.m. for the front line, arriving at 10:30 p.m. Relieved the 20th Battalion on duty. Rain at night. We are in front of Neuville Vitasse. The Canadians who were here will not forget this front, [where they staged] a raid almost every night.

April 25, 1918: Stood-to from 4:30 a.m. to 5:30 a.m. and stood-to from 6:00 p.m. to 8:00 p.m. On day duty, slept all night. Sun was out, rain at night. Received letter from Bella.

188

April 26, 1918: Stood-to from 4:15 a.m. to 5.15 a.m. We were completely war sick by this time. Alex Armstrong was fed up. Sometimes he got a paper with rations and used to bring it down to me to read the war news.

We always look through periscopes in the daytime. A trench mortar shell came over and hit in the next bay to me at 7:00 a.m. Alex was badly wounded and Davie Bain and Sgt. Mickey Leanard. We brought Alex to my bay as there was more protection and after getting a stretcher made him as comfortable as possible. He was hit in the stomach. I knew Alex was gone. At 11:00 a.m. volunteers took him out overland. The Germans did not fire, they knew he was wounded. Poor Alex suffered.

Stood-to from 8:00 p.m. to 9:00 p.m. and was fish-tailed. Made you think of home. Wrote Lucy no. 59 and Bella.

Using periscopes to look over the parapet into No-Man's Land was a common way to keep an eye on the enemy without exposing yourself to sniper fire. Some officers' periscopes were sophisticated, fully enclosed devices, complete with eyepieces and so on, while others were simply a mirror that a soldier could clip to his bayonet and stick above the trench top at such an angle as to get a view of his immediate front.

It is not clear who Mickey Leanard was. Nobody with that name or a name that closely resembles "Leanard" appears on any of the surviving 19th Battalion rolls.

The "bays" that Deward refers to are features of trench design. Trenches were usually built in a zigzag configuration to contain and minimize the effects of a blast on any given stretch of trench. The part of the zigzag closest to the enemy was a "bay" or sometimes a "firebay."

Here we see again the effects on Deward of a year's service at the front ("we were completely war sick by this time"). Perhaps the Germans who let his wounded friend be carried away were, too.

April 27, 1918: Germans came up to the sa ˙ and they shot Ramsay through the shoulder. It was about 1:00 a.m. We killed one Hun and the rest got away. Stood-to from 4:15 a.m. to 6:15 a.m. Cold day. Alex died, did not get him out soon enough. Had a good funeral [for Alex] near Bailleulment. They had funeral [parties] to the cemetery from that advanced tent hospital when possible. Wrote Lucy green envelope no. 60 and Bella.

According to the battalion's *War Diary*, the German raiding party consisted of eight men. The diary also states the battalion did not suffer any casualties, so it is likely that Ramsay was treated at the Regimental Aid Post and then returned to duty.[203]

Alex Armstrong was laid to rest in the Bac-du-Sud British Cemetery near Bailleulval, France.[204]

April 28, 1918: Stood-to from 4:00 a.m. to 5:00 a.m. Dull and cold. At 1:30 p.m. the Germans made a daylight raid. They hid in the same sap they came up before and at 1:30 p.m. jumped into our trench (when everything was as quiet as could be). Not a shell fired. This sap was on the left of our platoon and they took Ben Moore, Nick Carter, and George Morrison prisoners. Two of them were sleeping in their funk holes and the Germans threw them out of our trench, they did not fire a shot and were after prisoners. Everything was timed. The Germans had to go overland a short distance to get into their own trench that led to their front line. There were about twenty-six of them. The minute it was pulled off the German machine gunners opened and skimmed all along our parapet. The unfortunate part of it, I had my gun down cleaning it. They got away except six.

Received letter and photo from Bert Marden.

Stood-to from 8:00 p.m. to 9:00 p.m. hard unlucky trip for "A" Company.

Five of the six Germans who did not make it back to their own lines were accounted for by Bert Sedore, a twenty-three-year-old farmer from Ravenshoe, Ontario, and a battalion sniper who was in an "isolated sniping post" and able to do "good work."[205]

Deward's sketch showing the disposition of the German raiders and the direction from which they came on the afternoon of April 28, 1918.

April 29, 1918: At 3:00 a.m. our artillery opened up and we pulled a raid off on them. Killed some Germans in outposts under the wire going out to their front line and took six prisoners and a machine gun. No casualties. Raids are quick. Stood-to from 4:30 a.m. to 5:30 a.m. On-duty, [kept a] keen watch on Neuville Vitasse. Stood-to from 8:00 p.m. to 9:00 p.m. Raining heavy all night. Relieved by the 24th Battalion and left the front line at 12:30 a.m.

Although Deward tells us there were no casualties in what was clearly a revenge raid, the battalion's *War Diary* records that eleven other ranks received wounds of varying severity, mostly in the hand-to-hand fighting that took place while overwhelming a machine gun post.[206]

April 30, 1918: Mud. Passed Wailly and Basseux to near Bellacourt, arriving at 5:30 a.m. Tired. Had good feed and slept to morning. Movies at night. "Punk." Cecil [transferred] to our section finally at Bailleulval.

May 1, 1918: Bath and cleaned gun. Went to Bellacourt, dandy night meal. Wrote Ira and sent photo, wrote Bert and sent photo, Nora, and Beatrice. Wrote Lucy no. 61.

May 2, 1918: Clothing parade, got new tunic. Cleaned gun and inspection. Corporal Book was made a sergeant. Peters staying out next trip, his luck. Finished Lucy's green envelope.

May 3, 1918: Up at 8:00 a.m. Packed guns and went downtown to Bailleulval. At 6:30 p.m. to Purple Line, arriving at 10:30 p.m. Cecil and I carried extra eats in a sandbag. We only get three or four days rest now. Just time to get a bath and get paid. On-duty (gas) from 10:00 p.m. to 12:00 p.m. We did not have much to do here except aircraft duty at certain hours, day and night. We had a late lunch every night and fired a few pans at Heiney every day, but missed. We slept and washed every day while here, using water [that had gathered] in shell holes. We got a paper nearly every day printed in Paris.

It is not known which Paris-based paper Deward received; however, James Pedley mentions that among the newspapers available to him was the Paris edition of the *New York Tribune*.[207]

May 4, 1918: On-duty from 6:00 a.m. to 8:00 a.m. Cleaned gun and slept until 12:00 noon. Wrote Lucy no. 63, Jessie, Ada, Frieda, Omer Rivett. Fired two pans [of ammunition]. Received nos. 73, 74, 75, 76 and from Nora and Beatrice. Eats at night. On-duty from 9:00 p.m. to 10:00 p.m.

May 5, 1918: On-duty from 4:00 a.m. to 5:00 a.m. Slept, cleaned gun. Wrote Lucy no. 64 and Nora. On-duty from 10:00 a.m. to 11:00 a.m. Eat at night. Nothing to do.

May 6, 1918: On-duty from 1:00 a.m. to 2:00 a.m. cleaned gun. Continued and finished Lucy's letter. Wrote Beatrice. On-duty from 8:00 p.m. to 9:00 p.m. Paper up. I did not bring my greatcoat, but leather one and sweater and trench cap.

The "greatcoat" was an army-issue topcoat that hung to below the knees. This was an awkward piece of clothing for the trenches because the skirts often became caked in mud and its length hindered a man's ease of movement in and out of the trenches. (Deward mentions cleaning his on April 8, above.) A popular alternative to the greatcoat was the leather jerkin, a thigh-length, sleeveless vest that fitted loosely enough to allow extra layers of warm clothing underneath. Soldiers were also issued with a cardigan sweater, which is likely what Deward is referring to here. Trench caps were a variation of the cloth uniform, or forage, cap with earflaps that buttoned on top of the cap when they were not in use.

May 7, 1918: On-duty from 3:00 a.m. to 4:00 a.m. rain. On-duty from 10:00 a.m. to 11:00 a.m. and from 7:00 p.m. to 8:00 p.m. Paper came up.

May 8, 1918: Breakfast at 6:15 a.m. Nice day. Fired one pan [of ammunition], cleaned gun. Wrote Lucy no. 66. Laced Canadian buttons on tunic, "industrious." Late lunch every night.

When out of the trenches, soldiers often had to keep the buttons on their tunics shone. This was a tedious and time-consuming task, and even when using a button stick (a slotted sheet of brass that shielded the fabric from excess polish), some of the cleaner would occasionally get onto the material and stain it. To avoid this, "industrious" soldiers used a bootlace to attach the buttons to the front of their coat (there were also several smaller buttons on the breast pockets and shoulder straps, but these were usually left sewn in place). They did this by piercing the fabric where the button normally was sewn, pressing the button shank through the hole, and then stringing a lace through the shank. Some really industrious soldiers even acquired a second set of buttons that they kept polished at all times and exchanged with their everyday buttons for special occasions. Afterward, they replaced the good set, then tucked it away for the next time.

Buttons on coats that came from imperial stores, which often supplied the Canadian Corps, bore the royal coat of arms. There was, however, a uniquely Canadian pattern button, which featured a maple leaf and which members of the corps wore with pride — when they were available. This is what Deward means above by "Canadian buttons."

May 9, 1918: On-duty from 12:30 a.m. to 2:15 a.m. Breakfast at 7:30 a.m. Slept and washed every day. Wrote Lucy no. 67. Fired one pan [of ammunition] Received box no. 21, it was grand, I needed everything [that was in it]. On-duty from 10:30 p.m. This was a lovely day. Sewed good conduct stripe on. Paper came up.

A good conduct stripe was an award granted to privates and lance corporals after two years of service with no convictions registered on their service record. The stripe was an inverted chevron (that is, with the point up) worn on the left sleeve, roughly halfway between the cuff and the elbow.

May 10, 1918: Breakfast 7:30 a.m. Stayed up (dull). Nothing to do. On-duty one hour at night. Started copying diary. Paper came up.

May 11, 1918: Dull. Slept all morning. We packed up ready to move up to close supports in the sunken road. Left Brigade reserve (Purple Line) at 9:00 p.m. arriving close supports in the sunken road at 10:15 p.m. by the cookhouse. Higgy [Higgins] and I slept sound in a good hole by crossroads.

Arthur Higgins was a forty-three-year-old leather dyer from Somerset, England. He and his wife, Annie, resided in York County, Ontario, when Higgins enlisted in the 198th Battalion (The Canadian Buffs) in February of 1916.[208]

May 12, 1918: Got rations at 1:15 a.m. stood-to from 4:00 a.m. to 5:00 a.m. On anti-aircraft duty 6:00 a.m. to 8:00 a.m. 12:00 noon to 2:00 p.m. 6:00 p.m. to 8:00 p.m. Finished copying the diary. Fired five pans [of ammunition], broke the striker. Stood-to from 8:30 p.m. to 9:30 p.m. Paper came up (some class). Salvaging. Three duds hit in the bank on the road opposite to us. We had plenty of practice firing gun every day. He came over in planes and it was a dull day and chilly. We stood-to nights and mornings.

In the Lewis gun, the striker was the firing pin. Each Lewis gun came with a fairly comprehensive selection of spare parts, including a tin full of small parts that consisted predominantly of spare strikers. The end of the striker was small and, considering that the gun's action could be violent at times, it could be easily broken when hot after prolonged firing.

Salvaging meant searching for and recovering lost and discarded pieces of equipment and other war-related material, both Allied and enemy. The salvaged items were either cleaned, repaired, and returned to stores or else concentrated in dumps, then sold for scrap. Salvage could include such diverse items as ammonal (a type of high explosive used in mining enemy trenches), balaclavas, fuse caps, underwear, revolver holsters, suspenders, bayonet frogs, nose bags for horses, rifles, bicycles, machine gun parts, saddles, burlap, camp kettles, petrol tins, rum kegs, lanterns, tent poles, butter, bandages, crowbars, rolls of camouflage netting, sledge hammers, sheet iron, water pipes, wheel barrows, tar paper, acetylene tanks, trench mortar bombs, flare pistols, and so on.[209]

May 13, 1918: On-duty from 12:00 midnight to 2:00 a.m. Slept. Stood-to from 4:00 a.m. to 5:00 a.m. Dull and rain and chilly. Wrote no. 68 to Lucy and also to Mrs. Stevens in England and Mrs. Fox. On-duty from 6:00 a.m. to 8:00 a.m. 12:00 noon to 2:00 p.m. Rain. On-duty again from 6:00 p.m. to 8:00 p.m. Played cards, 500, Bridge, and Rummy. Stood-to from 8:30 p.m. to 9:30 p.m.

May 14, 1918: On-duty from 12:00 midnight to 2:00 a.m. No paper. Stood-to from 4:00 a.m. to 5:00 a.m. On-duty from 6:00 a.m. to 8:00 a.m. 12:00 noon to 2:00 p.m. On-duty again from 6:00 p.m. to 8:00 p.m. Dull and muddy. Fired four pans [of ammunition]. Played 500. Put gas helmet on. Stand-to from 8:00 p.m. to 9:00 p.m. Three duds lit in the bank on the road. Cleaned gun.

Duds (artillery shells that failed to explode), such as the ones that Deward mentions above and on April 15, often buried themselves deeply into the soft ground, only to emerge decades later with the heaving action of the frost. Even today, eighty-five-year-old duds appear in French and Belgian fields every spring and pose a severe hazard to the farmers who work the land. When a shell is found, the farmer places it at a roadside collection point, where French and Belgian army patrols make regular rounds to pick up and dispose of this "iron harvest."

May 15, 1918: Lovely day. On-duty from 12:00 midnight to 2:00 a.m. Stand-to from 4:00 a.m. to 5:00 a.m. On-duty from 6:00 a.m. to 8:00 a.m. 12:00 noon to 2:00 p.m. and from 6:00 p.m. to 8:00 p.m. Cleaned gun, fired two pans [of ammunition]. Washed. Stand-to from 8:30 p.m. to 9:30 p.m. Nicest day yet. We left battalion supports for Bretencourt at 11:30 p.m.

May 16, 1918: Arrived at [Bretencourt] 1:30 a.m. Had breakfast and slept to 9:00 a.m. Received nos. 77, 78, 79, and 80. Bath parade at 12:00 noon. A real summer's day. Wrote Lucy no. 69. Paid 20 francs. Met Dick Holman. To bed at 10:00 p.m. Hot day.

May 17, 1918: Up at 7:00 a.m. and on fatigues from 9:00 a.m. to 10:30 p.m. Played cards. Wrote Bella, Nora, Aunt Minn. Started no. 70, Lucy's green envelope. Over to YMCA. Lovely day. Bailleulval. Met Tommy Dion.

"Tommy Dion" was almost certainly Thomas Patrick Dion. The forty-year-old woodworker from Montmagny, Quebec, was living in Toronto when he enlisted with the 81st Battalion during the summer of 1915. Although he was not serving in the 19th Battalion, Dion may have met Deward prior to the war at the coffin works where Deward worked.[210]

May 18, 1918: Up at 7:00 a.m. Battalion parade. Tailor parade. Played cards. Movies in afternoon. Met Moffat. Wrote to Lucy, finished no. 70. To Wailly YMCA one kilometre [half a mile] away. Lovely day.

"Moffat" was most likely Roy Moffat, another of Deward's chums from the 180th Battalion. The twenty-eight-year-old Moffat listed his occupation as "lumber shipper" when he was attested in late February 1916 and so may also have known Deward before the war.[211]

May 19, 1918: Lovely day. Church parade at 9:45 a.m. Washed, hair brush, etc. Dinner, met Clayton. Finished Lucy's letter. Played cards.

"Clayton" was probably yet another of Deward's friends from the 180th Battalion. The 180th Battalion had two Claytons on its roll, Frederick and William. Frederick Clayton was a stenographer from Whitby, Ontario, while William Clayton was a machinist from Birmingham, England. Both Claytons were twenty years old and both were living in Toronto when they enlisted in early 1916.[212]

May 20, 1918: Battalion parade, Lieutenant Colonel [Hatch] inspected. Company drill. Tailor parade. Played cards from 10:00 a.m. to 12:00 noon. To YMCA. Lovely day.

May 21, 1918: Went to the dentist at the 6th Field Ambulance and had a filling. It took nearly all day to go there and back, several towns away. Then you had to line up and wait your turn. Sewed [the battalion's] colours on my tunic. Cleaned gun. Played cards. Received nos. 81, 82, 83, 84. Wrote Lucy no. 71, sent field post cards to Bea, Nora, May. Lovely day.

The "colours" that Deward sewed onto his tunic were the 19th Battalion's distinguishing patches (these patches were also called battle patches, battle colours, or Somme patches — after where they were first used). In late August 1916, the Canadian Corps adopted a system of cloth formation patches that used a combination of colour and shape to help an observer quickly identify other, neighbouring units. For example, the 19th Battalion's patch was a blue rectangle with a green hemisphere on top. The blue rectangle

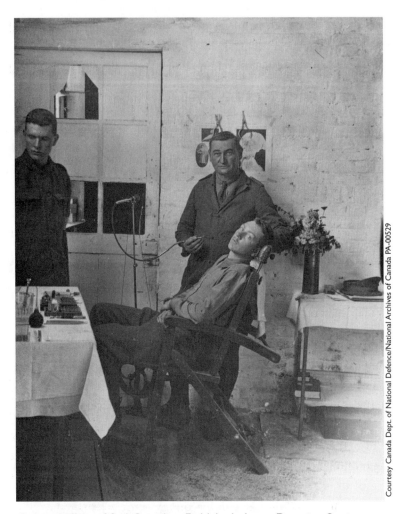

Courtesy Canada Dept. of National Defence/National Archives of Canada PA-00529

Dentist office of 3rd Canadian Field Ambulance Dressing Station, Vlamertinge, August 1916. Notice the foot-powered dental drill and the homey touches — flowers in a shell casing vase and photos on the wall — perhaps calculated to put the patients at their ease. Not all field dentists had such plush surroundings, which likely means this office was intended for the sole use of officers. Deward probably received his filling in a much more rustic set-up.

was common to all 2nd Division units, while the combination of green over blue indicated the 4th Brigade. The green hemisphere above the divisional patch meant the battalion was the second lowest numbered battalion in the brigade. Within the 4th Brigade, that was the 19th Battalion. In addition to the blue rectangle, the other 4th Brigade battalions wore the following: the 18th Battalion — a green circle; the 20th Battalion — a green triangle; and the 21st Battalion — a green square. This pattern of geometric shapes over rectangles was repeated in every other Canadian brigade and division, but with different colour combinations. Originally, the patches could be worn either centred on the back, just below the collar, or on both sleeves, at the divisional commander's discretion. By 1917, however, the patches were worn exclusively on the arms, where they were more visible.[213]

Each soldier had to sew his own patches or arrange to have someone else do it for him. An adequate supply of coloured cloth was frequently difficult for the quartermasters to maintain, and this meant that it might be several weeks before reinforcements and veterans with new coats could badge themselves (recall that Deward had received a new tunic three weeks earlier, on May 2).

May 22, 1918: Battalion parade. Lovely day. Lewis gun inspected by Lieutenant Colonel Hatch. From 9:30 a.m. to 11:30 a.m. we played cards. Discarded paper loaded ammunition. Book went on Lewis gun course. Received letter from Bert. Left Bretencourt at 8:00 p.m. Through Wailly to front-line Neuville Vitasse arriving at 11:30 p.m. that nerve-wrecking place. From now on we are in the trenches most of the time. In for two weeks and out for three days or sometimes four days. Just long enough to get paid and cleaned up. On-duty in the front line from 12:00 midnight to 1:45 a.m. Stand-to from 3:30 a.m. to 4:30 a.m. On-duty from 4:30 a.m. to 6:30 a.m. Dull, windy and cold. Tea and ham for breakfast. Same post as last time. Stand-to 9:00 p.m. to 10:00 p.m.

Paper loaded ammunition was a type of blank ammunition. The battalion was practising platoon and company attacks on May 20 so the ammunition that Deward discarded was probably the leftovers.[214]

May 23, 1918: On-duty from 12:00 midnight to 1:45 a.m. stand-to 3:30 a.m. to 4:30 a.m. then on duty again from 4:30 a.m. to 6:30 a.m. Dull, windy, and cold. Tea and ham for breakfast. On-duty from 12:30 p.m. to 2:30 p.m. and from 8:30 p.m. to 9:00 p.m. Stand-to 9:00 p.m. to 10:00 p.m.

May 24, 1918: Rained all day and had to stand-to 3:30 a.m. to 4:30 a.m. then on duty again from 4:30 a.m. to 6:00 a.m. On-duty from 12:00 p.m. to 2:00 p.m. and from 8:00 p.m. to 9:00 p.m. Stand-to 9:00 p.m. to 10:00 p.m. Received letter from Nora. No chance to write. Rain all day and cold. Miserable day.

May 25, 1918: Started Lucy's green envelope no. 72. Same duties but it was a nice day. Relieved by "B" Company at 10:15 p.m. Then went to battalion supports. On gas guard and shelled by 5.9's and minnenwerfers. This is an awful place for minnenwerfers. Stand-to 3:30 a.m. to 4:30 a.m. on duty 10:30 a.m. to 12:30 p.m. 6:30 p.m. to 9:30 p.m. stand-to 9:00 p.m. to 10:00 p.m.

A "5.9" was a type of German howitzer. It fired a shell 5.9 inches (15 centimetres) in diameter, weighing 95 pounds (43 kilograms). *Minnenwerfer* was the German term for a trench mortar.

May 26, 1918: With Peters on SOS post for four hours; Huns are expected over in the morning. Stand-to 3:30 a.m. to 4:30 a.m. on duty 10:30 a.m. to 12:30 p.m. 6:30 p.m. to 9:30 p.m. stand-to 9:00 p.m. to 10:00 p.m. Wrote Lucy a line, shelled heavily.

The SOS post that Peters manned was probably at or near the company signals station, where messages to and from battalion headquarters and other neighbouring formations were sent and received. This is the most likely spot from which, during an enemy attack, someone would launch the multi-coloured flares that would call on the local supporting artillery battery to lay down a barrage immediately in front of the battalion requesting assistance. Since Peters was a Lewis gunner and not a signaller, he was probably standing sentry duty.

The 19th Battalion's intelligence report for the twenty-four-hour period that ended at 6:00 a.m. on May 26 noted an unusual amount of enemy troop movement in his rear areas. This, combined with a particularly active programme of artillery fire on the Canadian-held front lines and heavy machine gun barrages on the parapets of the front-line trenches, led the battalion's scout officer, Lieutenant R.L. Dinsmore, to conclude that there was "something unusual [going on] in this sector." This is probably why Deward tells us that the "Huns [are] expected over in the morning."[215]

May 27, 1918: Stand-to 3:15 to 4:30 a.m. on duty 5:30 a.m. to 7:30 a.m. We were shelled heavily all morning. On SOS post 11:00 a.m. to 12:00 noon, stood-to from 9:00 p.m. to 10:00 p.m. Cold at night and rum every morning. Received letter from Ira.

May 28, 1918: The 22nd Battalion pulled off a raid. Huns retaliated 1:15 a.m. to 1:45 a.m. Stood-to from 3:05 a.m. to 5:15 a.m. On-duty at the SOS post, 11:00 a.m. to 12:00 noon. Lovely day. Early in morning I went to see the boys in the SOS post, when a shell hit [close by]. I couldn't hear anything after. Goodman and Coates were wounded. Higgins was blown off the firing step and I wasn't touched (very lucky).

  We were relieved by the 20th Battalion and left for the Purple Line supports at Ficheux Switch, Telegraph Hill.

May 29, 1918: Arrived at 2:30 a.m. Had to dig a dug-out and gun post and finished it at 7:00 a.m. having worked hard. Slept until 11:30 a.m. and then on duty. It was a nice day. Wrote Lucy no. 73, Nora, Beatrice, Bert M. and Omer Rivett. I found a piece of shell had gone through my respirator sideways and took a piece of my tunic with it. I had to go to Agny for a new one [respirator].

Deward was lucky that he was not hit by the piece of shell that ripped his tunic and damaged his respirator. He's even luckier that he did not need the respirator before he noticed the damage. Since he doesn't write about it, we can only conjecture how Deward might have felt as he hurried his way to Agny, praying, perhaps, that he would not be caught in a gas barrage. Many soldiers reported feeling "naked" when, to their horror, they discovered that they were without their respirators.[216] This is borne out by an examination of photographs taken at or near the front lines. Even when the soldier is wearing no other piece of equipment, he is invariably carrying his respirator bag.

May 30, 1918: Up at 7:00 a.m. no rum. This is the nicest day yet. Duty since coming here: two hours on and four hours off. They wanted volunteers for a 4th Brigade raid. Rum every morning. Nothing to do but anti-aircraft duty, no fatigue. Wrote May Chubb, Ira, and Lucy no. 74.

May 31, 1918: Nice day. On-duty from 4:00 a.m. to 7:00 a.m. Curtain on fire, one end of funk hole fell in. Huns expected over on June 2. Fritz says he will blow us off the earth, ho ho. The Germans advanced on south. Lovely day. Wanted volunteers for Brigade raid, "no compré." Wrote Mabel Daly and Aunt Stevens. Read book, "Tommy." Lovely day.

Presumably Deward means it was one of the anti-gas curtains that was on fire. Since the weather over the previous few days had been fair, a bursting shell, and not a deluge of rain, probably brought down one end of the funk hole.

This time, the battalion intelligence summary does not hint at why Deward believed the enemy was expected to attack on June 2.

The German advance in the south was the opening phase of the Third Battle of the Aisne, which was the third major German offensive in the spring of 1918. Like the first two, this operation enjoyed initial success, pushing the French back to the banks of the river Marne; also like its predecessors, the attacks petered out when the German supply lines could not keep up with the advancing troops.

This was the second day in a row in which an appeal went out for men to volunteer for a raid. Deward's "no compré" indicates a general attitude among the war-weary front-line troops toward placing themselves in danger unnecessarily.

The book Deward read could have been *Brother Tommy, the British Offensives on the Western Front January to June 1917*, by Henry Ruffin and André Tudesq (first published in 1917 in French and translated into English the following year). It might also have been *As Tommy Sees Us, a Book for Church Folk*, by A.H. Gray, a book of religious meditations with a war theme. Reading was a common pastime for soldiers, among whom literacy was far higher during the Great War than in any previous conflict.

June 1, 1918: My hours are long: 4:00 a.m. to 6:00 a.m. 10:00 am. to 12:00 noon, 4:00 p.m. to 6:00 p.m. and 10:00 p.m. to 12:00 midnight. Four of [the Lewis gun] crew on night fatigue. Shelled heavy every day. Tired. Huns advanced to a sixty-mile front, [but were] checked at Reims. Raid cancelled. Read book, "White Army."

The book Deward read was probably *The Great White Army*, by Max Pemberton. This novel appears to have been an extremely popular piece of historical fiction during the Great War. It was first published in 1915 and by the end of 1916 had undergone three printings. The story dramatized Napoleon's occupation of Moscow and his subsequent retreat from Russia in 1812.

June 2, 1918: 2:00 a.m. shelled heavy, gas. Wore gas mask for one hour. Lovely day. Wrote Lucy no. 75 and cousin Barnes, "Australian." Received letter from Nora.

June 3, 1918: A windy day. Left Telegraph Hill at 11:15 p.m. to Bellacourt, passed through Wailly, Bretencourt. Shell came over, blew one man's leg off. I can't think who's it was. Had bully and tea. Slept till 10:00 a.m. had breakfast and bath parade at 11.30 a.m. Nothing else to do.

Deward's almost offhand comment about one man losing his leg and his inability to remember the man's name suggests that he has become inured to the almost daily maimings that he is witness to, and perhaps also to the steady stream of anonymous faces that wash in from the reinforcement camps on a weekly basis.

June 4, 1918: Arrived at Bailleulval 2:30 a.m. Bully and tea. Up at 10:00 a.m. breakfast. Bath at 11:30 a.m. Finished Lucy's letter. Nothing to do. Band here.

June 5, 1918: Lovely day. Up at 7:15 a.m. Rifle inspection at 10:00 a.m. [Lewis] gun post inspection at 1:30 p.m. Played cards. Ho ho. Compulsory parade to concert, "See Twos," was good.

June 6, 1918: Battalion parade at 10:00 a.m. Lewis gun cleaning at 10:15 a.m. Gas lecture at 1:30 p.m. in a woods where they kept a lot of horses. This gas officer was from the gas school and he thought it would be a good place, nice and cool and shady. We all got nicely seated on the ground and he let us smoke. I guess he was lecturing about fifteen minutes when shells came, killing four horses close by. He says "I guess we had better call it off." Wrote Lucy no. 76, received letter from Bella.

June 7, 1918: Battalion parade and Lewis gun inspection. Afternoon off. Received letter nos. 86, 87, 88, 89 from Goodman. Wrote Lucy no. 77. Wrote Beatrice.

June 8, 1918: Battalion parade, inspection of [Lewis] guns by Brigadier Rennie at 11.30 a.m. "C" Company gun won. We then had a quick gun assembly contest, the Headquarters Company gun section won using a spare pinion, I was second (one and a half seconds behind). I should have got it. Afternoon off, played cards. Ball game at night, 19th Battalion versus 20th Battalion. We lost, 19 to 1, ho ho.

Attached to No. 4 Platoon.

It must have galled Deward, who took pride in his martial skills, to place second in a competition to the Headquarters Company Lewis gun section, instead of, say, a section from another front-line company. The pinion is part of the Lewis gun's mechanism that helps to automatically re-cock the gun after each round is fired. Deward implies the HQ company cheated by having a replacement.

June 9, 1918: Turned kits in. Bath parade. No. 2 Platoon stays out, but my section still goes in with No. 4 Platoon. Left Bailleulval at 8:15 p.m., passed through Bretencourt and arrived at the intermediate supports in front of the Purple Line, right at the front, at 11:30 p.m. Gas guard for my men. Sergeants Hatherly and Cox in charge.

Deward's No. 2 Platoon was designated left out of battle on this trip to the support lines, but Deward's section, being the Lewis gun section — and therefore needed — still had to make the trip.

June 10, 1918: Breakfast at 7:00 a.m. Received box no. 22, just in time — it was lovely. Wrote Lucy no. 79. As a non-commissioned officer, no duty. My men on two hours, six hours off, two at a time. Not a bad day.

Deward tells us that he was excused duty "as a non-commissioned officer." At some point during the previous few days, he had been made a temporary or acting lance corporal. This means that Deward had some of the privileges and all of the responsibilities of a non-commissioned rank, but was still drawing the pay of a private. This was often the first step toward a permanent appointment or promotion, a kind of trial period.

June 11, 1918: Put on fatigue as non-commissioned officer in charge of no. 5 section, sixteen men. Dug cable trench. Left at 10:00 p.m. back at 2:00 a.m. Started Lucy's green envelope no. 80.

June 12, 1918: 2:00 a.m. made coffee, slept until 12:00 noon. Huns strafed all day long. Took four men on fatigue, and then did gas guard from 12:00 midnight to 2:00 a.m. Windy day. Finished Lucy's green envelope.

That the "Huns strafed all day long" tells us that the Germans were shelling the area Deward was in throughout the day. The word *strafe* comes from the German verb *bestrafen*, which means "to punish."

CHAPTER 8

Preparing for Open Warfare,
June 14 to August 7, 1918

*"He said that we did not want any prisoners,
which meant kill them all."*

June 14, 1918: Gas guard from 12:00 midnight to 4:00 a.m. No duty during the day. Three [more men from my section were] on gas guard. Started green envelope to Lucy.

June 15, 1918: Gas guard from 2:00 a.m. to 4:00 a.m. by Headquarters. In charge of water fatigue from 11:00 a.m. to 12:15 p.m. Moved to front line by the creek. Left at 10:00 p.m. arrived at 11:15 p.m. [I am now an] acting non-commissioned officer attached to No. 3 Platoon.

June 16, 1918: Stood-to from 2:30 a.m. to 3:30 a.m. Good rations, dull and windy day. Quiet front. Stand-to from 9:15 p.m. to 10.15 p.m. Our post is near a creek, a dandy spot and quiet.

June 17, 1918: Our left front [is in front] of Boisleux-St. Marc and right front in front of Maveatelle. Received letters from Aunt Stevens, Lucy — no. 87, wrote Lucy no. 82. Nice day.

June 18, 1918: Rum at stand-to, from 2:30 a.m. to 3:30 a.m. Lovely day and very quiet every day. Left the front line at 11:15

p.m. for close supports, first sunken road. Arrived at 11:45 p.m. Gas guard only, still with No. 3 Platoon.

June 19, 1918: Stand-to from 2:30 a.m. to 3:30 a.m. Rum, rain. 21st Division (Imperials) pulled raid off. We were shelled heavy and he sent gas, Company Sergeant-Major Graham had both legs broken, shell lit by his dug-out and caved in. No gas guard, no duty at all. Wrote Lucy no. 83.

June 20, 1918: Rum. Dull day, rain. At night, "D" Coy raided the enemy. No prisoners. Shelled very heavy. Continued to write green envelope called no. 84.

The terseness of Deward's comment on the "D" Company raid belies its cost. Three prisoners were in fact secured, but they were shot dead when they tried to overpower their guard, who had been wounded by a shrapnel burst. The 19th Battalion lost two men killed: Maj. Armour Miller, formerly the commanding officer of the 134th Battalion, who, like Major Denison, had taken a demotion to serve in a front-line unit; and Harold White, a nineteen-year-old surveyor's assistant from Brantford, Ontario, whose body was never recovered. The battalion also lost six men as prisoners, which must have rankled. These included an officer, Lieut. Abraham Pike, who had gone in search of the missing Miller, and Art Cane, who had rejoined the battalion only the previous week after recovering from

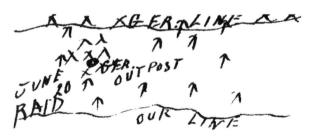

The 19th Battalion's June 20, 1918, raid, in which the battalion lost eight men: two were killed and six more were taken prisoner of war. The raid's main objective was to take German prisoners and destroy the outpost that Deward has drawn in the left centre of this sketch.

the trench foot he had contracted at Passchendaele. Another of the prisoners, George Tucker, died in captivity the day before the armistice. He, too, has no known grave. Both Tucker and White are commemorated on the Canadian Vimy Memorial.[217]

June 21, 1918: Lance-Corporal Sayers was wounded and later died. Stood-to in the communications trench. It was thought that the Germans were massing. Rain all night. Left close supports at 11:45 p.m. for Bellacourt. Arrived soaking wet at 4:00 a.m. Received letter from Nora.

June 22, 1918: Bath parade and cleaned gun. Windy day. Our casualties for those few days were around 75. Received a box from Bea and box from Lucy, no. 23. Received letter nos. 99, 100, & no. 1 and a letter from Holy Trinity.

It appears that Lucy began renumbering her letters at one after she reached one hundred. "Holy Trinity" is probably a reference to the Church of the Holy Trinity, an Anglican church in downtown Toronto.

June 23, 1918: Church parade. Paid twenty francs. Inspected the [Lewis] gun and my SBR. Wrote Lucy no. 85, Omer, Bella. Cold day.

The respirators required regular inspections and maintenance to keep them effective. Filters, for example, had to be changed after forty hours of use. Initially, the soldier was required to fill out a log whenever he wore the respirator, to keep track of how long the filter had been used. This was a highly impractical scheme under trench and battle conditions, so the army simply took to replacing the filters whenever possible. For soldiers out of the line, it meant frequent parades to the gas stations to have their SBR tested and the filter replaced. Most soldiers, however, did not seem to mind the extra work. As one veteran put it, "Our lives depended on our gas masks being in tiptop shape when needed."[218]

June 24, 1918: Physical drill 8:00 a.m. to 9:30 a.m. Company inspection. Lewis gun drill from 10:00 to 12:30 p.m. Wrote Cousin Mable, Harold Stephens, Ada, Jessie, and Frieda. Received letter from Nora. Started green envelope for Lucy, no. 86.

June 25, 1918: Physical drill. [Practised] artillery formation. Nicest day this month. Wrote Lucy no. 87.

"Artillery formation" was a tactic used by advancing troops to lessen the effect of a bursting artillery shell. The formation required the men to stay dispersed instead of clumped together, which is a natural tendency when in danger and why it needed to be practised.

June 26, 1918: Physical drill. Inspection. That's all. Nice day. Wrote Mrs. Field. Off in afternoon.

June 27, 1918: Nice day. No parade. Ready to move on. Left Bellacourt at 4:00 p.m. Marched to Basseux, two kilometres [one mile]. Took narrow gauge railway to Habarcq, arrived at 10:00 p.m. and marched to billets.

June 28, 1918: Up at 7:15 a.m. Packed up ready to move (cancelled). Nothing to do, court martial on. Received letters from Jessie, Ada, Frieda, H. Chubb, Lucy no. 4. Wrote Nora and Beatrice.

June 29, 1918: Company inspection 8:15 a.m. Inoculation and off until Tuesday. Wrote Lucy no. 88. Nice town with billets in barn. Received letters from Nora and Ira. To bed at 7:30 p.m.

This inoculation was probably another typhus shot.

June 30, 1918: Brigade Church parade 8:45 a.m. Marched to Lattre Saint Quentin, two towns away. Mr. Rowell addressed us.

Bath parade 1:15 p.m. Received no. 2. Sick today. Picture of section taken. Started green envelope no. 89.

The Honourable N.W. Rowell was president of Canada's privy council. He was on a tour of the front with Robert Borden and other members of the cabinet.

Deward's Lewis gun section, June 30, 1918. No. 8 Section, 2 Platoon, "A" Company, 19th Canadian Infantry Battalion. Back row, left to right: Wilson, Arnold, Latimer, Roberts, and Higgins. Front row, left to right: Peters, Book, Barnes, and Barker.

July 1, 1918: Holiday. Up at 5:00 a.m. Left in trucks at 8:55 a.m. for Corps sports at Tincques fourteen kilometres [eight miles] away. Had a good day, a terrible crowd. Met C. Martin and bunch, waited three hours in line for eggs and chips. Arrived home at 8:00 p.m. Received letter no. 8. Present were General Haig, Premier Borden, Mr. Rowell, and General Currie.

Many veterans remembered fondly that day they spent at Tinques. Canadian historian John Swettenham describes it thus:

> Dominion Day was especially well celebrated that
> year. The Corps was in reserve. On that day the 2nd

211

Division returned and fifty thousand Canadians assembled for sports at Tinques, 22.5 km (fourteen miles) west of Arras. A stadium had been knocked together by the engineers complete with a platform for distinguished guests. Sir Robert Borden, Gen. John Pershing (Commander-in-Chief, American Expeditionary Forces) and the Duke of Connaught all attended. There were marquees for refreshments and an open-air theatre where the "Dumbells" gave continuous performances. Planes hovered overhead to protect the Corps from enemy bombing. That night the "Volatiles," the concert party of the 1st Division, presented its revue, Take a Chance ... The [entire] week was peacetime soldiering, brass and weapons twinkling in the sun, flags, massed bands and stirring music.[219]

July 2, 1918: Lovely weather. Up at 6:00 a.m. I was mess order-ly. Company paraded, went for a swim in trenches that were filled with water. Wrote Lucy no. 90 and Nora. Dandy, nice day and hot. Cleanup and to bed. Never felt better.

While staying at nearby Acq, James Pedley paid another visit to his friend Arthur Duncan, and left us with a fascinating portrait of the 19th Battalion as it appeared shortly after rejoining the Canadian Corps from their sojourn with the Imperials:

It was Ostic who rode with me to Habarcq, to visit the 19th Battalion, which I had last seen at Bracquemont. Along with the rest of the 2nd Division, the 19th had spent May and June in the line south of Arras. One judged it had been no quiet front — the Division put on an average of two or three raids a week during a stay of a couple of months. Now, out of the line at last, the 19th officers were enjoying themselves. I found Art Duncan, second in command of a company, and under his escort did a tour of the mess billets. Like the rest of the 19th crowd, Art was gaunt and hard, the result of hard line work.[220]

July 3, 1918: Up at 7:00 a.m. Physical drill from 7:45 to 8:30 a.m. Company and Battalion inspections; inspection of guns from 2:00 p.m. to 4:00 p.m. Wrote Lucy two pages. Sick. Headache. To bed at 6:00 p.m.; fever and cold chills.

Deward was suffering from the Spanish Flu, which was working its way through the battalion in early July. (It was called "Spanish" because of the high death rates first reported in that country.)[221] In the spring of 1918, a potent strain of influenza appeared in the Middle East and spread quickly to the west, reaching Europe in the early summer. At first, the symptoms were fairly mild, much as Deward describes above, and most people who contracted the flu recovered from it. By mid-August, however, the virus was more virulent. It first appeared in Canada in the autumn of 1918, where it was ultimately responsible for an estimated fifty thousand deaths — almost as many victims as the total Canadian battle deaths. In mid-1919, mysteriously, the disease disappeared. Globally, the influenza claimed in excess of 70 million lives in less than eighteen months, far more than perished on the battlefields in four years of war.

July 4, 1918: Paraded sick. Got medicine and duty; mess orderly. Dull day and not feeling good. Wrote Freda, Jessie, and Ida. Kit inspection. Our Transport section won the Division inspection.

Although an infantry battalion travelled mostly by foot, it still required transportation for its equipment and supplies. A typical battalion transport section consisted of one transport officer, a transport sergeant, eleven drivers, thirteen riding horses, twenty-six draft horses, eight heavy draft horses, nine pack horses, sixteen various carts and general service wagons, and nine bicycles. The competition took place at the 2nd Divisional horse show, where the 19th Battalion represented the 4th Brigade. By winning the show, the battalion earned the right to represent the 2nd Division at a VI Corps horse show on July 10.[222]

July 5, 1918: Spent the whole day until 9:30 p.m. cleaning and scrubbing equipment and polishing brass.

July 6, 1918: Inspection by Brigadier Rennie through at 11:00 a.m. Paid twenty-five francs. Wrote Lucy no. 91.

July 7, 1918: Church parade in a field at 10:00 a.m. Not much sleep. Wrote Lucy no. 92 green envelope. Bacon, Book, and Gerry Anning under arrest.

Louis Bacon's service record does not register a conviction, so he was acquitted of whatever charges were brought against him. Roy Book was charged with being drunk while on active service and with conduct prejudicial to good order and military discipline for proceeding out of his billeting area without a pass. Gerry Anning was also charged with being out of his billeting area without a pass. Book and Anning were convicted and received fourteen days of Field Punishment Number One.[223]

July 8, 1918: Physical drills. Had charge of the platoon. Very warm. Battalion parade. Drill of a different kind. Company drill in the afternoon. Wrote Lucy no. 93, received letter from Bella, received nos. 5 and 6.

The 19th Battalion's training syllabus for July 8 indicates that "A" Company spent part of the morning practising platoon attacks, most likely studying the infiltration methods used by the Germans in their spring attacks, which were strongly advocated by General Currie. By 1918, platoons had become self-contained fighting units, able to call on their own machine guns and artillery (in the form of rifle grenades) and on those of other, nearby platoons for support.

The variety of weapons at a platoon's disposal gave it the flexibility to employ the tactics of fire and movement that had eluded the infantryman earlier in the war. To keep up with the rapidly evolving tactics in the final year of fighting, the men would have to learn many drills "of a different kind" while on the road to victory.[224]

July 9, 1918: Battalion parade and general drill. Paraded in the afternoon for one hour, from 1:30 p.m. to 2:30 p.m. Very warm. Started Lucy's no. 94. Wrote Ira, Chubb, Harold, and Rivett.

July 10, 1918: Battalion parade and general drill. Lewis gun classes. Paraded in the afternoon for one hour, from 1:30 p.m. to 2:20 p.m. Rained a little. Finished Lucy's no. 94.

July 11, 1918: Battalion parade. Route march to ride on tanks near Lattre Saint Quentin. Back home at 2:15 p.m. Rain showers. Bath parade. Received letter from Nora. Jim McFadden rode up to see me.

In the summer of 1918, the infantry spent a good deal of time learning how to move in conjunction with tanks. Infantry was taught to advance in front of the tanks, which only leant their aid when called upon. With no direct way for the infantry on the outside to communicate with the tank's crew on the inside (who were deafened anyway by the roar of the motor and the concussions from the firing guns), the careful coordination between the two that was necessary to ensure success, not to mention safety, required a lot of practice.[225]

July 12, 1918: Rain. Went to Lattre Saint Quentin, inspected by General Currie and he gave out medals. This was the first time we had been inspected by General Currie and of course we looked for a little speech from him. We got it. He told us how far the Germans had advanced and he said how we were to stay at our posts. If we got killed those at home would not miss us. He said that we did not want any prisoners, which meant kill them all. He did not appear to me as a soldier, big, fat, and flabby — his belt away up on his stomach. We got back at 5:00 p.m.

Currie was one of the ablest generals of the Great War, notwithstanding Deward's reflections on his appearance. He was the mastermind behind the Canadian victory at Vimy Ridge, and later, as commander of the Canadian Corps, his strategic grasp and meticulous planning ensured the corps would achieve an unbroken string of victories.

Despite his success, rank, and stature, Currie was a shy man who "in front of a large audience ... became abrupt, formal, and often spoke inappropriately ... Currie did not seem to have the gift for stroking fur the right way [and he had] a talent for picking just the wrong phrase in addressing troops."[226]

His gift for winning battles earned him a measure of respect from his men, but his seeming discomfort in their company made it hard for them to love him. We see this in Deward's reaction to Currie's 19th Battalion speech, which drew heavily from the Special Order that he issued at the end of March 1918 — during the height of the German offensive: "To those who will fall I say 'you will not die, but step into immortality. Your mothers will not lament your fate, but will be proud to have borne such sons. Your names will be revered for ever by your grateful country, and God will take you unto Himself ...'"

These words were meant to inspire, but instead they left Deward, and many other weary veterans, cold. Pedley observed that his men "laughed and sneered" when he read them the order. "He won't die, not likely!" jeered one man, while another added "Bloody old bomb-proofer, trust him for a safe billet!"[227]

Currie's role as Corps Commander certainly did keep him in "a safe billet," but he never forgot that the men under his command did not share the same advantage. In the words of Gen. "Ox" Webber, one of Currie's senior staff officers, and an Imperial, "I never met a man who took such trouble to safeguard the interests of his troops in action and in billet." Another Briton on Currie's staff, George Farmar, added, "No commander took a greater interest in the welfare of his men or felt losses more keenly." Andrew McNaughton, who commanded the Canadian Corps' Heavy Artillery at the end of the war, observed of Currie many years later, "[He] consistently sought to pay the price of victory in shells and not in the lives of men."[228]

Currie might not have been a charismatic orator, but Deward and his comrades could not have been in better hands.

July 13, 1918: Left Habarcq at 10:00 a.m. for Berneville, six kilometres [three miles]. Arrived at 1:00 p.m. Dinner and supper. Passed Warlus. Wrote Bella, Nora, Bea. Received nos. 7, 8, 9, 10, 11. Received from Aunt Minn, Nora, Cousin Mable.

July 14, 1918: Paraded in fighting order at 9:30 a.m. Church parade, inspection of haversacks. Left Berneville at 8:30 p.m. and marched to Arras passing Dainville on the way, arriving at 11:00 p.m. Dandy big city, billeted in stores. I lived in the shop. Big cathedral here and some civilians. Met Nash.

Again, it is likely that Deward met up with one of his 180th Battalion chums, as there are two Nashes that appear on the Sportsmen's nominal roll: Alfred Nash, a thirty-eight-year-old printer and ex-Imperial force cavalryman; and Laurie Nash, a twenty-four-year-old accountant. Both Nashes were English-born and residing in Toronto when they enlisted in the winter of 1916.[229]

July 15, 1918: Not allowed on streets in the day-time. Received a letter from Mrs. Field. Started no. 96. Rain. We did not do much here, only eat and sleep. A big bunch together. Had boot and bath parades at the market square and gun inspections. Received box no. 24, dandy.

Paragraph 10 of 19th Battalion Order No. 81, July 14, 1918, stipulates that "movement while in Arras is to be reduced to a minimum, all troops remaining under cover during daylight." The order does not tell us why this was necessary, but perhaps parts of the city were under observation by the enemy and it was thought that movement might draw shelling.[230]

July 16, 1918: Boot parade, Lewis gun lecture. Nothing to do. Very hot. Wrote Lucy no. 98 and Nora. Received letter from Nora.

July 17, 1918: The boys got two hundred bottles of wine, all drunk all night long. ("Why go to Paris when there is such a place as Arras" … ho ho!) Most places here have a double cellar, one below the other. The boys went out and into these wine cellars with sacks. They got red and white wines and some champagne. The whole battalion was practically drunk. I was sober, of course (… I had *some*). The military police caught some of a certain bunch up a lane taking sacks home and one of them got away and ran to his billet and got his pistol. He went back and held the police up and the fellows got away. It was dark, he would have killed them.

It appears not all "the fellows got away" since at least one eyewitness, George Marshall of "C" Company, noted a large number of arrests among Deward's "A" Company in his diary. The wine stash was looted from "C" Company's billet, a large mansion described by Marshall several days before the incident as having "wine cellars conveniently attached." Marshall goes on to tell us that on the night of the rampage "bottles by the hundreds [decorated] our quarters," and hints that trouble might have been brewing for some time when he confides that "the peace lovers [sought] the sanctuary of the [billet's] garret as night [descended] upon the ancient city."[231]

Drinking to excess created a serious problem for the military authorities, and it posed a real threat to discipline. As Edwin Vaughan, an officer serving with an Imperial battalion recalled, however, not all cases of mass drunkenness turned ugly:

> And when we went on parade at 7:00 am we had
> a terrible shock. There were numerous absentees

and nearly everybody was tight. They were reeling about and laughing and presented such an extraordinary sight in two swaying lines that we hurried them off at once and marched unsteadily up the Doint road. They were immensely happy and greeted everyone we met — including mules — with most amusing remarks. Corporal McKay in particular kept me choking with laughter ... He kept trying to shout the step and mixed up his "Lefts" and "Rights" indiscriminately. But he and all the others were very good humoured and cheery.[232]

July 18, 1918: The whole battalion had to parade on a grounds selected. It was raining and we had to wear rubber sheets and caps. The military police went down each row and we had to open our coats up. They could not recognize any of the men, not one. The Colonel says he does not know what will happen now. Left Arras at 10:00 p.m. arrived at "Y" Hutments three kilometres [two miles] from Mont-St. Eloi at 12:30 a.m. Received letters no. 12 & 13.

Presumably, the military police had the men open their coats to see if they were hiding any illicit bottles of wine on their persons.

July 19, 1918: Had breakfast at 1:00 a.m. On anti-aircraft duty. Left at 6:00 p.m. Marched five kilometres [three miles] to Gouves, next town to Habarcq. Arrived at 6:45 p.m. Very hot in stables. Received letter from Rivett.

July 20, 1918: Up at 6:00 a.m. Company inspection. Musketry practice in orchard. Went to church. Lieutenant Bell back. Paraded from 1:30 p.m. to 2:00 p.m. Wrote Lucy no. 99, received letter from Mabel.

July 21, 1918: Church parade at 10:00 a.m. between Gouves and Habarcq. Drill. Windy day. Continued Lucy's letter, wrote Harold.

July 22, 1918: Swell day. Physical drill at 8:00 a.m. Company inspection at 9:00 a.m. then bayonet fighting, musketry, squad drill, then route march. Wrote Mable, Rivett, Lucy no. 100, Nora then a field post card to Beatrice.

July 23, 1918: Left Gouves 8:15 a.m. arrived at Ambrines at noon. Rained all the way. Dinner and that is all. Received nos. 14 and 15 from Lucy.

July 24, 1918: Mess orderly. Kit inspection, 2:30 p.m. Muster roll cancelled. Received letter from Nora.

July 25, 1918: Dorothy's birthday. Physical training, company and battalion parade. General rain. Wrote Lucy no. 1, wrote Nora. Received letter from Bea, Martha and children. From Lucy, I received letter nos. 16, 17, 18, 19.

July 26, 1918: Bath parade, and general drill. More shooting practice. Muster parade by APM (Assistant Provost Marshall) about Arras. Wrote Beatrice, received letter from Fred (Ohio). Rain.

The provost was searching the ranks for more of the looters from the Arras incident.[233]

July 27, 1918: Physical training at 7:30 a.m. Rain. Bath parade at 9:30 a.m. Wrote Lucy no. 2. Rain. Started no. 3 green envelope. To bed, had cocoa.

July 28, 1918: Church 9:30 a.m. Gun inspection. Finished no. 3 letter, twenty-one pages. Received letter from Nora, received parcel from Holy Trinity.

July 29, 1918: Battalion parade. General and Lewis gun courses. Received letter from Bella, received box no. 25. Wrote Lucy
no. 4.

July 30, 1918: We left Ambrines at 2:30 a.m. Marched to near
Saint Pol, fourteen kilometres [eight miles]. Left there on train at
6:00 a.m. Went fast and got off at Hangest-sur-Somme at noon.
This is the farthest south yet that the Canadians have served. We
rested and then marched twelve kilometres [seven miles] to
Briquemesnil and arrived about 6:00 p.m. It was a good day's
hike and very hot. We passed Crouy and Cavillon. Going by train
we often went in passenger cars but more often we went in boxcars — and they always put about ten too many in a car which
meant you had no room to lay out or sit down properly. We
always had our full kit; we were packed in worse than cattle.

On July 21, General Currie attended a conference at Fourth
Army headquarters where he learned the Canadian Corps (along
with the Australians) had been chosen to spearhead an offensive
operation southeast of Amiens on August 10, a scant three weeks
away. At the conference, Rawlinson, commander of the Fourth
Army, stressed the need for extreme secrecy — not even the
Canadian Corps' four divisional commanders were to know the true
nature of the operation until the end of July. This presented Currie
with a difficult problem: how could he secretly prepare an army corps
for offensive action while at the same time moving them thirty miles
(forty-eight kilometres) to the south (the Canadians were east of
Arras), without alerting the Germans, and do it in less than three
weeks? Currie tackled this dilemma by devising a two-part plan: he
ordered his divisional commanders to begin planning an attack on
Orange Hill, an area near Arras that was similar to the ground over
which the Corps would attack at Amiens. He then sent two infantry
battalions, several casualty clearing stations (whose presence always
suggested an impending offensive), and a group of signallers north to
Mont Kemmel, Belgium. There, they made their presence well
known to the Germans by staging numerous raids and dispatching a

stream of dummy wireless messages in an easily broken code. With
the Germans now looking for the Canadians to show up at either
Orange Hill, east of Arras, or further north at Mont Kemmel, Currie
told his divisional commanders of their real destination, after which
they swiftly began their move south.

In the meantime, however, rumours had spread quickly through
the ranks, and most of the men assumed they, too, were headed to
Belgium. It's not surprising, therefore, that the 19th Battalion's Joe
O'Neill registered a high degree of astonishment among his men as
their train pulled into the station at Hangest-sur-Somme: "They
looked out the windows and they saw the name on a station, and oh,
if you could have heard their real old soldier stuff about the blankety
blank staff that got us on the wrong trains and shot us south when
we should have been going north."[234]

July 31, 1918: Got breakfast. Hot day. Wrote Bella. Had foot
inspection and went for a swim in Oissy — next village,
three kilometres [one mile] away. Best pool in France I had
seen. There was a big chateau and at the back in the grounds
was a pool. A big one and very large grounds. It was a deep
pool but you could have a real swim and by the time you got
home you could do with another bath. It's all hills and hot.
This is south of the Somme river. Drinking water is scarce.
Drank rainwater.

This day was intentionally devoted to rest after the long hot
march the previous afternoon.[235]

August 1, 1918: Platoon and company inspections and went
eight kilometres [five miles] away to practise with tanks.
Waited one hour to get barnyard water in well; made me sick.
Took our dinner away all day. Fifteen kilometres [nine miles]
altogether. Back at 5:00 p.m. we had supper, then went for a
swim. Very tired and very hot weather. I am not eating much,
water is sickening.

Northwestern France, including the war zone, experienced below average rainfall during the summer of 1918. The demands of the resident population, combined with those of millions of transient soldiers and transport horses, put a tremendous strain on the water supplies, at times creating acute shortages. Three weeks earlier, on July 11, the 19th Battalion had issued orders against wasting drinking water, threatening disciplinary action in all cases where waste occurred.

The same order also drew attention to the problems of drinking water becoming contaminated when horse lines, horse troughs, and latrines were placed too close to springs. The order stipulated that a minimum distance of 300 yards (275 metres) must be kept between wells and horse lines or other contaminants. In light of this order, it is surprising that the men were allowed to drink from a barnyard well. While this incident could be an indication of how severe the water shortages were in early August, it nevertheless stands as an indictment of the Battalion Medical Officer and those responsible to him for testing drinking water that the well was used without undergoing either analysis or even rudimentary sterilization precautions.[236]

August 2, 1918: Rain all day. Wrote Lucy no. 5. Paid twenty francs. Wrote Martha, wrote Mrs. Langmuir at Holy Trinity. Sick, to bed early.

August 3, 1918: Physical drills and company inspection, followed by Battalion parade and platoon drill. Rain. Lewis gun lectures. Rain. In billets from 10:30 a.m. to 12:00 noon. Wrote Lucy no. 6, left it in pack (forgot it). Moved and marched fourteen miles away, about twenty-three kilometres. Left Briquemesnil at 10:40 p.m.

All movement of troops and supplies had to take place at night after August 1. During the day, the men and their equipment were hidden away in woods and villages, or camouflaged in fields. And to ensure that nothing was revealed, the air force stood constant patrols over the area (which almost gave the game away when the Germans noticed the increased air activity) to chase off enemy reconnaissance and to keep a watchful eye on the ground for breaches of cover.[237]

August 4, 1918: Arrived at the outskirts of Cagny at about 5:00 a.m. Went through Amiens. Tired and sleepy. In tents. Had dinner. Wrote Lucy no. 7. Left tents at 9:30 p.m.

August 5, 1918: Marched to a wood outside of Villers-Bretonneux, arriving there at 3:30 a.m. Tiresome and slow journey. The roads were jammed with traffic. Heavy transports, two lines going one way and two lines coming back on the one road. We had to stop every four minutes or so. It was raining and I was sick. I found some shelter. Rain. Got rum at 4.30 a.m. and slept. I have a sick stomach and a bad cold. We moved to another part of the wood at 8:30 p.m. I was in a trench where there is no shelter. Rain. I slept warm but never was so sick.

The 19th Battalion was concealed in the Bois d'Aquenne, west of Villers-Brettoneux.[238]

August 6, 1918: We are just laying in these woods, waiting to go over-the-top. There are some dead Frenchmen around and a few high [German] boots sticking out of the ground. The woods are so full of trenches. I got up at 6:30 a.m. feeling better. Still raining. Corporal Bartlett and I made a bed on top of the ground out of hay and grass and put a cover on it. Of course it wasn't shell-proof but we took a chance. The trench wasn't far away. Feeling a shade better but not well yet. Posted letters and wrote a field post card to Lucy, Nora, and Bea. Rain all day.

Because secrecy around this operation was so important, the men were only finding out about their objectives now, barely thirty-six hours before zero-hour (the date of the operation was moved forward to August 8 at a conference held on July 27).[239]

One wonders what Deward might have written about on the eve of the pending offensive and if he felt that, perhaps, these might have been his last letters home.

August 7, 1918: Nice day. We got all the necessary ammunition and signals for going over-the-top and left the woods near Villers-Bretonneux at midnight for the line.

As the 19th Battalion advanced up to their start-line on the south side of the Amiens-Chaulnes railway embankment (which was the Canadian Corps' northern boundary) there was no moon to betray their movements, but the darkness that hid them from the enemy also made it difficult for the men to keep in touch with each other, as Deward notes later. To make matters worse, a dense fog had crept up the valley of the nearby river Luce and spilled onto the 19th Battalion's lines during the pre-dawn hours of August 8. By 3:30 a.m. however, all companies reported they were on their assembly positions, which consisted mostly of shell holes and shallow trenches.[240] Formed-up and waiting on the opposite side of the railway line was the 21st Australian Battalion, and to the south of the 19th Battalion lay their comrades from the 18th Battalion.

As dusk was falling on August 7, General Currie went out to watch the men moving up to their start positions. He had been under tremendous pressure to prepare the Corps for this operation quickly and was anxious that some vital detail of planning had been neglected. He was heartened, however, by what he saw. As Daniel Dancocks describes it: "One unit, well to the rear, marched past singing, 'Hail, hail, the gang's all here; what the hell do we care now!' Suddenly, Currie's worries were forgotten. Standing in his stirrups, he turned to his staff and declared, 'God help the Boche tomorrow!'"[241]

CHAPTER 9

Amiens and Arras,
August 8 to August 23, 1918

"Bell wanted to say for sure that he killed a German and so he shot a prisoner point-blank."

August 8, 1918: At 3:00 a.m. we started to mass between the railway and the road, it was pitch dark. We sat by a mound and got issued rum. The Germans must have got wise, because we were not too quiet (it was dark and we were trying to keep in touch). His batteries opened up and he made an awful mess of us. A large number of us were wounded or killed. Some ran and stumbled into shell holes they could not see for the darkness. I ran too, but fell into a narrow trench. Some other fellows were in there too, so we waited there for the fire to stop.

The shells that fell on the 19th Battalion, and on their Australian cousins just to the north, were not part of an enemy counter-preparatory barrage, as Deward feared, but instead belonged to a program of harassing fire the German artillery had been shooting all night long. Andrew McNaughton, who at Amiens served as the Canadian Corps' counter-battery officer, was nearby writing a letter to his wife. He noted the harassing fire and the barrage that landed on Deward:

> 2:25 a.m. … everything is OK. The harassing fire had died away to nothing and the ceaseless roar of tanks and transport moving up continues unabated.

3:27 a.m. ... A little more bombarding of our front lines going on. I will not open up [counter-battery fire] unless it becomes very heavy and general. I can start the guns in a moment by a signal which all can see if it is necessary. About 20 to 30 shells a minute now, but local, opposite ——, largely trench mortars, I think. Just been outside, it is off our sector and to the north and dying down.[242]

The German barrage lasted almost until zero hour.[243]

At 4:20 a.m. Zero hour. Our guns opened up and we got out of our holes and started toward the German lines. The guns were to play on his front lines for three minutes and then [move on to his rear lines] — we had to keep close [to the barrage] but not too close, otherwise we would run into our own barrage. I never went over unless I lit a cigarette. The Germans are too excited to notice a little thing like a lit cigarette.

J.S. Macklin, a veteran of the 19th Battalion, later commented similarly, "the shells came over our heads with an appalling shriek into the fog ahead. We simply lit cigarettes, shouldered our rifles, and walked after the shells, and this is what we did until we reached the objective."[244]

When I was about half way across No-Man's Land I got one of our shrapnel [balls] in the back. I thought I was wounded but Cecil Arnold looked and said no.

Evidently, in his excitement, Deward started to get ahead of the advance and into the barrage line. This was probably a result of the fog and the difficulties it created for the men trying to gauge the pace of the barrage.

We got to their front line and dozens of Germans put their hands up and said "mercy," "kamerad." Some got back [to our lines], but not all; we shot them down like dogs. We kept going and came to their support lines where we killed some more. By this time it was light but still very misty. You could not see ten feet [three metres] in front of you for the mist. We had to go through a wheat field and we came upon some Germans hidden in the wheat. We kept on going and came to some more trenches. One trench had a rifle sticking up high with a man's cap on it. We put a Mills bomb in that trench. We later found the occupants all huddled in the corner — dead.[245]

We came to another bunch afraid to come out and did the same thing. It was getting quite light by now and the Germans came running at us, shouting "mercy" and "kamerad." One fellow made signs with his hands that he had a wife and family. Some of the fellows swore at him, then pointed back toward our lines. The Germans ran back and were shot in the backs.

"Llandovery Castle" was the code word used by the Canadian divisions on August 8 to signal Corps headquarters that the men were on their start positions. The *Llandovery Castle* was an eleven-thousand-ton Union Castle passenger liner that had been working as a Canadian hospital ship when she was torpedoed on June 27, 1918, by the German submarine U86, with the loss of 234 lives, including 14 Canadian nursing sisters. Although most of the crew and hospital staff survived the sinking and made it into the lifeboats, the U-boat commander, Ober-Leutnant zur See Helmut Patzig, ordered his boat to ram them. Patzig then had the survivors machine gunned. Only one of the lifeboats escaped, by slipping into the fog. News of the sinking reached the Western Front on July 6 and, perhaps, explains Currie's attitude toward prisoners, which he conveyed to the 19th Battalion in his July 11 address to them, and which is echoed in the words of Canadian Brigadier George Tuxford: "I gave instructions to the [3rd] Brigade that the battle-cry on 8 August should be 'Llandovery Castle' and that that cry should be the last to ring in the ears of the Hun as the bayonet was driven home."[246]

The heavy fog had so reduced visibility that many pockets of German soldiers were missed by the leading waves of infantry and were not revealed until they began firing into the backs of the front-line men. These pockets of resistance were subsequently dealt with by the support and reserve troops who followed on the heels of the main advance.

Our objective lay across a road and through the village of Marcelcave. We were to dig in on the other side of it. We came to the road and could see Germans running back into the village. We opened a sweeping fire on them. We continued forward and entered Marcelcave. I went down the main street while others took the side streets. There were German dead lying in the streets. We went through the town, firing into every house or store. We found a German [regimental] headquarters, but left it for those behind us to clean out. At 7:10 a.m. we dug in on the far side of Marcelcave. We used our entrenching tools to do that by first filling the sandbags and putting them in front of us until we could dig a hole big enough for cover.

On the "other side" of Marcelcave lay the Green Line, which was the day's objective for the entire 4th Brigade. Here, the 4th Brigade units halted their advance to consolidate the position and reorganize their companies. The second phase of the battle started on the Green Line just over an hour later, when the 5th Brigade passed through and began moving toward their objective, the Red Line, some three miles (five kilometres) further to the east.

While we were digging in, a hidden German machine gun began firing. We made for it but it fired point-blank at us — it wasn't any farther than fifty yards [forty-five metres] away. It killed the fellow next to me. The tanks came up and over us and went back and forward in front of the wood that was in front of us, cleaning it out.

The tank that Deward saw in action was probably under the command of Captain Percy-Eade, who at the time was advancing parallel to the railway embankment. He was flagged down by men from the 26th Australian Battalion, whose advance was held up by machine gun fire coming from the outskirts of Marcelcave. The tank soon silenced the opposition, as Deward describes above, then entered the north end of town where it and the Australians quickly cleared that end of the village. In the meantime, as described by the Australian official history, the 19th and 20th Battalions mopped up the south side of town and "an uproar of shots and bombs resounded. Then, out came the Canadians, to the admiration of all, advancing as if on parade to their objective."[247]

> After our holes were made we connected them up and made a trench. Of course, that was some time later, about 10:00 a.m. About that time, the cavalry came with their small guns behind them and the big push was on. Our support companies — I was in the attacking wave — went through the German headquarters and took the whole staff prisoner — before they even knew anything had happened. The officer in charge got a medal.

It is not clear exactly what Deward is referring to by the cavalry coming through "with their small guns behind them." This could be a reference to the Royal Canadian Horse Artillery, which passed just south of Marcelcave during its early morning advance with the Canadian Cavalry Brigade toward Beaucourt and Cayeux. It might also have been one of the Canadian Field Artillery "contact batteries" moving forward. Contact batteries were sections of horse-drawn guns that moved forward with the infantry to provide close support. At least one of these contact, or "mobile," batteries was in action on the 4th Brigade front on August 8.[248]

The 19th Battalion's entry into Marcelcave came so quickly, the German staff — who were occupying the regimental headquarters that Deward mentions above — did not even have time to eat their breakfast. As Fred Stitt, an original 19th Battalion man recalled many years after the war, "After we got the betabbed generals up the stairs from this deep dugout, we investigated the place and found the porridge warm on the table, that's how badly we surprised them."[249]

To this, Joe O'Neill added, "I had my breakfast that morning in a German engineer's dugout with hot coffee still on the stove."[250]

The shrapnel that hit me went through my haversack and a bully beef tin (iron rations) and went right through my tunic and made a hole in my undershirt and a left a bump in my back.

On this occasion, Deward's full haversack proved a blessing. He was likely hit by a shrapnel ball from one of the 18-pounder field guns providing the rolling barrage that led the 19th Battalion's initial advance. Marcelcave itself, however, was beyond the range of most of the field artillery, and a special shoot by the Canadian Corps heavy artillery was laid on to help subdue the town's defences. Had Deward been struck by one of these larger calibre shrapnel balls, he would most likely have been killed.

Bell wanted to say for sure that he killed a German and so he shot a prisoner point-blank. It worried him later though.

Later that day, Bell was wounded by a shell fragment and evacuated to England. He recovered fully and returned to duty with the 19th Battalion in late September.[251]

Lieutenant Bell was exploring in a surface dug-out beside the road and found a German flare pistol. It went off and shot him in the knee. He later lost his leg.

Corporal Bartlett, who was a friend of Lieutenant Bell, reached the objective, although wounded, and then went back. He later won the Military Medal.

Our company officer, Lieutenant Herbert, was wounded, and Harry Dibble was killed along with another officer from our company. Captain Applegath got up high on a railway bank and signalled our objective. He was killed.

Harry Dibble had served alongside Deward in the ranks of the 180th Battalion. After he was posted to the 19th Battalion, he was awarded the Military Medal for bravery in the field and subsequently received a field commission.[252]

Deward must have added the detail about Captain Applegath at a later time and confused the dates. Gordon Applegath, of Toronto, another former 180th Battalion man, was killed on August 27, during the operations around Arras. He was twenty-

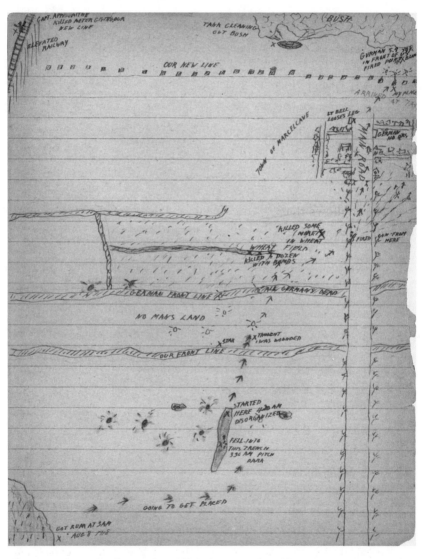

This map, drawn by Deward in 1926, shows in detail his movements in and around Marcelcave on August 8, 1918.

three. Deward may be thinking of Lieutenant Thomas Allan, a twenty-eight-year-old druggist from Varney, Ontario, who was killed in action with the 19th Battalion that day. Today, lieutenants Allan and Dibble lie almost side by side in Crucifix Corner cemetery at Villers-Brettoneux.[253]

Despite the relative ease with which the 19th Battalion secured their objectives on August 8, the battalion lost 158 men killed, wounded, or missing — of whom 11 were officers.[254]

August 9, 1918: Had tea at 3:30 a.m. Slept. Was very tired. We moved a little in advance at 11:00 a.m. Had dinner and then supper. Saw Fletcher taking prisoner out, he had him by the back of the neck and he, Fletcher, had a rag around his head. Prisoners were always sent back alone, they were glad and were picked up and maybe one or two men would take fifty or one hundred back farther. By that time all their belongings were taken from them by our fellows that met them first as prisoners. Received photos and letter, no. 20.

Canadians were notorious and inveterate souvenir hunters. James Pedley's experience on August 8 was probably typical: "...prisoners ... still dribble past us in little knots, their hands up in the air. 'Mercy!' 'Mercy!' they cry to every one. 'Souvenir!' [our] troops call out and each [prisoner] has his pockets felt into, and turned out."

Some of Pedley's experiences with souvenir hunting that day, however, were more macabre: "My batman [offered] to cut me off a dead German's finger for the ring on it."[255]

August 10, 1918: Wrote Lucy no. 8. Nice day. Moved to Caix, five kilometres [three miles]. We were bombed by aircraft every night.

August 11, 1918: Nice day. Breakfast at 5:30 p.m. Received letter no. 21, 22, 24 from Lucy. Received letters from George Field, Ira, and J.W. Barnes. Wrote Lucy no. 9. Left Caix at 7:00 a.m. for the trenches near Caix, about one hour's march, we arrived at 8:00 a.m.

August 12, 1918: Mailed letters and field post cards. We left the support lines for the front line about 8:00 p.m. The day was hot and we marched through Rosières taking our time. The Canadians captured plenty of guns. We arrived at front line about 9:30 a.m. Received letters from Bea, two from Nora, Harold (with photo), Rivett, May Chubb, and a field post card from J.W. Barnes.

While moving up to the front, Deward probably passed a dump containing some of the Canadian war trophies taken during the recent fighting, prompting his comment on the number of captured guns. During the Amiens offensive, the Canadian Corps captured 190 pieces of artillery and over 1,000 machine guns and trench mortars. They also pushed 22.5 km (14 miles) into enemy territory, liberated 27 villages, and took more than 9,000 prisoners into custody.[256]

August 13, 1918: We arrived in the front line about 4:30 a.m. Post safe. Troops tired. No shelling. Received nos. 26, 27, 28, 29 from Lucy. Appointed lance-corporal.

Deward was appointed lance corporal in place of twenty-four-year-old L/Cpl William Cresswell, who was wounded. Notice that Deward tells us he was "appointed" a lance corporal. Lance corporal was not a rank, per se, but an appointment. This meant Deward received the pay of a private, but was expected to fulfill command duties and was the man designated to replace the section corporal, should he become a casualty. Should Deward not be able to fulfill the duties of the lance corporal, the appointment would be quickly cancelled.[257]

August 14, 1918: Two men are kept on duty during the daytime and six at nights. Had tea. No shelling. The troops are tired.

Stand-to from 8:30 to 9:30 p.m. and from 4:30 a.m. to 5:30 a.m. Made my own tea. Very tired. Received cards and letters from Mable, Ira, Cpl. F. Barnes, George Field.

August 15, 1918: Beatrice's birthday. We are very tired. Only three to four hours sleep a night. We must always take special precautions against surprise. The German unit opposite was relieved by Alpine troops, Germany's raiders.

The German Alpine Corps had a reputation as an elite unit and was operating in the area as early as August 10, which may be the reason that Deward noted earlier that more men were on duty at night than during the day.[258]

August 16, 1918: My crew had to guard a sap the first day. I put up a trench block of dirt and any old thing we could find so any raider would have to jump over it. We then gathered old tin cans and spread them up the sap so at night, if anyone came along they would kick the cans and make a noise. I put the Lewis gun on the trench parapet and the bombers at the sap head. The nights are pitch dark.

By employing these little tricks of the trade, Deward is showing the value of his sixteen months of front-line experience.

We are looking for raids as the Alpines are all young fellows. Our officer's winds are up. At 4:30 p.m. we received orders to prepare to go over-the-top. This time it is without a barrage and [unlike August 8] today is a nice, bright sunny day. We started (no cigarette this time) but had to crawl to take the German front line. We crawled through fields. I crawled, dragging the Lewis gun after me. Three or four of our platoon got shot through the top of the head near me but we had to keep going. There was some barbed wire in front of us where we had to find the openings, which zigzagged through the belts of wire, and kept on crawling until we came to a trench. When we got to it, our officer looked his map over to see where he was. We split up the platoon, the officer took a party one way and I took the remainder the other way. We were to meet in the German front line. We found a half dozen or so dead Germans in the trench and then came upon a machine gun post. We captured the crew and sent them back with a couple of men and kept on going. We finally got to the German front line with only a few casualties. The officer gave us the devil for not killing the German machine gun crew.

As soon as we got to the front line we started to dig in, as it was 5:30 p.m. now. I had to dig in at three different places as they kept making us move, trying to get the Lewis gun posts, bombers, and rifleman evened out so we could set up a crossfire and not bunch together too much. We were relieved at 3:00 a.m.

"A" Company did not report themselves consolidated on their objective until 6:45 p.m., a full hour and a quarter after Deward dug his first hole. The uncharacteristic confusion after they reached their objective was probably the result of having to stage this minor operation on only a few hours' notice.[259]

This action, to seize the German positions around the village of Fransart, marked the final Canadian operation east of Amiens. Within a few days the Canadians began moving north again, to Arras.[260]

A sketch showing the trench at Fransart where Deward's party captured a German machine gun post on the afternoon of August 16, 1918.

August 17, 1918: Marched to just outside Caix. We passed Rosières and Vrély and got tea and cigarettes at the YMCA while on our way. Had breakfast and dinner and rested. Got orders to move to Weincourt and left camp at 4:00 p.m. and marched to outside Weincourt. There, I made a hole in the ground and put a sheet over it for a shelter. We had a bath in Caix on the way. We arrived about 8:00 p.m.

From now on we are generally just left in a field and told to stay here. I never hesitated, if they were waiting for orders, to dig a hole for protection. I knew the value of a good hole. They kept us out of towns.

By keeping the men out of towns, the army was probably trying to keep them safe from German long-range artillery, which could more easily register on a town than a field.

August 18, 1918: Breakfast at 8:00 a.m. Wrote Lucy no. 10. Very hot, but the nights are cold. Received a letter from Lucy, no. 24. Paid twenty francs. Wrote Nora, Bea, Rivett, George Field. Later, received letter nos. 29 and 30.

August 19, 1918: I got a new mess tin to replace the one wrecked by the shrapnel ball. Wrote Harold, Corporal Fred, Mable. I was warned for an advance party. We went to Weincourt at 9:30 p.m. and then marched to Boves. We stopped four kilometres [two miles] from Boves and had an hour-long sleep. I was made a full corporal.

Deward was promoted to full corporal to replace Corporal Leslie Haider, aged twenty-four, an original 19th Battalion man who was killed in action on August 8.[261]

An "advance party" was a small group sent on ahead of the main battalion to prepare the destination for its arrival.

August 20, 1918: Arrived at Boves 3:00 a.m. Slept and had breakfast in the field at 6:30 a.m. Left Boves on a train (we rode in boxcars). Train got in at 3:00 p.m. left at 5:00 p.m. and passed through Amiens, Vignacourt, Candas, Doullens. Arrived at Estrée-Wamin, got off and marched to Écc᾽᾽res, arriving at 7:00 a.m.

The tiny French boxcars, well worn after four long years of war service, were inevitably marked "40 hommes–8 cheveaux" (forty men or eight horses), a paradox that was seldom lost on the poor, tightly packed infantrymen.

The 2nd Division was heading back to its old stomping grounds around Arras, where it would soon be taking part in active operations once again.

August 21, 1918: Slept in a barn and had breakfast at 10:30 a.m. and dinner at 5:00 p.m. Wrote Lucy no. 11, Joe W. Barnes, and Winnie. To bed early after having milk and pears from a tin.

August 22, 1918: Kit inspection, rifle inspection, respirator inspection. Wrote Bella, Ira, May Chubb, Fred, and Nora. Received letter nos. 31 and 32, and from Nora, Hazel Chubb. Received a card from "Wee" Ira and a letter from Harold. Started green envelope no. 12.

August 23, 1918: We received moving orders, which meant we had to be up at 4:30 a.m. I took the Lewis gun to the transport, then had breakfast at 5:00 a.m. We left Écoivres at 12:30 p.m. and marched through Héricourt and Siracourt to Wavrans, arriving at 3:30 p.m. Left Wavrans by train at 6:30 p.m. (we rode in boxcars again). We Passed Saint Pol and Mont-St. Eloi, arriving at Noyelles at 11:00 p.m. We then marched to the Oxford Circus Huts at Warlus, arriving there at 2:00 a.m.

CHAPTER 10

On Leave,
August 24 to October 8, 1918

"I am fed up with war and have neglected my diary."

August 24, 1918: We had dinner at 3:00 a.m. and then slept. We had breakfast at 10:00 a.m. then washed and shaved. I finished Lucy's no. 12. We left Warlus at 9:30 p.m. and marched to the same billets in Arras [that we had occupied in July]. We arrived at 11:00 p.m. and slept.

August 25, 1918: We ate breakfast at 8:30 a.m. I wrote Lucy no. 13. We had nothing to do. No mail has been collected yet.
The mail was just finally collected.

The Canadian Army Postal Corps was the military organization responsible for handling mail for Canadian troops overseas. Under normal circumstances, mail was delivered to, and collected from, front-line units on a daily basis. Through his unit's field post office, every Canadian soldier had access to a full range of postal services, including postal money orders (bought and cashed), registered letters (inbound and outbound), and stamps. Despite the extended lines of communication between France and England, most letters posted to addresses in England arrived the following day — letters to Canada usually took a bit longer.[262]

I received a letter from Lucy (who was writing from Buffalo, New York). We left Arras at 10:00 p.m. for the front line on the right of Arras, arriving there at 11:00 p.m. Raining. I slept sitting up. We got word that we are going over-the-top again.

On August 14, Haig received a letter from Currie arguing that further operations around Amiens should be cancelled, due to mounting German resistance. Currie recommended, however, that if further operations at Amiens were necessary, they should be delayed, to give the attackers a chance to re-establish the element of surprise. Currie also recommended that it would be better still if the Canadian Corps was withdrawn entirely from the line, rested a few days, and then used in another surprise attack east of Arras. Currie submitted that a British advance there, combined with French advances planned for further south, might well compel the Germans to withdraw from their lines west of the river Somme without forcing the allies to mount an all-out frontal assault in that direction. Currie's plan made sense from a number of standpoints. The Canadians had held numerous sections of the line in the Arras sector almost exclusively for the past year and a half (since the battle of Vimy Ridge, except for a brief sojourn at Passchendaele), and they knew the area intimately. Also, the Canadian Corps' staff had drawn up plans for an attack east of Arras as a cover for the Amiens operations only three weeks earlier.

Currie's suggestion was in line with Haig's own thoughts that the time was right for a determined strike against the enemy, and he readily accepted Currie's proposal.

The Canadians, however, were not going to have an easy time of it. The enemy's positions east of Arras were constructed in depth and exceptionally strong. The landscape was well suited to defence, featuring several heavily fortified ridges. In front of the Canadians lay no less than five defensive lines: the old British and German front lines, overrun during the German advances in March 1918; the Fresnes-Rouvroy Line, which lay to the east of these; the Drocourt-Quéant Line (D-Q Line) beyond that; and then finally the long stretch of the unfinished Canal du Nord.

The D-Q Line was the most formidable of these defensive lines. It formed the southernmost extension of what the Germans called the *Wotan Stellung*, one of the fortified positions that formed the greater Hindenburg Line. The D-Q Line had been under construction for almost two years and consisted of thick belts of barbed wire, deep trenches, and even deeper concrete shelters. The Germans understood that the Hindenburg Line formed their best chance of stopping any combined Franco-British advance toward the Rhine, and they were prepared to defend it vigorously.

Currie's job, along with the British XVIIth Corps operating on his right, was to punch through these lines on a relatively narrow front and turn southward, denying the benefit of these defensive lines to the enemy and forcing him to withdraw.

The first phase of the operation was set to begin on August 26.[263]

August 26, 1918: Zero hour 3:00 a.m. No barrage (delayed). We went over-the-top at 4:00 a.m. Rain. Alongside the Cambrai Road (right) to first objective in front of Fosse Farm. Got there at 6:00 a.m. in shell holes. Soaked through. Sun came out at 3:00 p.m.

British attacks usually came at dawn, but since Currie could not achieve surprise through concealment, as he had done at Amiens, he chose instead to surprise the Germans by attacking at an unusual time — in the middle of the night. The tactic worked, and no serious German opposition developed until after sunrise.

Although zero hour was set for 3:00 a.m., the 19th Battalion formed the 4th Brigade's reserve, and therefore did not start their advance until an hour after the attacking waves (the 20th and 21st Battalions) had gone forward.

It is not clear what Deward means by "no barrage." There was quite a heavy, and effective, barrage as the attacking waves went forward at 3:00 a.m. He may mean there was no barrage as the 19th Battalion moved off an hour after the main attack.

At 4:30 in the afternoon we advanced another thousand yards [nine hundred metres] in battle formation. Sergeant Newell gave us each a drink of rum on the way over. He was feeling good. We couldn't make our objective but got in a half kind of trench and waited for a counter-attack. We would have been lost if he [the Germans] had come then, we had to get out of there and get back where we started. We did not get back until 2:00 a.m.

In the late afternoon, "A" and "B" companies of the 19th Battalion were ordered to advance and take up positions in two locations, marked Panther and Egret trenches on their maps. The advance had to be made over open ground, and the companies suffered several casualties from enemy artillery while advancing. When they reached an intermediate position, Curlew Trench, they found it occupied by "B" and "D" companies of the 27th Battalion, who through confusion had also been ordered to take Egret Trench. The whole advance, however, was held up by heavy machine gun fire coming from Egret Trench and other positions flanking it. After advising 4th Brigade Headquarters of this situation, "A" Company was ordered to return to the positions they had occupied at 4:30 p.m. while "B" Company was told to stay put and come under the orders of the nearby 18th Battalion.[264]

August 27, 1918: Sergeant Newell and a private went out investigating the enemy front lines. They had had too much rum to drink.

We went over-the-top along with a tank, but the Germans were using these anti-tank guns (cannons) and anti-tank rifles that have an immense cartridge. One of our fellows got shot by one of the rifles; it made a terrible hole — big enough to put your two fists in. But the guns! The shells from them burst just in front of the tank, close to the ground, and the shrapnel spread. Oh my! I dreaded them. You just heard the burst of the shell and then the shrapnel flew.

The Germans introduced a bolt-action anti-tank rifle in February 1918. It was designed to kill the tank's crew by firing a

13.2-millimetre (.519-inch) bullet through as much as 25 millimetres (1 inch) of steel plating.

While early tanks could also be disabled by a direct hit from an ordinary high-explosive shell, it is unlikely that shrapnel would have much effect on them. By firing shrapnel shells directly at the tanks, the German artillery was probably trying to kill the infantry that were advancing alongside the tanks and sheltering in their lee.[265]

We later found Sergeant Newell in the corner of a trench we had taken. He had been shot through the back of the head and his pockets were empty. The Germans let him get past them, then they ambushed him. When they captured him, they found his souvenirs, which were German photos of their families — and he had his pockets full of them.

This was another, less obvious danger of souvenir hunting. If the enemy caught you with their fallen comrades' personal possessions they were far less inclined to treat you with leniency.

Sketch showing where Deward saw the body of Sergeant Newell, who had been captured by the Germans then shot execution-style through the back of the head.

At 8:30 a.m. we went over-the-top again but this time with a barrage (the Battalion was pretty well cut up by now). Those machine guns of his played havoc with us. We got nearly to our objective, but could not make it. So, we held a river bank — it had been a river once but was now dried up. It had willow trees along both sides. We couldn't dig in there, only watch for the enemy to come. We couldn't hold the bank and had to retire at 11:00 p.m. It was heavy fighting, mostly with rifles and machine guns. Our battalion lost heavily. Nearly half of us were killed or wounded and only three officers came out who were not wounded.

Deward's account of this day's advance does not quite match with the 19th Battalion and 4th Infantry Brigade records. According to these sources, zero hour for the 4th Brigade units on August 27 was 10:00 a.m. and the first objective, the bank of the river Sensée, was achieved with relative ease. Deward also reports that the bed of the river they held was dry. In fact, the Sensée was flowing. However, to reach the Sensée, the 19th Battalion earlier in the day had to cross the river Cojeul, which was dry at the time. Given the sustained nature of the fighting over this period, it is unlikely that Deward was able to keep his diary up-to-date, and he probably made these entries several days later, while in rest billets. This might explain some of the confusion and inaccuracies that have crept in.

For some reason, on this day the artillery failed to provide the effective support that the infantry needed to overcome the strongly organized system of trenches in front of them. This had disastrous repercussions for the attacking troops, as both Deward and the official records note:

> Just beyond the first objective [the river Sensée] the battalion was held up by severe machine gun fire from a strongly organized system of trenches and from the flanks.
>
> ... Throughout the advance, the artillery barrage was very poor, the line of barrage was very irregular, and some guns were about 30 seconds after others in lifting, which caused many casualties. These operations were very costly to the Battalion, casualties were severe and at the end there were only five company officers left."[266]

Among the 19th Battalion's wounded on August 27th was Louis Bacon, who had performed so valiantly as a stretcher-bearer at Hill 70. His wound was not serious, however, and he returned to duty with the battalion on September 20th.[267]

> **August 28, 1918:** They sent gas shells over at 12:30 p.m. We went over-the-top again with a barrage, but lost many men and could not make our objective. The Germans were bound to hold on. We are held up by machine guns. We stayed in shell holes, then we got into a trench. It was a crime to stay here so we got ready for another attack, but we got word that the Germans were coming. I'm in charge of half a company here, there are no other NCOs. Everyone has to make steps so they can get up to fire over-the-top, as it is a deep trench. One or two of the draftees, although the majority were good men, refused and I threatened to shoot them if they didn't dig. We had only a few men left and everyone was needed to do their part. Some of us piled German dead on top of each other and stood on them so we could see over-the-top of the trench. I thought for sure we were gone. The Germans came on but at our particular part of the line they seemed to have slowed up. We had to retire again at 7:00 p.m. — to where we started from. At one point during the day, we were almost surrounded.

That a corporal was in charge of half a company gives us some insight into the number of casualties the battalion had suffered up to that point and how it was the senior NCOs (sergeants and sergeants major) and junior officers (second lieutenants and lieutenants) who bore the highest casualty rates per capita.

The draftees to which Deward refers were men who had been conscripted under the Military Service Act, which Deward had supported by voting for the Unionist Party during the federal election the previous December.

The 4th Brigade that attacked in the early afternoon of August 28 was only a ghost of the formation that had taken the field barely forty-eight hours before. The heavy fighting of the previous two days had bled the battalions almost white. In addition, the surviving men had not been able to sleep more than a few hours, nor could they be properly re-equipped. To make matters worse, again, on the morning of August 28, the artillery failed to properly soften up the objectives, leaving many heavily wired points and machine gun posts intact. It was upon these rocks that the decimated brigade's attack soon foundered. Although attempts were made for many hours to overcome the enemy's defences, "the advance was brought to a halt … Numerous attempts were made to gain ground but only succeeded in increasing the casualty list. Nearly all the officers and section commanders were killed or wounded making reorganization in the face of the devastating fire of the enemy a hopeless task."[268]

Later in the day the enemy began reinforcing his front lines, which probably accounts for the advancing enemy troops that Deward observed. At about the same time, adding to the 4th Brigade's misery, the enemy also laid down a heavy barrage of high explosives and gas along the valley of the Sensée.[269]

> On one of our over-the-top trips we had to skirmish over, that is, run for a hole and then get down and look for another place to run to, then make for that. We had a new officer leading our platoon, a big, tall fellow. It was his first trip up the line. He would run and then get down on one knee. I said he won't last long. He didn't.

The new officer may have thought it unbecoming to fling himself in the muck. Whatever his motivations, his courage was not in question. As mentioned above, junior officers sustained some of the highest casualty rates among the fighting men. Will Bird arrived at the front about the same time as Deward in 1917, and by the time of the Amiens battle sixteen months later, he had had fourteen different officers command his platoon.[270]

> I have had thousands of bullets whistle past my head, it's a nice sound, but … We went on and there was a machine gun post we tried to get. It played on a gap in the wire. There must have been forty men all heaped up dead in that gap. We had to get past the machine gun to get behind a bank for cover. A half

This drawing was created by Deward in 1926 and depicts the action south of Vis-en-Artois during the Arras battles of 1918. Shown here is the lead-up to the incident in which the Germans counterattacked Deward's half-company late in the afternoon of August 28.

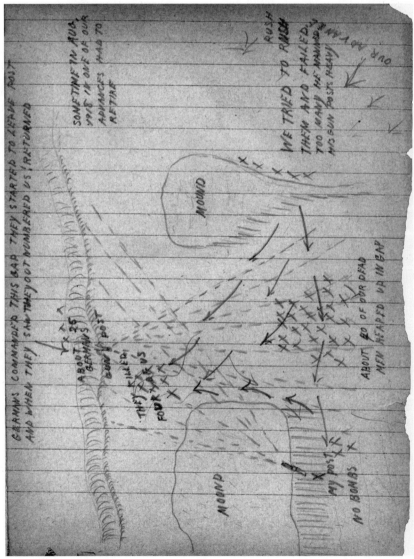

dozen of us made it and we tried to plan to get the machine gun post. Unfortunately, we had no bombs, which you could have tossed into the post easily. So, we planned a rush, which we did, some from the other side and us from where we were. We jumped into a kind of trench and rushed them. They killed the first four men and we saw that we couldn't make it. The Germans, however, started to jump out of the trench, but when they saw that we were beat they stopped, jumped back in the post, and started firing again.

This passage helps to reveal the benefit of the time the Canadians spent in training. Notice the lack of reference to the chain of command, "we tried to plan to get the machine gun post" and "we planned a rush," and so on. There was no thought here of waiting to receive orders from higher up. Even with most of the senior section, platoon, and company leaders out of action, it is clear that Deward and his men continued to display initiative and a dogged determination in the face of a very serious threat. This kind of performance only occurs when morale is high and the troops have confidence in each other, their junior leaders (lance corporals and corporals), and the soundness of their training.

August 29, 1918: We were relieved by the 1st Division coming in after a month's rest. At 3:00 a.m. we went halfway to Arras. Monchy le Preux is just to the left of us. Had three meals and left for Arras at 3:00 p.m. arrived at 5:00 p.m. Had supper, cleanup, feet are sore. Had my first sleep since Sunday. This is Thursday. Received a letter from Omer Rivett and box no. 26 from Lucy (for my birthday and a dandy!). Feet sore.

The remnants of the 19th Battalion were relieved by the fresh 8th Battalion during the early hours of August 29. Although the 1st Division units had not yet been committed to this battle, they did not have a month's rest as Deward claims. Many 1st Divisions units were active on the Amiens front as late as August 16.

The four battalions of the 4th Brigade had suffered severely at the hands of the enemy, so much so that the surviving officers of the 19th and 21st battalions had to form a composite battalion from what was left so they could hold their final line before they were relieved. In all, the 19th Battalion lost 295 men in those three days of fighting. Their sister unit, the 20th Battalion, had suffered even more severely, losing 437 during the same period.[271]

These losses, however, were not in vain. Although the 2nd and 3rd Divisions failed to take all of the Fresnes-Rouvroy Line and the subsequent D-Q Line, they penetrated deeply enough to provide a good jumping off point for the 1st and 4th Canadian Divisions when they renewed the attack on September 2. By September 4, these formations had punched through the D-Q Line and were crouched on the west bank of the Canal du Nord. Daniel Dancocks tells us that by breaking through the Hindenburg Line, the Canadian Corps:

> ...achieved two things: it had forced the enemy to abandon all the ground won at such enormous cost during the first half of 1918, and it wrecked [German commander General] Ludendorff's plan to conduct a gradual, fighting withdrawal to the Hindenburg Line.
>
> The Canadians also gave Kaiser Wilhelm a nervous breakdown. "Now we have lost the war!" Wilhelm wailed when he received the bad news from the D-Q Line. "Poor Fatherland!" The distraught Kaiser thereupon went to bed and refused to get up for twenty-four hours.

Lucy's package arrived a few days early; Deward's birthday was not until September 2, when he turned thirty.

During the previous three days of fighting, Deward has been transformed into a true infantryman. After all that he has been through, the one thing that he makes a point of complaining to his diary about is his sore feet.

▨ **August 30, 1918:** We are in the same billets in Arras where we usually stay. We had a good sleep but it was cold. Omer Rivett came to see me. Wrote Lucy no. 14. We left Arras at 8:00 p.m. marching through Berneville, and arrived at Simencourt where we were put into huts. We marched twelve kilometres seven miles]. I made myself some cocoa. I wrote Nora, Wee Ira. Canadians took Wotan Woods and a Hindenburg switch line.

When Deward tells us the Canadians took Wotan Woods, he is probably referring to Upton Wood, which was taken by the Canadians on August 30. Upton Wood lay just in front of the D-Q Line, or Wotan Stellung, which could be the source of the confusion. The Canadians also captured part of the Vis-en-Artois switch line, which connected the D-Q Line to the Fresnoy-Rouvroy Line (a switch line was a trench system that joined up two main lines — something like a communication trench only more elaborate and on a much larger scale).

▨ **August 31, 1918:** We had a bath parade and a clothing parade. We were kept busy with training all day. Later, I went downtown with Cecil.

Even though the battalion had just come through an intense period of fighting, it had to keep up a regimen of training to help integrate reinforcements and to allow newly promoted NCOs to exercise their authority. By keeping the men busy, it also helped to distract them from the trauma they had just endured.

▨ **September 1, 1918:** I was warned that I was to go on a gas course and I was paid. I left Simencourt at 11:30 a.m. and walked through Berneville to the Warlus gas school, three kilometres [one mile] away. Wrote Lucy no. 15, Bella, Harold, Mable. Later, I went to bed and slept cold.

September 2, 1918: We paraded from 9:00 a.m. to 12:00 noon. I bought tickets for the See Too's concert. After gas school, I left

Warlus at 2:30 p.m. and walked through Berneville, half a kilometre [a third of a mile], then to Wailly four kilometres [three
miles], Agny three kilometres [two miles], and to Beaurains
three kilometres further. I arrived at 5:30 p.m. only to find the
battalion had moved into dug-outs elsewhere. I waited at the
cross-roads until 7:00 p.m. then slept with Sergeant Farr.

It's difficult to know for certain how Deward knew the dis-
tances between each of these villages, but it's likely there were
signposts along the way that stated the distance to the next village.

September 3, 1918: Received letter nos. 33, 34, 35, 36 from
Lucy. I also received photos and a letter from Bella. We left
Beaurains at 2:00 p.m. and marched through Wancourt, to a
position two ridges in front of that town. We arrived there at
6:00 p.m.

It was slow going as the roads have heavy traffic. We were
put in shell holes and trenches. We were issued ammunition
and told that we might have to move on one hour's notice. I
slept all night.

The battalion was now moving back into the general area that it
had fought over from August 26 to 28, although it was well back from
the ongoing operations further east, in front of the Canal du Nord.[272]

September 4, 1918: We ate breakfast at 7:30 a.m. then got
more ammunition. I finished letter no. 15 and left at 2:30 p.m.
for the Brigade support lines. We marched past Hendecourt,
arriving at 5:00 p.m. I slept in a dug-out and it is a real long
one. I was down near the end of it and when you had to go out
at night for gas guard, you had to go over-the-top. It was a deep
tunnel. You had all you could do to not slip on someone while
getting out.

On September 4, the 19th Battalion moved up into the support
lines to relieve a battalion from the 6th Brigade. They took up their

support positions in an old German trench system, which is where Deward encountered the long, deep dugout.[273]

September 5, 1918: Breakfast was ready at 7:30 a.m. I wrote Lucy no. 16, Bella, Ira, Nora, Hazel Chubb, and received a letter and some photos from Mable. I was warned that I had to go for gas instructions at Brigade Headquarters near Hendecourt the next day.

September 6, 1918: I left the trenches for gas instructions at 8:15 a.m. and arrived at Brigade at 9:00 a.m. We had lectures and rain. I came back to the trenches at night. Wrote Lucy no. 17.

It appears that Deward had been appointed "A" Company's gas NCO. After attending a course of instruction at the brigade's gas school, the company gas NCO became responsible for enforcing good gas discipline among the men of his company. In addition, the gas NCOs had to hold gas drills, inspect the company's anti-gas equipment — including the men's respirators — and otherwise assist the battalion's gas officer.[274]

September 7, 1918: I was down at Brigade gas school all day, then came back at 4:00 p.m.

September 8, 1918: Rain. We had a rifle inspection. I was at school all day, then back at 4:00 p.m. I was able to take a bath. Rain.

September 9, 1918: Rain. I sheltered in a dugout in the morning. Wrote Lucy no. 18. I was at gas school for most of the day and back at 4:30 p.m. I received two letters from Lucy, nos. 40 and 41. I started a letter for a green envelope, no. 19.

September 10, 1918: I was down at Brigade again (my last day), and back at 4:00 p.m. Rain. Received letters from Nora, Corporal Fred, Harold. I received letters from Lucy.

While Deward was attending gas school, the rest of the battalion remained in the support lines, training and scouring the recently fought over ground for salvageable equipment and supplies.[275]

September 11, 1918: I inspected the respirators for our company. Rain. I was warned that I was going to be sent on leave.

I saw a pretty aeroplane fight. They were using tracer bullets. Our men brought the German plane down. I had seen several planes come down while at the front.

I went to see the Medical Officer, got paid £20 and 10 francs, then left with the transport at 7:30 p.m. and got a ride on a truck back to Arras, eighteen kilometres [eleven miles] away. I walked a little more and got a ride to Agny, another five kilometres [three miles] away. I traveled twenty-seven kilometres altogether, sixteen miles — I was lucky to get that far in one evening. I arrived at the train station at 12:00 midnight.

September 12, 1918: There was no place to sleep here so I got in a box car and slept cold. It was raining until 6:30 a.m. I reported to the RTO (Railway Transport Officer) and left on the train at 8:00 a.m. arriving at Saint Pol at 11:30 a.m. I then marched to rest billets, got some blankets and slept. Later I shaved and washed. I left Saint Pol on a train at 4:00 p.m. passing through Étaples, arriving at Boulogne at 9:30 p.m. We were marched to rest billets, had a free dinner and got our bed boards, then went to bed.

At the rest billets, then men had to turn in the boards from the bed frames each day and draw them again in the evening. This might have been to stop the men from using the boards for firewood, but more likely was intended to make the beds unusable during the day — to cut down on malingering.

September 13, 1918: Up at 5:30 a.m. I got cleaned up and had a free breakfast. I left the rest billets at 10:00 a.m. and marched down to the boat, which left Boulogne at 12:30 p.m.

253

The trip was rough and I was sick. We arrived at Folkestone at 3:30 p.m. I arrived at London's Victoria Station at 7:00 p.m. and made my way to the Maple Leaf Club. I had a bath and got a new pair of underwear.

September 14, 1918: Rain. I bought some clothes, then went into a tailor's and a girl fixed [the shrapnel hole in] my tunic while I waited. I went to the Strand Theatre, then left for Glasgow from Euston Station at 11:30 p.m.

September 15, 1918: I arrived at Glasgow's Central Station at 9:15 a.m. I met Dick and went to communion in the afternoon. We went to Baird's that night. It rained. I had my photo taken.

September 16, 1918: Rain. I stayed in and wrote Lucy no. 1.

It is not clear why Deward has started to renumber his letters. Previously, he started to renumber his letters after he reached one hundred, but that is not the case here.

September 17, 1918: Still raining. I posted a view book of Arras.

September 18, 1918: I left Glasgow.

September 21, 1918: I arrived at Euston station at 7:30 a.m.

September 22 to 25, 1918: I left Paddington Station at 11:30 a.m. and arrived in Bristol at 1:30 p.m. Mable gave me a swell time. We saw Clifton Bridge and went all over Bristol to shows and, later, we went to a place called Bath. I also saw my father's brother, and then went to Alverton to see father's sister. I left Bristol at 8:00 p.m.

Clifton Bridge is a suspension bridge that spans the Avon gorge at Bristol. Built in the 1860s, it is an engineering marvel. The current trustees of the bridge liken it to Bristol as the Eiffel Tower is to Paris.

Deward's photo, September 15, 1918. In this photo you can make out the battalion colours that Deward had sewed to the top of his sleeve back in June and the edge of his corporal's stripes.

September 26, 1918: I arrived at Paddington Station, London at 11:40 p.m. I was late arriving on account of getting on the wrong train, which took me away up by the Australian's camp. I put myself up at the YMCA.

September 27, 1918: I left Victoria Station at 6:30 a.m. and arrived at Folkestone at 9:30 a.m. After crossing the channel, I went to the Boulogne rest camp.

September 28, 1918: After breakfast, I went to Dainville, Arras, the Chelsea Huts, and Wancourt. I was put up at a rest camp for the night. The rest camps were really just dug-outs.

October 1, 1918: It took me three days to find the battalion. When I discovered their location, I left to join them at once, that was around 7:00 p.m. travelling by the Cambrai-Arras Road through Agny to Inchy-en-Artois where I found the battalion. Later that night, we went over the Canal du Nord and bivouacked in a field.

While Deward was on leave, the 19th Battalion had spent most of its time in Brigade reserve, providing working parties and resting at various locations in what had been the Hindenburg Line and in old German trenches on the west bank of the Canal du Nord. Earlier, on September 27, the 1st, 3rd, and 4th Divisions had crossed the Canal du Nord, seized the east bank, and were now working their way through the enemy's defences in front of Cambrai. On the evening of September 30, the 2nd Division, which until now had been in Corps reserve, itself crossed the Canal du Nord in preparation for offensive operations against Cambrai.

October 2, 1918: We moved up the Arras-Cambrai Road and bivouacked by a farm four kilometres [two miles] from Cambrai. We are staying here right beside the road in holes. I am fed up with war and have neglected my diary.

The 4th Brigade was being held in divisional reserve from October 2 until October 9 and was spared the heavy fighting that took place in front of Cambrai.[276]

It is no coincidence that Deward declares he is "fed up with war," only seven days after returning from leave. While the anticipation of leave gave the men something to look forward to, the realization of it only emphasized the misery in which they existed at the front. Deward might even have been suffering from mild depression triggered by his return to a hellish and uncertain existence at the front. Clearly the extraordinary experiences of battle and the fantastic world of the trench and No-Man's Land by now had become commonplace for him and no longer had the same power they once had to motivate his diary-keeping.

Courtesy Canada Dept. of National Defence/National Archives of Canada PA-003246

View of Cambrai from Canadian front line, advance east of Arras, October 1918. This is how Deward most likely saw the city of Cambrai on October 2, just before its fall to the Canadian Corps. The fighting has recently swept past this location, as evidenced by the German corpse in the foreground.

October 7, 1918: We moved to the other side of Douai Road and stayed in railway-bank funk holes. I had to make a [Lewis] gun post here. Later, we moved through a part of Cambrai that is burning. We made a post the other side of the city. I got some souvenirs from abandoned houses. We moved again at night.

The Germans had planned to destroy Cambrai by fire before their withdrawal, and for several days before the Canadians entered the city, huge columns of smoke could be seen rising as entire blocks

257

burned. Cambrai was not completely cleared by the Canadians until October 9. To help facilitate this, the 2nd Division was ordered to pass north of Cambrai and then strike east of the city to seize the bridges over the Canal de l'Escaut, cutting off the defenders' line of retreat. The attack took place at 1:30 a.m. October 9 with the men wearing white arm bands to distinguish them from the Germans in the darkness. The unusual hour of the attack again caught the Germans by surprise and in the middle of their final withdrawal from the city. The operation was a complete success. The 4th Brigade was in divisional support and was not called upon to take part in the fight. Their part in the active operations around Cambrai, however, would come soon enough.[277]

My nerves were always good untill I had my last leave from France Sept 1918 maybe on account of the war lasting so long the thought of what was in front of us I then started to get the wind up have never got over it, since I came home I have always tried experience, but could never do it, so I class myself as a war wreck, which people will never understand

CHAPTER 11

The Armistice,
October 9, 1918, to February 10, 1919

"My rifle was slung over my shoulder and the bullet went through the butt and through my right thigh."

October 9, 1918: During the day, we received orders to go over-the-top tomorrow morning. We have had no sleep for three days. Again, we stayed in the railway embankment dug-outs all night, about one hundred yards [ninety metres] from our morning jumping-off place. During the night we were given our rations.

After the fall of Cambrai, the Canadian Corps continued its attacks, pushing back the Germans ever eastward. In support of these operations, the 19th Battalion received orders in the early hours of October 10 to seize Naves and the high ground about one thousand yards (nine hundred metres) to the northeast of the town, overlooking the river Erclin.[278]

October 10, 1918: Raining, very misty. We were not told what we were going to do until it was near daybreak. We had to take their front-line trenches and then a town [Naves]. We went over-the-top at 6:00 a.m. The 21st Battalion was holding our front lines, in shell holes. There are no trenches here, just shell holes. We passed over [the 21st Battalion] without a barrage and had no trouble until we got into a hollow before the town. [The Germans] opened up a fire and we sent up our SOS flares (red over red over red) but the artillery could not see them for rain and mist and did not open fire. We wasted time there under whatever protection we could get, then received orders to advance. But, in the meantime, the Germans had retired and all we did was just go through the town, shooting into houses and looking into barnyards.[279]

The attack on Naves was lead by "A" and "B" companies accompanied by what the 19th Battalion's *War Diary* describes as a "very light" barrage. So light was the barrage that it apparently went unnoticed by Deward. In spite of the delay that Deward experienced in front of Naves, the 19th Battalion secured its objective northeast of the town by 8:30 a.m.[280]

We went over a bridge that had a mine under it but it did not work (it was in the bank under one end). We dug in on the other side of town, into a ridge.

In the afternoon the cavalry came up to advance on the next ridge. They went over us about 2:00 or 3:00 in the afternoon. They had to go down a hill and up another. A creek [the river Erclin] ran between them and the Germans, who were on the other side in trenches in the hill. The cavalry went forward, the horses ringing wet [with sweat]. My, but it is a pretty sight as they dashed down the hill and over the creek ... then the Germans opened up on them. It was a shame. They could not help but hit them with machine guns. All the men out of seventy-five or so went down but one, and he finally went. But the horses were not all killed. That attack was a failure. Cavalry were not much good in this war.

With the fall of Cambrai and the resulting breakthrough into more open country it was hoped that a mobile force of cavalry and armoured cars could be used to secure certain key objectives ahead of the advancing infantry. On the previous day, October 9, the Canadian Light Horse (CLH) had crossed the Canal de l'Escaut to seize the high ground northwest of Naves. Their attack was halted, with heavy losses, by concentrated machine gun fire coming from Naves and nearby Iwuy. The action that Deward describes on October 10 was mounted by "A" and "C" squadrons of the CLH (approximately 280 mounted men), with similar results.[281]

As Deward notes, not all of the horses were killed, but they did suffer a disproportionately higher number of casualties. The charge on October 10 cost the regiment seventy-one animals, of which sixty-six were killed. The losses among the men were considerably lighter, five killed and seventeen wounded.

At night, we moved up the road farther to make another advance and to try and get Fritz's trenches, as he was quite a distance from us. We got in our assembly place and started over-the-top at 10:00 p.m. I knew we would never get there, but the Imperials were going over to take the top of the German hill at 5:30 a.m. next morning, relieving the Canadians. And the Canadians, I guess, wanted to give them a flying start as the Imperial jumping-off place was maybe 500 yards [450 metres] behind us.

We started. No artillery and pitch dark. We extended out in line just far enough so as you could see the man next to you. We went very slowly, orders passing down the line so as not to get one flank too far ahead of the other. An officer was on each end. We kept going, no shelling, but nice and quiet. I judged we had been going nearly two hours when we heard the Germans talking and clicking [cocking] their guns to get ready. We were practically on them. Their trench was only a few yards from us. They heard us. I got down quick. Their machine guns opened up but as luck had it, no one opened up in front of me. When they swept I was down close to the ground. The second fellow from me got it and was groaning. I passed the word along to try and stop if he could. He did.

I don't know how many men we lost. Some were shot through the heels and most through the head while getting down. We waited for orders and they came. Crawl to the next man and retire to the road again! We went back, maybe about 1:00 a.m. and when we were told about so many getting killed and wounded we all had to go back and get (and bring out) all the wounded we could.

We spent most of the rest of the dark hours going back and forward getting the boys. We stayed on this main road in funk holes. The road ran directly into the German lines. Cecil Arnold and several more were killed that were pals of mine.

In all, the 19th Battalion made three attacks on October 10. The morning attack secured the town of Naves as Deward outlines above. At 2:00 p.m. the battalion advanced another one thousand yards (nine hundred metres) and established two of its companies on the far side of the river Erclin. The final operation carried out by the 19th Battalion on October 10 began at 5:15 p.m. and saw "A" and "B" Companies advance another 1,500 yards (1.3 kilometres) in the face of heavy machine gun fire. They reached their objective, the jumping-off positions for the Imperial attack planned for the following morning, by 7:45 p.m.

It isn't clear what Deward is referring to when he tells us that they started over-the-top at 10:00 p.m. Again, this may be a detail that Deward added later, but remembered incorrectly. In mid-October, the 19th Battalion's 5:15 p.m. attack would have started in twilight and ended only after the full darkness of night had descended. This may at least in part explain the confusion.

During the night of October 10–11, the 19th Battalion was placed into Brigade reserve. From there it was to support an attack the following morning by the 20th and 21st battalions on the high ground to the east of Iwuy.[282]

This sketch shows, on the left, the twilight attack made by the 19th Battalion on October 10, 1918, and, on the right, the disposition of the 19th Battalion in funk holes along what was probably the Cambrai-Saulzoir road on the morning of October 11.

October 11, 1918: Captain Duncan took some men out to find out where the Germans were but was wounded and taken prisoner.

Arthur Duncan died of his wounds while a prisoner of war and has no known grave. Of Duncan's loss, James Pedley laments, "He was reported missing near Cambrai in October, and no authentic trace of him remains. One hopes that the end came quickly, that he was not lugged wounded into the German lines, questioned and goaded by German Staff officers before he died. One does not know."

This is an astonishing statement in light of what we know was Duncan's fate. It may be that Pedley knew Duncan was captured, but chose to disguise the truth as conjecture. This might have been wishful thinking on Pedley's part, but more likely he wanted to protect Duncan's loved ones from the unpleasant truth of his death.[283]

The West Yorks went over us at 9:00 a.m. The Imperials are so much different than us. Their non-commissioned officers kept them in dead straight lines, there must have been six waves of them as far as you could see both ways. (The Canadians may go over in bunches any old way, but they always get there.) They passed us and kept going and reached their objective about 10:00 a.m.

The "West Yorks" were one of the West Yorkshire Regiment battalions of the 146th Brigade, 49th (West Riding) Division, a unit of the Imperial Army.

It is interesting to note Deward's description of Imperial tactics, which seem to still feature rigid waves of advancing infantry, even at this late date in the war. Officially, these type of "parade ground" manoeuvres were passé, and their use by the West Yorkshire battalions might indicate the majority of their men were fresh reinforcements who had been rushed to the front and had not yet received more advanced training. If these troops were indeed green, it could also explain their behaviour later in the day, which Deward also notes below.

We had to dig a post for the [Lewis] gun in the meantime, in case of an emergency, about ten yards [nine metres] off the road. When we did that we went back to the road. The whole battalion was on this main road in funk holes. The Germans all the time had been getting ready for a drive timed for 10:00 a.m. That was the reason his trenches had been full of men during the night. The Germans started shelling, it was awful. This was a hard road. I had no funk hole, so got into the gutter. My back was on a level with the road. The shells would come straight down the road. Overhead [there were exploding] shells and shells that did not explode until they hit [the ground], making only a small hole and bouncing down the road, sometimes half a shell. It would make an awful noise twisting through the air. Men were cut to pieces in the funk holes which were higher than the road. A shell lit a foot [thirty centimetres] from me but I missed its blast.

One veteran noticed that the small shells fired from German tanks, "bounded along the ground like stones skipping on water," an interesting observation in light of what was to happen next.[284]

About 10:30 a.m. we saw the Imperials coming back on the mad tear. We got in position and waited and they finally came back to where we were, all in a panic. Down the road and through the fields as far as you could see saying "for God's sake get out of here, they are coming tanks and all." I never saw a more frightened crowd. We went back with them to a cross road. They were coming alright.

Our officers began to figure it out and then yelled "come on Canadians." We went and the Imperials as well, we were all mixed up, and the rally was followed up all along the line. It was in the open and there were thousands of men. The Germans were thick, too. They had two tanks on our front. Great big square tanks. We went on to meet them and about halfways several of the tanks were shot by bullets. By now, the Germans had stopped and were starting to go back.

> Their machine gunners covered them. I had a few rounds at
> them with the Lewis gun.

The German counterattack at Iwuy was the first and only time
that Canadian infantry encountered German tanks in battle. It was
most likely Captain Shiell, the officer commanding "A" Company,
who uttered the rallying cry that Deward tells us of above. Shiell
was credited with saving the situation by rushing forward the
Lewis gunners from "A" and "C" companies (including Deward's
crew) to a position overlooking the German advance. There, they
opened a fusillade on the tanks and the supporting infantry. At the
same moment, Lieutenant Vincent Crombie, of "C" Company, also
appeared on the scene with a captured German anti-tank rifle,
adding the sting of armour-piercing bullets to the stream of lead
pouring from the battalion's Lewis guns. Much credit for stemming
the German attack must also go to the timely arrival of a Canadian
field battery and the added weight of concentrated machine gun
fire from the nearby 2nd Canadian Motor Machine Gun Brigade,
who raked the advancing German infantry at ranges of less than
400 yards (370 metres). Those enemy machines that were able to,
withdrew in the direction of Villers le Cauchies, whence it was
believed they came. Sadly, the resourceful Crombie was wounded
later in the day and died in hospital several weeks later.[285]

The confusion caused by the unexpected appearance of tanks
is perhaps best reflected today in the uncertainty of just how many
the Germans used on that day. Deward saw two tanks, but General
Currie's report on the action mentions seven. J.F.B. Livesay, writing less than a year after the attack, put the number of tanks at
five. The official historian of the Canadian Expeditionary Force,
G.W.L. Nicholson, mentions "some half dozen tanks," while the
history of the 20th Battalion states there were only four of the
machines. The 20th Battalion's history also disagrees about the
direction from which the tanks came, claiming they came from the
direction of Avesnes-le-Sec. All accounts agree, however, that it
was a mixed force of German-built and captured British tanks that
carried the attack (over the course of the war, the enemy captured

and refurbished nearly one hundred damaged British tanks that had been abandoned on the battlefield). Germany was uncharacteristically slow to develop the potential of this new weapon, and while orders had been placed for one hundred German-designed tanks, only twenty had been delivered by the war's end.[286]

This episode is also peculiar because it saw an officer of the British Empire employing a captured, German-made rifle to help drive off a German attack consisting mainly of captured, British-made tanks!

I was up in the front with Captain Shiell and we were both making for a slight railway bank for cover, not any more than seventy-five yards [seventy metres] from the Germans when I got hit. It was about 2:00 p.m. October 11th. My rifle was slung over my shoulder and the bullet went through the butt and through my right thigh. I yelled and reeled a couple of times, then went down. I ditched all I had and drank all my water but had no cigarettes. I had no field dressing and was bleeding, my leg was numb. I dragged myself along to a sunken road and got in. An Imperial man saw me and told me to come into in a square cut-out alongside of the road with him. He says, "You'll be alright here." The Germans had passed him earlier and gave him water and cigarettes, which he gave a couple of to me. He says, "You won't have to worry about the Germans, they use you good."

After passing through the butt of his rifle, the bullet struck Deward in the front, upper third of his right thigh, passed through his right buttock, and exited from the gluteal cleft (or "bum crack" in less clinical parlance).[287]

It is strange that Deward did not have a field dressing (large bandage). Each soldier was issued with one and was supposed to keep it for himself, should he become wounded (the bandages were carried in a special pocket sewn into the lining of the coat skirt). Deward may have used his field dressing on a comrade while helping to evacuate the wounded the previous night. His generosity, however, could have cost him his life had his bleeding been profuse.

In the meantime the battalion had gone back to their original place, the main road. Captain Shiell sent two men up to take me out and with help I got back to our battalion Dressing Station, a couple of miles back. There were dozens of men lying around outside, as it was not a deep dug-out, on stretchers. Some dead and some nearly so. The captain came up and told them to look after me as dozens were there before me. I went down into the dug-out and got a heavy dressing on my wound and they told me, if I can possibly walk, to get out as it may be three days before you'll get out if you wait here. They couldn't get an ambulance up, because the was shelling too heavy. I went and walked three kilometres [one mile], just slowly. I dared not sit down. I tried to get in with the Imperials as the ambulance came there, but they wouldn't let me, they had too many serious cases of their own to get out. I walked about two miles [three kilometres] farther and then got a lift on a motor truck and went ten miles [sixteen kilometres] to a field ambulance in a big marquee. They had two long rows of stalls with nurses and orderlies dressing wounded.

Being able to walk three kilometres with a gaping bullet wound in his right buttock is a testament to the physical and mental toughness that a year and a half of front-line service had created in Deward.

A field ambulance was a mobile hospital that moved with and operated just behind the front lines. It was a concentration point for casualties who were too seriously wounded for treatment at the regimental aid post (first aid station). The field ambulance would dispense the most appropriate medical attention available, then either return the man to his unit when he was fit or, in the case of those more seriously wounded, evacuate him to a permanent facility either in France or England.

First you were inoculated. I saw two barrels of arms and legs. I got a new dressing and went outside. Got eats and candies and I went into tents where we were to wait for a train in the morning. It must have been 11:00 p.m. now. I was dead tired and laid down and slept. When I woke up (I was using my tin Lizzie for a pillow) a fellow had his foot on my face, we so were crowded in.

"Tin Lizzie" was soldier's slang for helmet.

I could not get up and they came around and put a label on me, "Serious." I was put on a stretcher and left on a train bound for a hospital at Étaples [No. 56 General Hospital]. I stayed there all night on a cot, and then was put on a train going to Calais, then on a boat for England. Serious cases were sent back to England as they had no X-rays in France. German [prisoners] carried us onto the boat at Calais and off again at Dover.

Deward was evacuated to England on board His Majesty's Auxiliary Transport *Stadt Antwerpen*.[288]

We were put on a swell train and given different things. I had been inoculated three times up until now. I was taken to Country of Middlesex War Hospital, Napsbury.

The County of Middlesex War Hospital was a relatively new facility, having opened in June 1905 as the Middlesex County Asylum, Napsbury. The hospital was situated on a 432-acre estate and included several buildings and informal gardens.

October 15, 1918: I had X-ray pictures taken and the doctors thought it remarkable that the bullet did not hit a nerve or bone as it went through the thick part of my leg. It was a lovely hospital and we had all we wanted.

Deward was indeed lucky. Wounds to the buttocks were serious, because of the threat from bacterial infection. If the wound became septic, amputation was not an option, and without the benefit of antibiotics there was little at that time the doctors could do to save you.[289]

October 17, 1918: I got up for the first time for a short time.

October 18 to 29, 1918: The next few days, I went down to the YMCA at Napsbury, walking with cane.

October 30, 1918: A concert is on and supper is at 5:00 p.m. I went down to Saint Albans on a bus and then walked a bit and got supper at a restaurant.

November 7, 1918: Press news says Germany has signed armistice terms.

Obviously, these reports were premature.

November 10, 1918: I went down to Saint Albans to a show and had supper at Napsbury.

November 11, 1918: 11:30 a.m. The doctor says the official armistice is signed. I went down to Saint Albans. Great doings. Girls were lined across the street, kissing soldiers. I had a free supper that was given to all soldiers who went to this one particular restaurant.

This is how my original section finished up at the end of the war.

No. 2 Platoon, seven Lewis gunners:
Lance-Corporal Cowan — sick.
McDonald — (gassed).
Horseman — killed August 15, 1917.
Higgins — wounded through lung.
C. Arnold — killed October 10, 1918.
Billy Bell — killed at Passchendaele November 11, 1917.
Barnes — wounded, shot through thigh October 11, 1918.

November 12, 1918: I was boarded for Epson. At night we had a party given by Sister Cavell.

November 13, 1918: I left the hospital at 10:30 a.m. by train to Epson via London, arrived at 1:15 p.m. Went to the movies.

Deward's wound had healed sufficiently that he was sent to the Military Convalescent Hospital at Woodcote Park, Epsom, where he was to be examined (or boarded) to determine his fitness category.[290]

November 14, 1918: Examined and marked Dl. General Turner told us we would be sent home soon. However, while here, we all had to be on parade grounds every morning, [buttons] shined up and boots dubbined (not shined). And those who could do work had to, once in a while. I had to take charge of a fatigue or something every morning. The huts were inspected and you had to be out of them, except the Orderly Corporal, that was me. We went to movies or a show every day.

Category D1 meant that Deward was well enough to be discharged from hospital, but did not possess the fitness level required for general service. Were hostilities still ongoing, Deward would have been put onto a training routine of route marches and physical drills to toughen him for front-line service. Instead, he spent his afternoons at the cinema.[291]

Lt. Gen. Sir Richard Turner was the Chief of the General Staff for the Canadian Expeditionary Force, the most senior Canadian soldier in Britain.

November 22, 1918: Marked for medical board and was warned for leave.

Deward passed his medical board and was discharged from the hospital the following day.[292]

December 23, 1918: Left Epson at 12:00 noon. Slept at Maple Leaf Club in London. Left London at 1:30 p.m.

December 24, 1918: I arrived in Bristol at 3:00 p.m.

December 25, 1918: We had pork, turkey, and pudding. Saw Fred Barnes, a cousin.

December 26 to December 28, 1918: Fred and I went to Bath and went to the show each night.

December 29, 1918: I left Bristol at 3:30 p.m. and arrived in London, Waterloo Station at 9:10 p.m. I left Euston Station at 11.30 p.m.

December 30, 1918: I arrived in Glasgow at 3:30 a.m.

December 31, 1918: Dick and I stayed out until after midnight. There were thousands on the street, I was the first one in the house. I went to bed at 4:30 a.m.

January 1, 1919: We got up at 11:30 a.m. and went to church at night. I saw all of Glasgow.

January 3, 1919: I left Glasgow 8:45 p.m.

January 4, 1919: I arrived Euston Station, London at 7:00 a.m. Left Waterloo. Station 4:55 p.m. arrived Milford 6:30 p.m. Walked to 1st Canadian Convalescent Receiving Depot, Whitley.

The Convalescent Receiving Depot was another facility for rehabilitating and reconditioning men who had recovered from their wounds.

January 18, 1919: Left 1st CCRD for the reserve battalion. I was put on a company draft for No. 11 Camp, Rhyl.

When the authorities at the receiving depot were satisfied that Deward was physically strong enough for regular duties, he was assigned to a reserve battalion stationed in Rhyl, Wales.

January 21, 1919: Left Whitley at 9:30 a.m. passed Oxford and Crewe, arrived at Kinmel Park, North Wales, 8:30 p.m.

Kinmel Park was the name of the Canadian staging camp situated just outside of Rhyl. This spot was chosen because of its access to railway lines and its proximity to Liverpool, which was the port of embarkation for Canadian troops heading home.

January 24, 1919: Signed LPC Rhyl. It was an awful camp. No pay and not much to eat. One day the camp broke into the stores and stole everything.

It is not clear what Deward means by "Signed LPC Rhyl."

The living conditions in most of these staging camps were substandard. Coal shortages, influenza, and dock strikes left thousands of men cold, sick, and stranded. With the war over, even strict military discipline was not enough to keep some men — impatient to get home — in check. In all, there were thirteen disturbances in Canadian camps between November 1918 and June 1919. The worst of these occurred at Kinmel Park in early March 1919, when some eight hundred soldiers rioted for two days, causing extensive damage to the camp and causing the deaths of five men and injuries to twenty-three others.

January 29, 1919: I was moved to No. 3 Dispatch Company.

January 30, 1919: I learned that I was on a boat roll for Saturday (Hurrah).

To be placed on a boat roll meant that Deward was assigned to a ship bound for Canada.

February 1, 1919: I left Kinmel at 10:00 a.m. and marched to Abergele. We got on a train and passed through Chester to Riverside, Liverpool. I boarded the ship at 4:00 p.m.

(*Carmania*). We left the dock at 5:00 p.m. at low tide, and cleared the bay by 8.50 p.m. A little sick.

R.M.S. *Carmania* was an eighteen-thousand-ton Cunard passenger liner. At the beginning of the war she was requisi tioned by the Admiralty for conversion to an armed merchant cruiser. While on patrol in the South Atlantic in September 1914, *Carmania* attacked and sank the German armed merchant cruiser *Cap Trafalgar*, formerly of the Hamburg Sud Amerika Line. Both liners had resorted to disguise as a ruse-de-guerre and, by an odd coincidence, had disguised themselves as each other. *Carmania* was severely damaged during the battle and underwent extensive repairs at Gibraltar before she was returned to passenger service in 1916. *Carmania* remained in commercial service until 1931, with a brief return to military duty in 1919 helping to repatriate Canadian soldiers from the United Kingdom.

February 4, 1919: We are said to have gone 1,200 miles [1,900 kilometres]. Liverpool to Halifax is 2,600 miles [4,200 kilometres]. There are concerts on board every night and gambling.

February 8, 1919: We arrived at Halifax at 5:00 p.m. and boarded our train at 6:30 p.m. We had the best of everything.

February 10, 1919: We arrived in Quebec City at 6:00 a.m. and got off at a rest camp. We stayed there about a week, taking in all of Quebec City. Concerts. One night they carried out ten men dead from poison alcohol. One night I had rheumatism in my shoulder for the first time.

We left Quebec and arrived North Toronto in the morning, after being away twenty-eight months.

I have written my diary and told of my experiences as nearly as I know how. There are many things I have forgotten at the time of writing but I have told the most important part of it. I can only say that war is an awful thing and the hardships are great. And there is something wrong if a man has seen as much of it as I have and wishes to see another.

In this, surely Deward speaks for almost all veterans. General Currie, who led the Canadian Corps through some of its toughest fighting and who knew the character of his men as well as anyone, perhaps summed up this point of view best in a speech at Toronto less than a year after the armistice:

> One, somehow or other, gets the impression that there is a great deal of glory and glamour about the battlefield. I never saw any of it. I want you to understand that war is simply the curse of butchery, and men who have gone through it, who have seen war stripped of all its trappings, are the last men that will want to see another.[293]

A man's nerves were never made to stand the shocks and concussions of shells, and sights and smells that go with war. I sincerely believe that the war has made me ten years older. It certainly has put my nerves on edge.

My nerves are gone.

APPENDIX

After Deward transcribed his diary in 1926, he created a series of notes, mostly observations and discussions, which he appended to the main text. These notes doubtless represent incidents and details that came to mind as a result of the transcription process.

In many cases you will recognize a reference to an incident described earlier in the diary. Other remarks stand on their own. The latter range from the quality of German weapons to the role the United States played during the closing chapters of the war.

The tone of the appendix is different from that of the main diary text: it reads less like the jottings of a journeyman diarist and more like the recollections of a veteran storyteller, hunkered down in a Legion hall on an Armistice Day afternoon.

In the original manuscript, the notes appear in no particular order. After reading through them, however, it became apparent there were certain themes to which Deward would return. To make these motifs more accessible to the reader, I have arranged the notes thematically and provided them with brief headings.

A War Wreck

My nerves were always good until I had my last leave from France, September 1918; maybe on account of the war lasting so long and the thought of what was in front of us. I soon started to get very nervous and have never gotten over it. Since I came home I have always tried to work hard and steady to get over this three year experience, but could never do it. So I class myself as a war wreck, which people will never understand.

Somersaulting Down

I was never in England at the time of an air raid, but we had a false alarm once while at West Sandling Camp and all had to get out of our huts and run for the woods. The raid was carried on farther away.

Bombs from planes were one thing that gave you a queer feeling, because you could hear them [falling] as they did not explode until they hit something. Shells from guns, if very close, you did not hear until after the explosion. You never hear a shell from a gun coming. The only shells you hear are bombs and trench mortars.

We were in Passchendaele six weeks and every day the Germans made several raids (bombing planes). The roads were thick with transports and troops and I can only remember one day when they hit the road. They came mighty close to the roads though. We used to run off the roads and get into any kind of hole, the smaller the better.

One day three of us ran, after hearing one coming, and got into a short piece of trench, very narrow. The bomb lighted about twenty feet [six metres] away. It almost deafened you.

We had aero (anti-aircraft duty) duty while on rest, day and night, two hours on, four off. We used to arrange it four on and eight off.

At Vlamertinge, ten miles [sixteen kilometres] from Ypres, our own planes carried a light at night until they got near the German lines. At Vlamertinge, water was scarce and we used to wash in a puddle at the side of our huts (filthy water).

On the Ypres front there were no dug-outs, just tents of course. If we stayed in tents at any one place very long we put a double row of sandbags around it about four feet [125 centimetres] high. But it seemed funny when they were bombing, as long as you were under a tent and could not see them you *felt* safe.

When a bunch of troops kept looking up [at aircraft], it was just like making a target. Their faces would show up.

In France, in October 1918, we were too far advanced and our own planes bombed us while we were at a crossroads and killed and wounded several until we put ground flares out.

Communication between troops on the ground and their own aircraft operating high above was difficult in 1918, as it remains today. In the summer of 1916, the 19th Battalion took part in several aircraft cooperation exercises in conjunction with the 2nd Canadian Division School. In these exercises, the troops on the ground signalled their location to circling aircraft using various devices, including: red and green flares, mirrors, tin discs (tied to the men's backs), and umbrellas (painted black and white). The pilots reported the discs, mirrors, and umbrellas were all good, but the mirrors proved best at attracting their attention on sunny days. Surprisingly, perhaps, the flares were totally missed by the aircraft on at least one occasion. The report on this exercise concluded the use of mixed signals was the best way to ensure aircraft could spot the men on the ground.[294]

In Belgium the German planes kept very high. They must have been a kind of aluminium silver colour for they certainly showed up. Although the main roads were long and straight, at that height, allowing for wind and the speed of plane, it stands to reason that it wasn't easy to hit a mark.

In France they took more chances and used to fly over in a low cloud and then suddenly dropped low out of the cloud and flew back again.

I saw some beautiful aeroplane fights, especially the one where they used tracer bullets. It was late in 1917 and our plane gave fight and kept Fritzie from going back. You could follow the bullets and they kept getting near until our man brought him down. Another time there was a fight on up in the clouds. We heard it but could not see it. All of a sudden a plane [came] somersaulting [down with] a wing off. It was our plane.

It was in the summer of 1917 before the British started to get the best of the German planes. Before that he had what we called the Little Red Devils. My, our planes looked as though they were standing still, they made rings around us. At one place he used to come over every evening and then dart low and fire all along the trenches. Everyone used their rifles and guns, but he always got away.

At one time, in the evening, he used to come over and bring a balloon down, sometimes two, but our anti-aircraft guns could not get him. One evening, about 5:00 p.m. he came and brought two observation balloons down and next night he brought five down all in a row. Of course the men in them had to jump with their parachutes. It was pretty to look at.

At La Targette one Saturday, we put up a dummy observation balloon filled full of high explosives. He always flew over them and fired. Of course, they expected him to hit it. On this one it would have made such a huge flame that he could not have escaped it. He came over as usual and brought three more down passing right over the dummy and did not fire at it. So whether he could smell a rat or not I don't know.

Some of the balloons, not all of them, were fastened on an auto specially built, and of course they had a telephone from there to the balloon. But they kept moving it from place to place, especially when the Germans were shelling it. They found out a lot of information from these balloons, which were more for the artillery. They could see where troops were massing and could see exactly where our shells were hitting and give directions.

At the Vimy show, our anti-aircraft guns forced a German plane down behind our lines. He just glided down. Our men wanted to kill him. As we had Military Police at different corners and at crossroads (during advances), to give directions, the police saved [him].

Nine Times Out of Ten

It doesn't seem possible, but if you stand behind a big gun, a 9.2, you can follow the shell when it leaves the gun as far as you can see.

A "9.2" was a British heavy howitzer. It fired a shell 9.2 inches (23 centimetres) in diameter. According to Empey, the muzzle blast of a 9.2 could knock the roof tiles from nearby houses.[295]

We were going into the line one time on the Lens front at night. There was a bush alongside the road. All of a sudden I saw a red flash, heard a terrible noise, and felt a great heat. A gun was in there and opened up, I was directly in front of it. Was deaf for five minutes and it made me jump.

The naval guns were about ten miles [sixteen kilometres] behind the front lines for long distance firing. They didn't fire many shells but oh my, they could hit their target! One [gunner] told us they could hit their target nine times out of ten.

Then there were the extra heavy guns. They were on flat-cars on a train. At night, if they had a particular mark to hit such as a building, they were taken up to near the front and only fired one shot and were taken out again.

Morale and keeping up high spirits is everything in war. That's why an army will shell and shell even if you don't see many killed. The shelling continuously gives you a terrible feeling. It isn't so bad if it only lasts a half hour or so, but when it keeps up as before a battle for ten or twelve hours before, there is nothing more nerve-wracking.

On a main road I saw a French shell dud that had just force enough to go through a tree, about four inches [ten centimetres] of the nose sticking out and four inches of the base showing.

In 1917, at one particular part of the Lens front, he used to shell the front-line trench at 6:00 p.m. every evening, regularly. We had communication trenches back to another trench about one hundred yards [ninety metres] back where we used to move about 5:30 or so and wait until it was all over; and then go back to our front line. They used to sure tear it up too, believe me.

There Were Hundreds of Them

Machine guns made a terrible racket when you were in front of them, as at Lens in the Hill 70 scrap. There were hundreds of them there and you couldn't hear yourself think when they were in action. It was deafening with their sharp cracks. And when you are being fired at by them it just sounds like bees buzzing with a kind of ping sound. I've had hundreds pass my ear (especially in 1918 open warfare). They were a dangerous weapon in this war but not nerve-wracking like shells. They were all placed where each one could crossfire. But at Lens they were in houses up high and all over. They were the recognized things during the latter part of the war — as in open warfare. They did away with trenches of men, and the Germans had machine gun posts all over [the countryside], with seven or eight men to a post.

When he says "They did away with trenches of men" presumably Deward means that trenches, which were full of men, were no longer used, that is, done away with, because the advancing British and French armies had broken through old trench systems.

Although all of the German [regiments] had machine guns, we had a special Machine Gun Corps, which were behind the frontline battalions. Each battalion also had Lewis guns, which one man could carry. It took two or more to carry a machine gun. A Lewis gun weighed twenty-six pounds [twelve kilograms] and many a time I have dragged that after me in crawling over-the-top in the afternoon, on an advance, besides your other equipment.

In the Rifle Butt

The Germans were well equipped with machine guns and pistols. He had a long-barrelled pistol with a frame handle. He could either use it as a pistol or attach the handle and make a rifle out of it.

While out on rests, we used to practice target shooting. I was very good, but it is surprising how many cannot hit a target with a revolver.

Our rifles (Lee Enfield) were the best we had. They were not as good as Ross rifles for target shooting, but far superior otherwise. Although our rifles jammed on us after firing two or three shots at the Fresnoy scrap, they were good on the whole. They had to be kept cleaned and we had what we called a "pull-through" for cleaning them: a cord with a weight on the one end and a loop on the other, where you put a piece of waste cloth. And a brass oil bottle, which were all kept in the rifle's butt. If our rifles were on the ground a couple of days they would be corroded.

The German rifles were better. They were nickel plated and could be left lying around in rain and would not rust. They had ramrods. One German would have one part and another the other part. They worked in pairs. Our bayonet was short and wide and his was long and narrow. I found one of his saw bayonets, a very thick one with a saw on one edge.

The "ramrods" that Deward refers to in the German rifles were actually cleaning rods. Instead of using a cord to pull strips of cloth through a rifle, the Germans used stiff rods for pushing the cloth through the barrel. Each rod was not long enough on its own and had to be joined with the rod from a second rifle to be effective (each rod was tapped on one end and threaded on the other so that two rods could screw together).

The saw bayonets were issued to special "pioneer" troops. The purpose of the saw blade was to make it easy for the pioneers to crawl out into No-Man's Land and saw down the posts on which the enemy barbed wire was strung. The advent of steel wire posts made the saw blade somewhat less effective.

It Made a Terrible Noise

Our Mills bombs were more effective than his egg bombs. Ours were larger and could not be thrown as far. They were perforated in squares and his were smooth and small and could be thrown a long way. But he also had a cylindrical stick, with a tin can full of explosives on one end. It was used for concussion. It made a terrible noise in a trench and many of our men got concussions through one of these. But we had a larger bomb (Stokes Bomb) that we used on raids and threw down his dug-outs. It had both and blew everything up.

The Stokes bomb was designed originally to be fired from a Stokes trench mortar.

It Was Surprising How Fast You Could Dig

I could not stand our gas helmets, although we had to use them several times. Coming out of Hill 70, after being relieved, we were being gassed and had to put them on. It was pitch dark and I just put the mouthpiece in my mouth and the clippers on my nose and left the face piece off.

Earlier in the war we had the PH helmets that went right over the head and tucked under the coat. The German gas helmet looked like a tin can fastened on their mouth.

I don't remember seeing an entrenching tool in German equipment but we had one and I had to use it a couple of times. It was surprising how fast you could dig with it and then fill your sandbags for protection.

The German equipment did feature a small shovel, which hung from the waist belt.

The Germans did not have to wear their equipment in the front line and we did.

Dog Biscuits

At the latter part of the war, iron rations consisted of bully beef and hard tack all sealed in one tin. They were not to be opened until the last resort. I had to open mine on three different occasions, but the bully beef was salty and as you would not have any water you were worse off. Thirst is worse than hunger and I have had my mouth and tongue blistered from thirst. His iron rations were better than ours, at least his biscuits were. Ours were like dog biscuits and his were small and I liked them.

At one farm house, in the fall, the farmer used to boil vegetables for his cattle (without salt). We used to steal them and have a regular meal.

Drunk on Champagne

There is the immoral life of the army that I can't write about. I wasn't very bad. I was drunk four times. Once, I was drunk on beer and was picked up on the side of the road on the way to camp. And at Arras, almost the whole battalion was drunk on red and white wine. And once, at Christmastime, I got drunk on champagne and was picked up on a doorstep. And once at Shoreham-by-Sea.

There were good men and some very mean ones in France. When we go in equipped to go over-the-top we took two bottles of water (and had a good chance of running out of it). We went in this once and at night a schoolteacher used to steal the other fellow's water and save his own. And at different times some fellows would have their rations stolen.

Two Rubber Sheets

In Belgium it rained every day we were there. We were in bivouac most of the time and when we got back our blankets, and us, were always soaking wet.

I used to very often carry two rubber sheets, for you could bet in 1918 that you would be sure to have to dig a hole on top of the ground and stay in it. One sheet would do to put on the ground in the hole, and the other over you if it should rain, which it very often did. It was better and lighter than a greatcoat. The Germans had dandy ground sheets. I had one for a while. It was light and large and was cut so as you could make a bivouac out of it.

As a rule, Sunday was the day we had to move into the trenches. It always seemed nine times out of ten it rained. We had marched through some terrible rainstorms and going overland in clay is slippery and slimy; always slipping and getting stuck. It took all your strength. Sometimes you would step on the side of a shell hole and fall in the dark. There would not be a light anywhere but maybe away in the distance you would see the gun flashes.

We have been soaked through hundreds of times while in France and it is a wonder we are not all crippled up by now with rheumatism.

Left Out

In going in to the trenches only three platoons to a company were sent in, they always kept one out. In case a battalion was wiped out they would have a company left and would not lose their name as a battalion. I was never left out. At one time they tried to keep a whole platoon out at once and it did not work. Then they picked so many in a section from each platoon (four sections to a platoon) but I was never lucky.

The Suicide Section

They were always short of non-commissioned officers and as I was Number 1 on the gun I was always put in charge of my section of seven men and Lewis gunners. At one time I was going into the lines so regularly that I saw the captain to try to get a rest, and could not, owing to the non-commissioned office shortage and that there were so many new men with us. Three sections went into [battle from] a platoon: bombers, Lewis gunners and rifle grenadiers. Rifle grenades were fired from rifles and were similar to a bomb, but could be sent farther. The Lewis gunners were called the suicide section and always had to go in front of the company and in dangerous positions. We were used for covering the battalion if they were retiring in a battle. We had been in some of the most dangerous positions, in saps, and at the end of a German trench guarding a blockade.

You Could Put a House in Them

I was never in a place where the front line was a crater but there were some terrible big craters at one place on the Vimy front. There were three close together. I forget all the names but one was called Pulpit Crater. They were large; you could put a house in them.

There were some terrible big tunnels that the Germans had built. One was called the Zivy Cave. And they knew how to build them too! Some were very deep and a couple of battalions could be hidden in them. Maybe there would be sixty or seventy-five steps to get to the bottom and narrow passageways. Zivy Cave had water in it and electric lights. One big tunnel was so big that they had different entrances about half a mile [eight hundred metres] apart.

You have heard about how hard it was to take a farm or sugar refinery. The reason why was on account of tunnels. When our side sent raids out, to find out things, they would never get back again. This happened two or three times at one refinery. So then they sent one raiding party out and followed it with another at the same time, so far back, to see what happened when the first party got so far. Just past a certain place, dozens of Germans came out of tunnels and captured them and, of course, when the Canadians found that out they knew what to do and soon took that refinery.

Dropping Badges

Strategy is everything in war, and surprise. Just before the big push in 1918 the Canadians sent a few men up to Belgium about two weeks before; and sent them over on raids. When they got into the German trenches they would drop a hat or a badge and then get back out again. Of course the Germans thought that the Canadians were up in Belgium, when in fact we made our big push at Amiens in the south of France.

You Dare Not Move

We used Very lights to show the ground up at night. You dare not move when they were up.

There were lights that they dropped from aeroplanes. They had a parachute on them and would stay in the air, maybe twenty minutes. And the Germans had a wonderful light that they dropped from their planes, a very big one. You could see for miles around. Troops dare not move while it was up.

I've looked over-the-top hours and hours, through the nights into darkness.

Even on Quiet Trips

No matter how quiet a trip was there was always so many got killed in a battalion.

We Had to Crawl

At one particular spot, the Germans had a rifle set in a hole in their trench — set stationary. The sniper looking over at our trench could see two places where the trench was torn away. When he saw a head passing the first space he knew how many seconds it took for him to get to the second space and timed his rifle accordingly. He generally killed them and that is why we had to crawl past these places. We had snipers too. They were under Battalion headquarters and could pick any good spot they wanted to on the battalion front.

Jake Places

We have been in all kinds of places to sleep. In barns, hay lofts, and pig pens; sleeping with chickens, pigs, and cows. Each farmer and house had to put up so many soldiers in the towns. A hayloft was a good place when plenty of straw was around. We had to be careful of matches and at one place the fellows burnt a barn down. We formed a bucket brigade but couldn't save it. They only had wells. Some places half the boards were off and you would nearly freeze and have to shave next morning in cold water or use your tea. We have often slept in a house upstairs on the floors or in stores. Some pretty jake places [compared] to trenches. I have slept in every position imaginable, cramped and otherwise. I have slept standing up while off-post duty in the trenches when it was too cold to lie down and I have gone four or five days in the trenches without any sleep. You can be surprised at what you can do under war conditions and are trained for it. But I have seen dozens of men collapse under the strain.

Most of our marches were done at night when it was cooler and as soon as you got a rest you would fall asleep and had to get up in five minutes. That was when you were not getting much rest and sleep. I have even marched sleeping, which I thought impossible.

On marching, the historian of the 49th Battalion observed:

This was the last war in which armies marched on their feet and as a consequence the last occasion on which men enjoyed the fellowship of moving together, shoulder by shoulder, knee by knee, mile after mile, hour after hour. There was something in the pulse and swing of marching that soldiers will never know again. For fifty minutes of every hour they moved as one, sometimes with song, sometimes as sight-seers in a strange land, sometimes sullen and disgruntled, sometimes spent, with a friend carrying his neighbours rifle or packsack, sometimes imbued with high cynicism, nearly always engaged in endless arguments. The marching column was a dynamic, integrated entity, with its unit figures deferring to its routines, yet fiercely retaining individual identities. At the ten minute rest periods there were those who threw off their packs and strode about stiff-legged, flexing their shoulders; there were those who lay on the pave pillowed on their packs, as though they had dropped in their tracks. There were a few who used the fall-out to clean their weapons or to mend their kit or clothing. But when the word came to fall in they were one once more and as they picked up the step they also picked up something of the strength and assurance acquired from their fellowship.[296]

Fun While Out on Rest

In real war the hardships are great. We had a non-commissioned officer's lecture in the field just about the time when draftees [conscripts] first came to us; they were watching them closely. They told us to impress on their minds that you had to keep going until you were good and tired, and then you were just started. It was true.

The infantry is the hardest and worst part of an army. There is no other branch that has to go through the hardships and trials that they do. I had my share and stood the test. I will not take my hat off to any soldier, no matter how long he was in France. I saw as much fighting and hardship as anyone. I don't know what ever made me so tough but I have never fallen out of any march or trip and many a time have carried another fellow's pack or rifle. On one occasion going into the front line, I carried Billy Bell's gun magazine carriers, eight pans, two hundred rounds of ammunition, beside my own four pans and extra ammunition and bombs.

Of course, we had fun while out on rests. Games, shows, and it certainly used to be a treat. A funny thing was that as soon as you came out of a battle you would soon forget about it until it was time to go in the lines again.

We were in a hut in England and there used to be a little officer that we detested. He came around about midnight inspecting and a blind was up. He made me get up to pull it down. Another night the same officer was on again and as soon as he opened the door the fellows made noises at him. One fellow got another one's boot and let it go at him. The fellow that owned the boot was really asleep. There was a rumpus around that but he couldn't find out anything.

To a Crisp

To my mind, and from what I saw, the tanks were a failure. Mind you, they had a nerve-wracking effect when one was coming towards you as at the Naves scrap, with hundreds of Germans as well. I'll never forget how that German square tank looked so big.

In Belgium I saw dozens and dozens of tanks out of action; stuck in the mud. I saw men in them burnt black to a crisp. What chance did they have, as they were full of gasoline and shells?

On one occasion, on August 8, we had taken the town of Marcelcave and had to dig in so many hundred yards in front of the town. Just where we dug in a German [machine] gun was right in front of us, in front of a woods. They were firing point-blank at us and killed two men beside me. Later on, one of our tanks came up, went past us and cleared the [machine] gun post out, then went on, and up and down in front of the woods firing, cleaning it out.

Their Heads Were Out of Shape

I saw the cavalry in action once. That was another bunch of the army that had not much chance in this war. We had just taken some more ground that morning and dug in on top of a hill. In the afternoon the cavalry came up. A [cavalry] sergeant inquired just where the Germans were. The cavalry had to go down this big hill and over a stream in the hollow. The Germans were in trenches about halfway up the other hill. The cavalry started. The horses were all sweating, the men excited; about seventy-five or one hundred of them. At the top of the German hill was a town. They wanted to get to the outskirts of that and were feelers. It was a lovely sight to look at. The Germans let them get down the hill and across the stream and then opened up with their machine guns. They could not help hitting them and not a man came back. The horses were not all killed. There were quite a lot of German dead around and the strange part was that, I noticed that most of their heads were out of shape. Some peculiar shapes that I could never understand. Maybe from fright, or hoses trampling them down.

For God's Sake, Get Out!
Some people say that war is not picturesque. I admit it was not all picturesque, but three battles I saw were. Photos cannot explain a battle. At a real scrap there are no war correspondents or reporters there to take a picture, or anything.

At Fresnoy we went into the front line through a steady rain and under heavy shellfire. At 4:30 a.m. we saw masses of Germans, four thick lines of them (the last line just coming over the hill) coming towards us, then jumping into our trenches; some getting bayoneted. The Germans always came over in mass and did not seem to work independent of each other. And then later in the day, when ordered to fall back, I was trying to miss stepping on faces and hands where some men had fallen; and trenches caving in and half-burying them in such sticky mud that you sank up to the top of your boots. And it was still raining.

At Hill 70, there were the grandest artillery duels that have been witnessed all through the Canadian Army. Each side had hundreds of guns. No sooner would one side open up and the other would, too. This happened dozens of times. All kinds of shells, rockets, Very lights, and SOSs of all colours. You could see shells bursting at night. I was in the front line and had some good views.

Many veterans spoke of a strange and spectacular light created by the artillery at night. Will Bird remembered:

> ... and from a shell opening in the rear wall came a glow of red as the sky behind it was lit by gun flashes. The glows played on the walls of the next ruin with a fascinatingly bizarre effect. The batteries were not a great distance behind us, and for fifteen minutes we stayed and watched the light flicker, dance, vanish, and reappear. Then the shelling stopped and a waiting silence ensued.[297]

At the battle of Naves, everything was in the open. Thousands of men were on both sides, and two of his tanks. The Imperials passed over us after our battalion had lost two-thirds of our men. And later on in the day when the Germans counter-attacked, the Imperials came back in disorder and panic. Hundreds of them saying, "For God's sake get out. Get back. The Germans are coming in thousands." And they were! I was wounded the same day, after we had counter-attacked together and drove them back. It was picturesque enough for me!

Extra Weight
I had many opportunities to get souvenirs, but had enough to carry! [Souvenirs] were extra weight. I did get a German belt, tassel, holster, pistol, and two clips of shells off a dead German non-commissioned officer. I gave the pistol to Dick Gaunt while on leave and intended to get another, but got wounded.

The tassel, or *Troddel*, that Deward mentions above was a decorative cloth strap that looped around German bayonet frogs (the holder that attaches the bayonet scabbard to the soldier's belt). A Troddel helped to distinguish the company the soldier belonged to within a specific regiment as well as his rank, and as such were often multicoloured and elaborately woven. This made them a prized souvenir.

I had many narrow escapes but was always lucky.

The Hindenburg Trench
The Hindenburg Trench (Line), the Germans thought, could never be taken. It was a wonderful trench system; very deep. You had to go up a ladder to get at [machine gun] posts. It was made for [machine] guns and the post positions were solid cement and reinforced about three feet [one metre] thick. He had tunnels leading up to it and brought his ammunition right up to it on miniature railways.

These German miniature railways, or *feldbahns*, were similar to the British narrow-gauge railways.

Three to One

It always took three to one to make an advance, as only about one-third ever got there. The Germans could come on us just as easily if he had the men and used our tactics. Everyone knows, who has been through a battle, it is better to go over-the-top and take a line (with a barrage) and then get relieved, than to go in and hold the line after it is taken. The Germans were very quick in counter-attacking, anywhere from one hour [after the first attack]. He would shell sometimes, then you would suffer. Surprise is everything.

It seemed a shame not to be able to help a dying man while in the first wave, but every man was always needed. It was considered cowardice to stop and help unless you were back farther [in the support or reserve wave].

On going over-the-top I never lagged. I was always in front. I believed in it. I missed the shells for one thing. Bullets were not nerve-wracking like shells.

Dig a Good Place

It paid to always dig a good place!

They Got Muddy

It was the easiest thing to get lost. In going in you [would try to] take notice of every landmark [but sometimes], when coming back, the landmarks were gone, all shelled down. On one trip, on the Lens front, we went into the trenches at night following white tapes that the scouts had laid. But they got muddy [and you couldn't see them anymore].

Counting the Trips

As nearly as I can find out, just counting the trips in and out of the trenches and from one part of the line to another while with the 19th Battalion, I was: in the trenches 248 days; in the front line 94 days; marched 882 miles [1,419 kilometres], mostly at night; on the trains 91 hours. I was in France eighteen months. [When on the move] I averaged two miles per hour [three kilometres per hour], sometimes we went three and sometimes we went less than two.

They Were Quite Black

One time in the big push, in 1918, we were going over and it appeared that the Imperials had tried before us. It was in the afternoon, and I noticed fifty or more Highlanders (Imperials) dead. They were quite black and must have been there a few days. But the strange part was that they were all laying in the same way (on their backs) and the same direction. Their kilts were blown back over them, possibly for burying, and all had their boots off, which the Germans took I guess.

Who Won the War

There has often been talk of who won the war. It is a well known fact that the Allies were at their last. They could not have stood much more war alone. In 1918, after the German push at the Amiens front, it looked as though we were beat. It looked as though men were scarce. Our big guns were pulling back and those in action had caterpillars there ready to hook up. It looked very bad to me and away back, men who were being sent to Canada were detained at different depots. And those that were able to march at all were sent back to the lines.

The Americans, two million of them, were behind us. The morale of the troops is a great thing and when we started our push, knowing that we had their backing was a great factor.

The Germans were disheartened; their morale gone. They did not have trenches full of men then. It was open warfare and he held us up with machine gun posts. The Germans were brave and most stuck to their guns until they saw it was of no use.

The Americans claim that they won the war, that they had two million troops in the field at that time. But they forget that Britain had lost a million men up until then, through four years of war, and those that were left were war-worn, not fresh troops; and that the British Navy practically guided the Americans across, safe from submarines.

My nerves were always good untill I had my last leave from France Sept 1918 & maybe on account of the War lasting so long & the thought of what was in front of us. I then started to get ... were never got over it. Since I came home I have always tried to work hard & steady to get over this three years experience, but could never do it, so I class myself as a war wreck, which people will never under-stand

ENDNOTES

1   Ian Hugh MacLean Miller, *Our Glory and Our Grief: Torontonians and the Great War* (Toronto: University of Toronto Press, 2002), 31—32.
2   Miller, *Our Glory and Our Grief*, 91.
3   Sidney Allinson, *The Bantams: The Untold Story of World War I* (London: Howard Baker, 1981), 23, 45, 178.
4   Miller, *Our Glory and Our Grief*, 91.
5   NAC, RG 9 III, vol 4702, folder 72, file 1, *180th Battalion Historical Record*.
6   NAC, RG 9 II B 3, vol 80, *180th Battalion Nominal Roll of Officers, Non-Commissioned Officers and Men*.
7   Desmond Morton, *When Your Number's Up: The Canadian Soldier in the First World War* (Toronto: Random House of Canada, 1993), 56.
8   D.J. Corrigall, *The Twentieth: The History of the Twentieth Canadian Battalion, Central Ontario Regiment, Canadian Expeditionary Force* (Toronto: Stone and Cox, 1935), 4–5.
9   Kim Beattie, *48th Highlanders of Canada 1891–1928* (Toronto: 48th Highlanders of Canada, 1932), 414.
10 David W. Love, *A Call to Arms: The Organization and Administration of Canada's Military in World War One* (Winnipeg: Bunker to Bunker Books, 1999), 50.
11 NAC, RG 9 III, vol 4702, folder 72, file 1, *180th Battalion Historical Record*.
12 *Canadian Soldier's Diary: From Belleville, Canada to Bramshott Camp, England* (Hasselmere: Gables Press, n.d.), May 21 to May 29, 1916; and; Sidney George Cane, *Diary of Our Trip*, August 9 to August 15, 1916.

13   Love, *A Call to Arms*, 103–105.
14   *Encyclopaedia Britannica*, 11th Edition, volume 5, See entry under Canada–Finance.
15   NAC, RG 150, 1992-93/166, box 445 file 5, 862690 *Barnes, Deward*.
16   Personnel record of Deward Barnes, as previously cited.
17   Miller, *Our Glory and Our Grief*, 25–26.
18   Personnel record of Deward Barnes, as previously cited.
19   Morton, *When Your Number's Up*, 87.
20   NAC, 1992-93/166, box 1814 file 29, 863159 *Clyde, Nat*; and box 8309 file 15, 862695 *Rivett, Omer.*
21   NAC, RG 24, National Defence, volume 1650, file HQ 683-292-6, *Inspection Report of 198th Battalion, Syllabus of Service Range Practices, Military District No. 2*, 24 June 1916.
22   Love, *A Call to Arms*, 62.
23   180th Battalion Historical Record, as previously cited.
24   Love, *A Call to Arms*, 92.
25   This information comes from correspondence received from Robert Mee-Gregory of Derbyshire, England, who is a member of the United Kingdom based Police History Society. The correspondence was prompted by an appeal for information on the Police History Society Web site.
26   Clive M. Law, *Khaki: Uniforms of the Canadian Expeditionary Force* (Ottawa: Service Publications, 1997), 31–32.
27   Brian Davis. *British Army Uniforms and Insignia of World War Two* (London: Arms and Armour Press, 1983), 166; and Law, *Khaki*, 33.
28   NAC, RG 24, National Defence, volume 1650, file HQ 683-292-6, *Inspection Report, 198th Battalion CEF, Syllabus of 5 Day Course for Brigade Bombing Schools*, 20 November 1916.
29   NAC, RG 150, 1992-93/166, box 109 file 30, 862727 *Allen, Thomas.*
30   D.J. Goodspeed. *Battle Royal: A History of the Royal Regiment of Canada*, 2nd ed. (Royal Regiment of Canada Association, 1979), 298–300.
31   *Encyclopaedia Britannica*, 11th Edition, volume B, See entry under Boulogne.
32   Rose E.B. Coombs, *Before Endeavours Fade: A Guide to the Battlefields of the First World War* (London: Battle of Britain Prints International, 1990), 124.

33 Tim Cook, *No Place To Run: The Canadian Corps and Gas Warfare in the First World War* (Vancouver: University of British Columbia Press, 1999), 88.

34 Will R. Bird, *Ghosts Have Warm Hands* (Nepean: CEF Books, 1997), 6.

35 James H. Pedley, *Only This: A War Retrospective* (Ottawa: Graphic Publishers, 1927), 19.

36 Bird, *Ghosts Have Warm Hands*, 7.

37 Morton, *When Your Number's Up*, 118–119.

38 G.W.L. Nicholson, *Canadian Expeditionary Force, 1914–1919* (Ottawa: Queen's Printer, 1962), 230 footnote; Love, *A Call to Arms*, 122.

39 Pedley, *Only This*, 19.

40 Nicholson, *Canadian Expeditionary Force*, 230.

41 Cook, *No Place to Run*, 72.

42 NAC, RG 9, Series III-D-3, volume 4928, Reel T-10725; *War Diary, 19th Battalion*, April, 1917; and Nicholson, *Canadian Expeditionary Force*, 262, map of Vimy Ridge operations opposite.

43 NAC, RG 9, Series III-D-3, volume 4928, Reel T-10725; *War Diary, 19th Battalion*, March and April, 1917.

44 NAC, RG 9 II B 5, vol 5, *Board of Officers, Canadian Expeditonary Forces, Report on 19th Infantry Battalion, 4th Infantry Brigade*, Toronto; January 29, 1915.

45 NAC, RG 9, Series III-D-3, volume 4928, Reel T-10725; *War Diary, 19th Battalion*, April, 1917 Appendix 3, "Secret, 19th Canadian Battalion Instruction for the Offensive No. 2"; and Volume 4919, Reel T-10712, *War Diary, 10th Battalion*, April 1917; Appendix 86, 30, "Battle Stops and Trench Police."

46 NAC, RG 9, Series III-D-3, volume 4928, Reel T-10725; *War Diary, 19th Battalion*, April, 1917.

47 NAC, RG 9, Series III-D-3, volume 4928, Reel T-10725; *War Diary, 19th Battalion*, April, 1917.

48 Veteran's Affairs Canada, http://www.vac-acc.gc.ca/general/sub.cfm?source = collections/virtualmem/photos&casualty = 65098, updated February 20, 2001, accessed February 1, 2004. (Note: double-click the photo of Denison to open an enlargement of his portrait that includes biographical details.)

49   NAC, RG 9, Series III-D-3, volume 4928, Reel T-10725, *War Diary, 19th Battalion*, March, 1918, Appendix 3, "Parade State 9/3/18".

50   Bill Rawling, *Surviving Trench Warfare: Technology and the Canadian Corps, 1914–1918* (Toronto: University of Toronto Press, 1992), 97.

51   The Empire Club of Canada, *Experiences of an Infantryman at the Front*, Major Wilfrid Mavor, M.C., speaker — January 31, 1918, 97–102.

52   General Staff, *Instructions for the Training of Platoons*, 7.

53   NAC, RG 9, Series III-D-3, volume 4928, Reel T-10725; *War Diary, 19th Battalion*, April, 1917.

54   NAC, RG 9, Series III-D-3, Volume 4920, Reel T-10712-10713, *War Diary, 10th Battalion*, May, 1917.

55   NAC, RG 9 II B 3, vol 80, *180th Battalion Nominal Roll of Officers, Non-Commissioned Officers and Men.*

56   Arthur Guy Empey, *Over the Top* (New York: A.L. Burt, 1917), 22.

57   Empey, *Over the Top*, 21.

58   G.W.L. Nicholson, *Seventy Years of Service: A History of the Royal Canadian Army Medical Corps* (Ottawa: Borealis Press, 1977), 89–90.

59   Nicholson, *Seventy Years of Service*, 88; and NAC, RG 150, 1992-93/166, box 1466, file 12, 799801 *Cane, Sidney George.*

60   Alexander Barrie, *War Underground* (New York: Ballantine Books, 1971), 159.

61   Nicholson, *Canadian Expeditionary Force*, 250.

62   Love, *A Call to Arms*, Appendix H, "Canadian Corps Trench Standing Orders, London, 1916; Section 12 Gas Alert, Paragraph C".

63   Cook, *No Place to Run*, 184–185.

64   Cook, *No Place to Run*, 45, 196, and 204.

65   Commonwealth War Graves Commission, http://www.cwgc.org/cwgcinternet/casualty_details.aspx?casualty = 167929, copyright 2000–2003, accessed February 1, 2004.

66   NAC, RG 9, Series III-D-3, Volume 4928, Reel T-10725-10726, *War Diary,19th Battalion* May 1917.

67   Ralph Barker, *A Brief History of the Royal Flying Corps in World War 1* (London: Constable and Robinson, 2002), 277.

68   P.J. Carisella and James W. Ryan, *Who Killed the Red Baron?* (London: White Lion, 1969), 54.

69   Barker, *The Royal Flying Corps in World War 1*, 278.

70   Nicholson, *Canadian Expeditionary Force*, 269–278; and NAC, RG 9, Series III-D-3, Volume 4928, Reel T-10725-10726, *War Diary,19th Battalion* May 1917.

71   General Staff, *Field Service Pocket Book 1914* (London: His Majesty's Stationery Office, 1914), 159; and J.A. Barlow, *Small Arms Manual* (London: John Murray, 1943), 68.

72   Nicholson, *Canadian Expeditionary Force*, 197; and Rawling, *Surviving Trench Warfare*, 71.

73   NAC, RG 9, Series III-D-3, Volume 4928, Reel T-10725-10726, *War Diary, 19th Battalion* May 1917 Appendix 2, "19th Canadian Battalion On the Left of Fresnoy, May 8th, 9th & 10th, 1917 (a report on the Fresnoy action)."

74   NAC, RG 9, Series III-D-3, Volume 4928, Reel T-10725-10726, *War Diary, 19th Battalion* May 1917 Appendix 2, "19th Canadian Battalion On the Left of Fresnoy, May 8th, 9th & 10th, 1917 (a report on the Fresnoy action)".

75   NAC, RG 9, Series III-D-3, Volume 4928, Reel T-10725-10726, *War Diary, 19th Battalion* May 1917.

76   Nicholson, *Canadian Expeditionary Force*, 278; NAC, RG 9, Series III-D-3, Volume 4928, Reel T-10725-10726, *War Diary, 19th Battalion* May 1917; and, RG 9, Series III-D-3, Volume 4928, Reel T-10725-10726, *War Diary, 19th Battalion* May 1917 Appendix 2, "19th Canadian Battalion On the Left of Fresnoy, May 8th, 9th & 10th, 1917 (a report on the Fresnoy action)."

77   Bird, *Ghosts Have Warm Hands*, 63.

78   NAC, RG 9, Series III-D-3, Volume 4928, Reel T-10725-10726, *War Diary, 19th Battalion* May 1917.

79   Editor's Note: In Deward's 1926 transcription, he wrote "… afterwards L/Corporal Cowan and I were recommended for the D.C.M.," but later crossed out the letters D.C.M.

80   NAC, RG 9, Series III-D-3, Volume 4928, Reel T-10725-10726, *War Diary, 19th Battalion* May 1917 Appendix 2, "19th Canadian Battalion On the Left of Fresnoy, May 8th, 9th & 10th, 1917 (a report on the Fresnoy action)"; RG9, Series III-D-3, Volume 4845, Reel T-1927-1928, *War Diary, 2nd Canadian Division–General Staff*, May 1917; RG9,

Series III-D-3, Volume 4926, Reel T-10721, *War Diary, 18th Battalion,* May 1917; RG9, Series III-D-3, Volume 4930, Reel T-10730, *War Diary, 20th Battalion,* May 1917 ; and RG9, Series III-D-3, Volume 4936, Reel T-10740-10741 *War Diary, 29th Battalion,* May 1917.

81   NAC, RG 9, Series III-D-3, Volume 4928, Reel T-10725-10726, *War Diary, 19th Battalion* May 1917.

82   Daniel Dancocks, *Welcome to Flanders Fields* (Toronto: McClelland & Steward, 1989), 234.

83   Kevin R. Shackleton, *Second To None: The Fighting 58th Battalion of the Canadian Expeditionary Force* (Toronto: Dundurn Press, 2002), 40.

84   NAC, RG 9, Series III-D-3, Volume 4928, Reel T-10725-10726, *War Diary, 19th Battalion* May 1917.

85   NAC, RG 9, Series III-D-3, Volume 4928, Reel T-10725-10726, *War Diary, 19th Battalion* May 1917 (including Appendix 2, "19th Canadian Battalion On the Left of Fresnoy, May 8th, 9th & 10th, 1917"); and RG9, Series III-D-3, Volume 4982, Reel T-10813, *War Diary, 4th Company, Canadian Machine Gun Corps,* May, 1917.

86   Morton, *When Your Number's Up*, 106.

87   NAC, RG 9, Series III-D-3, Volume 4928, Reel T-10725-10726, *War Diary, 19th Battalion* May 1917.

88   NAC, RG 9, Series III-D-3, Volume 4928, Reel T-10725-10726, *War Diary, 19th Battalion* May 1917, Appendix 2, "Field Messages May 8, 1917"; Fraser, *The Journal of Private Fraser*, 283; and Commonwealth War Graves Commission, Debt of Honour Register, Commonwealth War Graves Commission, http://www.cwgc.org/cwgcinternet/ casualty_details.aspx?casualty = 65098, copyright 2000-2003, accessed February 1, 2004.

89   NAC, RG 150, Accession 1992-93/166, Box 4064–36; *Harman, Huson Munry*, Major.

90   NAC, RG 9, Series III-D-3, Volume 4928, Reel T-10725-10726, *War Diary, 19th Battalion* May 1917, Appendix 2.

91   From information provided to the author by the Canadian Agency of the Commonwealth War Graves Commission on 25 September, 2003.

92   John Harold Becker, *Silhouettes of the Great War* (Nepean: CEF Books, 2001), 60; The author has both leather and

pressed fibres specimens in his personal collection; NAC, RG9, Series III-D-3, Volume 4929, Reel T-10727-10728, *War Diary, 19th Battalion,* April 1918, Appendix 4.

93   Reginald H. Roy (ed.), *The Journal of Private Fraser* (Nepean: CEF Books, 1998), 252.

94   Empey, *Over the Top,* 299.

95   Nicholson, *Canadian Expeditionary Force,* 274.

96   NAC, RG 150, Accession 1992-93/166, Box 9043–64, 214046 *Smith, George*; and Morton, *When Your Number's Up,* 58.

97   Commonwealth War Graves Commission, Debt of Honour Register, www.cwgc.org/. See entry for Lichfield Crater Cemetery, Thélus.

98   NAC, RG 9, Series III-D-3, Volume 4928, Reel T-10725-10726, *War Diary, 19th Battalion,* June, 1917 Appendix 2.

99   NAC, RG 9, Series III-D-3, Volume 4928, Reel T-10725-10726, *War Diary, 19th Battalion,* June, 1917 Appendix 2.

100   Roy (ed.), *The Journal of Private Fraser,* 78–80.

101   Roy (ed.), *The Journal of Private Fraser,* 78–80.

102   Morton, *When Your Number's Up,* 142.

103   NAC, RG 9, Series III-D-3, Volume 4928, Reel T-10725-10726, *War Diary, 19th Battalion,* June, 1917, Appendix 2; and General Staff, *Musketry Regulations, Part 1,* paragraphs 274 and 387.

104   Becker, *Silhouettes of the Great War,* 84.

105   NAC, RG 150, 1992-93/166, box 5972 file 17, 862742 *Martin, Cecil*; and box 6811 file 31, 862725 *Allen, Thomas.*

106   NAC, RG9 , RG9, Series III-D-3, Volume 4928, Reel T-10726, *War Diary, 19th Battalion,* July 1917.

107   A.B. Godefroy, *For Freedom and Honour? The Story of 25 Canadian Volunteers Executed in the Great War* (Nepean: CEF Books, 1998), 42–44, 81, and 84–85.

108   Karl Weatherbe, *From the Rideau to the Rhine and Back: The 6th Field Company and Battalion, Canadian Engineers in the Great War* (Toronto: Hunter-Rose, 1928), 253.

109   Jonathan F. Vance, *Death So Noble: Memory, Meaning, and the First World War* (Vancouver: University of British Columbia Press, 1997), 79.

110   Roy (ed.), *The Journal of Private Fraser,* 294.

111   NAC, RG9, Series III-D-3, Volume 4928, Reel T-10726, *War Diary, 19th Battalion,* August 1917, Appendix 7.

112 Bird, *Ghosts Have Warm Hands*, 123–124.

113 Cane, *Personal Diary*, hand-written note after the diary entries.

114 Corrigal, *The Twentieth*, 136.

115 Cook, *No Place to Run*, 119–121.

116 NAC, RG9 , Series III-D-3 , Volume 4930 , Reel T-10730, *War Diary 20th Battalion*, August 1917.

117 NAC, RG 150, Accession 1992-93/166, Box 7641–16, 213295 *Patterson, Harvey*; RG 150, Accession 1992-93/166, Box 7636–31, 213434 *Patterson, Charles*; and the personnel record of Deward Barnes, as previously cited.

118 Cook, *No Place to Run*, 133.

119 NAC, RG 9 III DI, Vol. 4692, Folder 51, File 18; *Notes on attack, 19th Bn., A., C., and D. Coys., N. W. Lens August 15–17 1917*, Unsigned.

120 NAC, RG 9 III DI, Vol. 4692, Folder 51, File 18; *Notes on attack, 19th Bn., A., C., and D. Coys., N. W. Lens August 15–17 1917*, Unsigned.

121 NAC, RG 9 III DI, Vol. 4692, Folder 51, File 18; *Notes on attack, 19th Bn., A., C., and D. Coys., N. W. Lens August 15–17 1917*, Unsigned.

122 NAC, RG 9 III DI, Vol. 4692, Folder 51, File 18; *Notes on attack, 19th Bn., A., C., and D. Coys., N. W. Lens August 15–17 1917*, Unsigned.

123 NAC, RG 150, Volume 19–19, 766109 *Abrahams, George Victor*.

124 John Swettenham, *To Seize the Victory: The Canadian Corps in World War I* (Toronto: Ryerson Press, 1965), 175.

125 Swettenham, *To Seize the Victory*, 177.

126 Cook, *No Place to Run*, 124.

127 NAC, RG 9 III DI, Vol. 4692, Folder 51, File 18; *Notes on attack, 19th Bn., A., C., and D. Coys., N. W. Lens August 15–17 1917*, Unsigned; and RG 9, Series III-D-3, Volume 4928, Reel T-10726-10727, *War Diary, 19th Battalion*, September 1917.

128 Swettenham, *To Seize the Victory*, 178 and 255, n. 47.

129 NAC, RG9, Series III-D-3, volume 4928, Reel T-10726-10727, *19th Battalion War Diary*, September 1917.

130 NAC, RG9, Series III-D-3 , volume 4928 , Reel T-10726-10727, *19th Battalion War Diary*, September 1917,

Appendix 3.

131 NAC, RG9, Series III-D-3, volume 4928 , Reel T-10726-10727, *19th Battalion War Diary*, September 1917.

132 Law, *Khaki*, 21; and Pedley, *Only This*, 150.

133 Cook, *No Place to Run*, 250 n. 31.

134 Cook, *No Place to Run*, 68; and Pedley, *Only This*, 211.

135 Morton, *When Your Number's Up*, see the photograph and caption between 210 and 211.

136 John Swettenham, *McNaughton: Volume 1, 1887–1939* (Toronto: Ryerson Press, 1968), 113.

137 Daniel Dancocks, *Legacy of Valour: The Canadians at Passchendaele* (Edmonton: Hurtig Publishers, 1986), 107.

138 A.J. Kerry. *The Corps of Royal Canadian Engineers* (Ottawa: Ottawa Military Engineers Association, 1962), 211, for list of materials hauled, see NAC, RG9, Series III-D-3, Volume 5006, Reel T-10854, *War Diary, 2nd Tramways Company*, May 1918.

139 W.J.K. Davies, *Light Railways of the First World War: A History of Tactical Rail Communications on the British Fronts 1914–18* (Newton Abbot: David and Charles, 1967.), 183.

140 Swettenham, *McNaughton*, 110 and 113.

141 Dancocks, *Legacy of Valour*, 124.

142 NAC, RG9 , Series III-D-3 , Volume 4928 , Reel T-10726-10727, *War Diary, 19th Battalion*, November 1917, Appendix 3.

143 NAC, RG9 , Series III-D-3 , Volume 4928 , Reel T-10726-10727, *War Diary, 19th Battalion*, November 1917, Appendix 1.

144 Godefroy, *For Freedom and Honour?*, 61–62.

145 Dancocks, *Legacy of Valour*, 110.

146 NAC, RG9 , Series III-D-3 , Volume 4928 , Reel T-10726-10727, *War Diary, 19th Battalion*, November 10, 1917.

147 Swettenham, *McNaughton*, 116.

148 RG 150, Accession 1992-93/166, Box 1466-3, 766144 *Cane, Arthur William*.

149 NAC, RG9 , Series III-D-3 , Volume 4928 , Reel T-10726-10727, *War Diary, 19th Battalion*, November 1917, Appendix 3.

150 NAC, RG9 , Series III-D-3 , Volume 4929 , Reel T-10727, *War Diary, 19th Battalion*, March 1918, Appendix 3.

151 Davies, *Light Railways of the First World War*, 79.
152 NAC, RG9 , Series III-D-3 , Volume 4928 , Reel T-10726-10727, *War Diary, 19th Battalion,* November 1917.
153 Pedley, *Only This*, 47.
154 Corrigal, *The Twentieth*, 136.
155 NAC, RG 150, Box 406 - 20 , 862959 *Bangay, Edward Albert*; and Commonwealth War Graves Commission, Debt of Honour Register, http://www.cwgc.org/cwgcinternet/casualty_details.aspx?casualty = 496919, copyright 2000-2003, accessed February 1, 2004.
156 NAC, RG 150, Accession 1992-93/166, Box 625–18, *Bell, William Douglas,* Lieutenant.
157 NAC, RG 150, Box 4116–6, *Harstone, John Archibald,* Lieutenant.
158 NAC, RG9 , Series III-D-3 , Volume 4928 , Reel T-10726-10727, *War Diary, 19th Battalion*, December 1917, Appendix C.
159 NAC, RG 150, Box 879 - 41, *210133 Book, Roy*.
160 NAC, RG 9 III DI, Vol. 4692, Folder 51, File 18; *Notes on attack, 19th Bn., A., C., and D. Coys., N. W. Lens August 15–17 1917*, Unsigned.
161 NAC, RG 150, Accession 1992-93/166, Box 331–21, 408737 *Bacon, Louis*.
162 Morton, *When Your Number's Up*, 84.
163 N.M. Christie (ed.), *The Letters of Agar Adamson* (Nepean: CEF Books, 1997), 101.
164 Morton, *When Your Number's Up*, 234 and 237.
165 Becker, *Silhouettes*, 93 and 98.
166 Vance, *Death So Noble*, 84.
167 Empey, *Over the Top*, 293–294.
168 NAC, RG 150, Box 879 - 41, 210133 *Book, Roy*.
169 NAC, RG 150, Accession 1992-93/166, Box 5709–28, 2095 *Lodge, Harold Edward James*.
170 Pedley, *Only This*, 128.
171 Godefroy, *For Freedom and Honour?*, 61–62; and NAC, RG9, Series III-D-3, Volume 4928, Reel T-10726-10727, *War Diary, 19th Battalion, November 1917*.
172 NAC, RG 150, Box 223-42, 862443 *Armstrong, Alexander*.
173 NAC, RG9, Series III-D-3, Volume 4929, Reel T-10727, *War Diary, 19th Battalion,* February 1918, Appendix 1.

174   Patrick B. O'Neill, "The Canadian Concert Party in France," *Theatre History in Canada*, Vol. 4, No. 2 (Fall 1983), 192–198.

175   Frederick George Scott, *The Great War as I Saw It* (Toronto: F.D. Goodchild, 1922), 153.

176   Rawling, *Surviving Trench Warfare*, 98.

177   NAC, RG9, Series III-D-3, Volume 4929, Reel T-10727, *War Diary, 19th Battalion*, February 1918, Appendix 4.

178   Becker, *Silhouettes of the Great War*, 84.

179   Cook, *No Place to Run*, 91.

180   Pedley, *Only This*, 81; and Victor Wheeler, *The 50th Battalion in No Man's Land* (Nepean: CEF Books, 2000), 75–76.

181   Christie (ed.), *The Letters of Agar Adamson*, 135–136.

182   NAC, RG 150, Box 4341 - 3, 862068 *Hiley, Frank*.

183   NAC, RG150, Series 8, File 602-19-255, Reel T-8693, records relating to courts martial of the First World War.

184   Pedley, *Only This*, 166.

185   NAC, RG9, Series III-D-3, Volume 4931, Reel T-10731-10732, *War Diary, 21st Battalion*, March 1918, Appendix B.

186   NAC, RG 150, Box 1009 - 49, 210138 *Brailsford, Harold*.

187   NAC, RG9, Series III-D-3, Volume 4931, Reel T-10731-10732, *War Diary, 21st Battalion*, March 1918, Appendix A.

188   Edmund Blunden, *Undertones of War* (London: Penguin, 2000), 27.

189   Nicholson, *Canadian Expeditionary Force*, 339.

190   NAC, RG 150, Accession 1992-93/166, Box 193–6, 766115 *Anning, Gerald*.

191   Godefroy, *For Freedom and Honour?*, 62; and personnel record Harold Lodge, as previously cited.

192   Pedley, *Only This*, 179.

193   Morton, *When Your Number's Up*, 251–252; and Christie (ed.), *The Letters of Agar Adamson*, 20.

194   Scott, *The Great War As I Saw It*, 214–215.

195   R. Ernest Dupuy and Trevor N. Dupuy, *The Encyclopedia of Military History: From 3500 B.C. to the Present* (New York: Harper and Row, 1970), 978; Nicholson, *Canadian Expeditionary Force*, 362–367; Swettenham, *To Seize the Victory*, 195–200; University of Calgary, Centre for Military and Strategic Studies, Publications, Occasional Papers, *Operation Michael, The Last Card*, http://www.stratnet.ucal-

gary.ca/publications/pdf/herwig_operation-michael_nov2001.pdf, Herwig H., copyright November 2001, accessed on February 2, 2004.

196   NAC, RG 9 Series III-D-3, volume 4929, Reel T10727-10728, *War Diary, 19th Battalion*, April, 1918, Appendix 1, "A" Company Work Report, April 1, 1918."

197   NAC, RG 9 Series III-D-3, volume 4929, Reel T10727-10728, *War Diary, 19th Battalion*, April, 1918; and RG9, Series III-D-3, Volume 4882 , Reel T-10679, *War Diary, 4th Canadian Infantry Brigade*, April 1918.

198   Cook, *No Place to Run*, 64.

199   NAC, RG 9 Series III-D-3, volume 4929, Reel T10727-10728, *War Diary, 19th Battalion*, April, 1918, Appendix 4, "Hostile Shelling Report April 11, 1918".

200   NAC, RG 9 Series III-D-3, volume 4929, Reel T10727-10728, *War Diary, 19th Battalion*, April, 1918, Appendix 4, "Secret memo from 4th C. I. B., 9th April 1918".

201   NAC, RG 150, Accession 1992-93/166, Box 896–6, *Borthwick, George Bruce, Lieutenant*; RG 9 Series III-D-3, volume 4929, Reel T10727-10728, *War Diary, 19th Battalion*, April, 1918, Appendix 5, "A list of men cited for conspicuous gallantry and devotion to duty during the counter-attack on April 16, 1918"; and Commonwealth War Graves Commission, Debt of Honour Register, http://www.cwgc.org/cwgcinternet/casualty_details.aspx?casualty = 557796, copyright 2000-2003, accessed February 2, 2004.

202   Love, *A Call to Arms*, 76.

203   NAC, RG 9 Series III-D-3, volume 4929, Reel T10727-10728, *War Diary, 19th Battalion*, April, 1918.

204   Commonwealth War Graves Commission, Debt of Honour Register, http://www.cwgc.org/cwgcinternet/casualty_details. aspx?casualty = 18525, copyright 2000-2003, accessed February 2, 2004.

205   NAC, RG 9 Series III-D-3, volume 4929, Reel T10727-10728, *War Diary, 19th Battalion*, April, 1918.

206   NAC, RG 9 Series III-D-3, volume 4929, Reel T10727-10728, *War Diary, 19th Battalion*, April, 1918.

207   Pedley, *Only This*, 299.

208   NAC, RG 150, Box 4330–36, 916144 *Higgins, Arthur*.

209   NAC, RG9 , Series III-D-3 , Volume 5023 , Reel T-10908, *War Diary, Canadian Corps Salvage Company*, April 1918, "Salvage Returns for Month Ended 30/4 1918."

210   NAC, RG 150, Accession 1992-93/166, Box 2530-79, 157571 *Dion, Thomas Patrick.*

211   NAC, RG 150, Accession 1992-93/166, Box 6276-13, 862495 *Moffat, Roy Clifton.*

212   NAC, RG 150, Accession 1992-93/166, Box 1779-23, 862453 *Clayton, Frederick*; and Box 1781-19, 863102 *Clayton, William George.*

213   NAC, RG9 III, Vol. 4117, Folder 8, File 1 *19th Battalion Correspondence Re: Cloth Badges*; and RG9 III C3 Vol. 4170, Folder 8, File 1, *2nd CMR Correspondence Re: Cloth Badges.*

214   NAC, RG9, Series III-D-3, Volume 4929, Reel T-10728, *War Diary, 19th Battalion*, May 1918, Appendix 3, "Schedule of Training, 19th Battalion, 16th to 21st May."

215   NAC, RG9, Series III-D-3, Volume 4929, Reel T-10728, *War Diary, 19th Battalion*, May 1918, Appendix 4, "Summary of Intelligence for 24-hours ending 6:00 a.m. May 26 1918."

216   Cook, *No Place to Run*, 94.

217   NAC, RG9, Series III-D-3, Volume 4929, Reel T-10728, *War Diary, 19th Battalion*, June 1918, Appendix 5, various reports on the raid of 21st June; RG 150, Accession 1992-93/166, Box 6173-20, *Miller, Armour Adamson*; RG 150, Accession 1992-93/166, Box 10290-39, 542251 *White, Harold Sydney* RG 150, Accession 1992-93/166, Box 7830-50, *Pike, Abraham Bowman*; RG 150, Accession 1992-93/166, Box 1466-3, 766144 *Cane, Arthur William*, and RG 150, Accession 1992-93/166, Box 9809-9, 228255 *Tucker, George Andrew.*

218   Cook, *No Place to Run*, 198.

219   Swettenham, *To Seize the Victory*, 205.

220   Pedley, *Only This*, 306.

221   NAC, RG9, Series III-D-3, Volume 4929, Reel T-10728, *War Diary, 19th Battalion*, Appendix 1, "Battalion Orders No. 70, July 5th 1918."

222   Love, *A Call to Arms*, 32; and NAC, RG9, Series III-D-3, Volume 4929, Reel T-10728, *War Diary, 19th Battalion*, Appendix 1, "4th Canadian Infantry Brigade ... In accordance with attached instructions for an Artillery and Horse Transport show ...19/6/18."

223 Personnel records of Louis Bacon, Roy Book, and Gerald Anning, as previously cited.

224 Rawling, *Surviving Trench Warfare*, 6; and A.M.J. Hyatt, *General Sir Arthur Currie: A Military Biography* (Toronto: University of Toronto Press, 1987), 111.

225 Hyatt, *General Sir Arthur Currie*, 195—196.

226 Hyatt, *General Sir Arthur Currie*, 109.

227 Pedley, *Only This*, 206.

228 Daniel Dancocks, *Sir Arthur Currie: A Biography* (Toronto: Methuen, 1985), 143; and Nicholson, *Canadian Expeditionary Force*, 315.

229 NAC, RG 150, Accession 1992-93/166, Box 7235–17, 862012 *Nash, Alfred Percival*; and Box 7237–6, 862270 *Nash, Laurie Elwood*.

230 NAC, RG9, Series III-D-3, Volume 4929, Reel T-10728, *War Diary, 19thBattalion*, July 1918, Appendix 2, "19th Battalion Order 81, 14 July, 1918."

231 Canadian War Museum Archives, "*Questionnaire for the 19th Canadian Infantry Battalion History*," Accession number 19740071-087.

232 Edwin Campion Vaughan, *Some Desperate Glory: The World War 1 Diary of a British Officer 1917* (New York: Henry Holt, 1988), April 27.

233 Canadian War Museum Archives, "*Questionnaire for the 19th Canadian Infantry Battalion History*," Accession number 19740071-087.

234 James McWilliams and R. James Steele, *Amiens: Dawn of Victory* (Toronto: Dundurn Press, 2001), 44.

235 NAC, RG9, Series III-D-3, Volume 4929, Reel T-10729, *War Diary, 19th Canadian Battalion*, August 1918.

236 NAC, RG9, Series III-D-3, Volume 4929, Reel T-10728, *War Diary, 19th Battalion*, Appendix 1, "19th Canadian Battalion Order No. 75, July 11, 1918."

237 Dancocks, *Spearhead to Victory: Canada and the Great War* (Edmonton: Hurtig Publishers, 1987), 31 and Hyatt, *General Sir Arthur Currie*, 115.

238 NAC, RG9, Series III-D-3, Volume 4929, Reel T-10729, *War Diary, 19th Canadian Battalion*, August 1918.

239 McWilliams and Steele, *Amiens: Dawn of Victory*, 59.

240 NAC, RG9, Series III-D-3, Volume 4929, Reel T-10729,

War Diary, 19th Canadian Battalion, August 1918.

241 Dancocks, *Sir Arthur Currie,* 152.

242 Swettenham, *McNaughton,* 142–143; and McWilliams and Steele, *Amiens: Dawn of Victory,* 74.

243 NAC, RG9, Series III-D-3, Volume 4929, Reel T-10729, *War Diary, 19th Canadian Battalion,* August 1918.

244 Dancocks, *Spearhead to Victory,* 40.

245 Editor's Note: In Deward's 1926 transcription he wrote, "we shot them down like dogs," but later crossed out "we" and wrote "they."

246 Edwyn A. Gray, *The Killing Time: German U-Boats 1914–1918* (London: Pan Brooks, 1975), 206–207; and McWilliams and Steele, *Amiens: Dawn of Victory,* 31.

247 McWilliams and Steele, *Amiens: Dawn of Victory,* 121.

248 NAC, RG9, Series III-D-3, Volume 4883, Reel T-10680, *War Diary, 4th Canadian Infantry Brigade,* August, 1918; Dancocks, *Spearhead to Victory,* 41; and J.F.B. Livesay, *Canada's Hundred Days* (Toronto: Thomas Allen, 1919), 72.

249 Dancocks, *Spearhead to Victory,* 41.

250 Dancocks, *Spearhead to Victory,* 41.

251 NAC, RG 150, Accession 1992-93/166, Box 619-10, 862801 *Bell, Leonard Clement.*

252 NAC, RG 150, Accession 1992-93/166, Box 2502–22, *Dibble, Harry,* Lieutenant.

253 NAC, RG 150, Accession 1992-93/166, Box 201–49, *Applegath, G. H.,* Captain; Box 109–37, *Allan, Thomas Amos,* Lieutenant; and RG9, Series III-D-3, Volume 4929, Reel T-10729, *War Diary, 19th Battalion,* August 1918.

254 McWilliams and Steele, *Amiens: Dawn of Victory,* 121; and NAC RG9, Series III-D-3, Volume 4929, Reel T-10729, *War Diary, 19th Battalion,* August 1918.

255 Pedley, *Only This,* 344–345.

256 Nicholson, *Canadian Expeditionary Force,* 419.

257 NAC, RG9, Series III-D-3, Volume 4929, Reel T-10729, *War Diary, 19th Battalion,* September 1918, Appendix 1.

258 Nicholson, *Canadian Expeditionary Force,* 414.

259 NAC, RG9, Series III-D-3, Volume 4929, Reel T-10729, *War Diary, 19th Canadian Battalion,* August 1918.

260 Nicholson, *Canadian Expeditionary Force,* 419.

261 NAC, RG9, Series III-D-3, Volume 4929, Reel T-10729,

War Diary, 19th Battalion, September, 1918, Appendix 1.

262 Love, *A Call to Arms,* 239–241.

263 Nicholson, *Canadian Expeditionary Force,* 422–423; and Swettenham, *Breaking the Hindenburg Line* (Ottawa: Canadian War Museum, 1986), 10–11.

264 NAC RG9, Series III-D-3, Volume 4929, Reel T-10729, *War Diary, 19th Battalion,* August 1918, Appendix 6, "Operations by the 19th Canadian Infantry Battalion, August 25th–29th 1918".

265 Royal Electrical and Mechanical Engineers' Museum of Technology, The Weapons Collection, Handheld Anti-Tank Weapons page, http://www.rememuseum.org.uk/arms/heavy/armhhat.htm, last updated September 8 2002, accessed January 4, 2004.

266 NAC RG9, Series III-D-3, Volume 4929, Reel T-10729, *War Diary, 19th Battalion,* August 1918, Appendix 6, "Operations by the 19th Canadian Infantry Battalion, August 25th–29th 1918."

267 Personnel record of Louis Bacon, as previously cited.

268 Corrigall, *The Twentieth,* 241.

269 NAC RG9, Series III-D-3, Volume 4929, Reel T-10729, *War Diary, 19th Battalion,* August 1918, Appendix 6, "Operations by the 19th Canadian Infantry Battalion, August 25th–29th 1918".

270 Bird, *Ghosts Have Warm Hands,* 104.

271 NAC RG9, Series III-D-3, Volume 4929, Reel T-10729, *War Diary, 19th Battalion,* August 1918, Appendix 6, "Operations by the 19th Canadian Infantry Battalion, August 25th–29th 1918"; and Corrigall, *The Twentieth,* 243.

272 NAC, RG9, Series III-D-3, Volume 4929, Reel T-10729, *War Diary, 19th Battalion,* September 1918.

273 NAC, RG9, Series III-D-3, Volume 4929, Reel T-10729, *War Diary, 19th Battalion,* September 1918.

274 Cook, *No Place to Run,* 73.

275 NAC, RG9, Series III-D-3, Volume 4929, Reel T-10729, *War Diary, 19th Battalion,* September 1918.

276 NAC, RG9, Series III-D-3, Volume 4929, Reel T-10729, *War Diary, 19th Battalion,* September 1918.

277 Nicholson, *Canadian Expeditionary Force,* 456–458; NAC, RG9, Series III-D-3, Volume 4883, Reel T-10680, *War*

Diary, 4th Canadian Infantry Brigade, October 1918.

278   NAC, RG9, Series III-D-3, Volume 4929, Reel T-10729, *War Diary, 19th Battalion*, October 1918.

279   Editor's Note: In Deward's 1926 transcription, he stated originally that the name of the town was Naves. Later, he crossed out Naves and wrote Hyon. Naves, however, is correct.

280   NAC, RG9, Series III-D-3, Volume 4929, Reel T-10729, *War Diary, 19th Battalion*, October 1918, Appendix 1, "19th Canadian Battalion, Report on Recent Operations, Oct 7th to Oct 10th."

281   NAC, RG9, Series III-D-3, Volume 4955, Reel T-10771, *War Diary, Canadian Light Horse*, October 1918; and Nicholson, *The Canadian Expeditionary Force*, 458.

282   NAC, RG9, Series III-D-3, Volume 4929, Reel T-10729, *War Diary, 19th Battalion*, October 1918, Appendix 1, "19th Canadian Battalion, Report on Recent Operations, Oct. 7th to Oct 10th"; and Volume 4883, Reel T-10680, *War Diary, 4th Canadian Infantry Brigade*, October 1918; and Livesay, *Canada's Hundred Days*, 310.

283   Pedley, *Only This*, 306.

284   Corrigall, *The Twentieth*, 262.

285   NAC, RG9, Series III-D-3, Volume 4929, Reel T-10729, *War Diary, 19th Battalion*, October 1918, Appendix 1, "19th Canadian Battalion, Report on Recent Operations, Oct. 7th to Oct 10th."

286   Corrigal, *The Twentieth*, 261; Dancocks, *Spearhead to Victory*, 178; Livesay, *Canada's Hundred Days*, 312; and Nicholson, *Canadian Expeditionary Force*, 459.

287   Personnel record of Deward Barnes, as previously cited.

288   Personnel record of Deward Barnes, as previously cited.

289   Susan Mann (ed.), *The War Diary of Clare Gass, 1915–1918* (Montreal & Kingston: McGill-Queen's University Press, 2000), 63.

290   Personnel record of Deward Barnes, as previously cited.

291   Love, *A Call to Arms*, 62.

292   Personnel record of Deward Barnes, as previously cited.

293   The Empire Club of Canada, *The Last Hundred Days of the War*, Lieutenant-General Sir Arthur Currie, speaker—August 29, 1919, 303–317.

294 NAC, RG9, III, C3, Volume 4115, Folder 1, File 1, *Programme of Experiment of Infantry Cooperation With Aircraft*, July 9, 1916.

295 Empey, *Over the Top*, 301.

296 G.R. Stevens, *A City Goes to War* (Edmonton: The Edmonton Regiment Association, 1964), 70–71.

297 Bird, *Ghosts Have Warm Hands*, 84.

My nerves were always good untill I had my last leave from France Sept 1918 I maybe on account of the war lasting so long & the thought of what was in front of us I then started to get over it, since I came home I have always tried to work hard & steady to get over this three years experience, but could never do it, so I class myself as a war wreck, which people will never understand

BIBLIOGRAPHY

The following is a list of the sources that I consulted while editing the diary and creating the notes.

Archival Sources

National Archives of Canada, *RG9, Militia and Defence*
National Archives of Canada, *RG 150, Ministry of the Overseas Military Forces of Canada*
National Archives of Canada, Photographic Collection
Canadian War Museum, *Questionnaire for the 19th Canadian Infantry Battalion History*, Accession Number 19740071-087
City of Toronto Archives, William James Photographic Collection

Unpublished Sources

Argyll and Sutherland Highlanders of Canada, *19th Battalion Personnel Database*. A list containing the service details of former battalion members compiled after the war by the 19th Battalion Association. The list is now in the possession of the Argyll and Sutherland Highlanders of Canada — who perpetuate the 19th Battalion.

Cane, Sidney George. *Diary of Our Trip (1916–1917)*. A description of the diarist's journey with the 134th Battalion from Camp Borden, Ontario, to Witley Camp, England, in the summer of 1916. The diary also contains extensive notes on the Lewis gun that appear to have been made during a course of instruction on the weapon.

Articles

Brown, Tom. "Shell Shock in the Canadian Expeditionary Force, 1914–1918." *Canadian Psychiatry in the Great War, Health, Disease, and Medicine*, Hannah Foundation (1984).

Herwig, Holger H. "Operation Michael: 'The Last Card.'" University of Calgary, Centre for Military and Strategic Studies, Occasional Papers (November 2001).

O'Neill, Patrick B. "The Canadian Concert Party in France." *Theatre History in Canada*, Vol. 4, No. 2 (Fall 1983).

O'Neill, Patrick B. "Entertaining the Troops." *The Beaver* (October-November 1989).

Printed and Published Sources

Allinson, Sidney. *The Bantams: The Untold Story of World War 1*. London: Howard Baker, , 1981.

Barker, Ralph. *A Brief History of the Royal Flying Corps in World War 1*. London: Constable and Robinson, 2002.

Barlow, J.A. *Small Arms Manual*. Revised ed. London: John Murray, 1943.

Barrie, Alexander. *War Underground*. New York: Ballantine Books, 1961.

Beattie, Kim. *48th Highlanders of Canada 1891–1928*. Toronto: 48th Highlanders of Canada, 1932.

Becker, John Harold. *Silhouettes of the Great War*. Nepean: CEF Books, 2001.

Bercuson, David J. and Granatstein, J.L. *Dictionary of Canadian Military History*. Oxford: Oxford University Press, 1992.

Berton, Pierre. *Vimy*. Toronto: McClelland and Stewart, 1986.

Bird, Will R. *Ghosts Have Warm Hands*. Nepean: CEF Books, 1997.

Blunden, Edmund. *Undertones of War*. London: Penguin, 2000.

Canadian Soldier's Diary: From Belleville, Canada to Bramshott Camp, England. Hasselmere: Gables Press, n.d.

Carisella, P.J. and James W. Ryan. *Who Killed the Red Baron?* London: White Lion, 1969.

Christie, N.M., ed. *The Letters of Agar Adamson*. Nepean: CEF Books, 1997.

Cook, Tim. *No Place to Run: The Canadian Corps and Gas Warfare in the First World War*. Vancouver: University of British Columbia Press, 1999.

Coombs, Rose E.B. *Before Endeavours Fade: A Guide to the Battlefields of the First World War*. Revised ed. London: Battle of Britain Prints International, 1990.

Corrigall, D.J. *The Twentieth: The History of the Twentieth Canadian Battalion, Central Ontario Regiment, Canadian Expeditionary Force*. Toronto: Stone and Cox, 1935.

Dancocks, Daniel. *Gallant Canadians: The Story of the Tenth Canadian Infantry Battalion 1914–1919*. Calgary: Calgary Highlanders Regimental Funds Foundation, 1994.

Dancocks, Daniel. *Legacy of Valour: The Canadians at Passchendaele*. Edmonton: Hurtig Publishers, 1986.

Dancocks, Daniel. *Sir Arthur Currie: A Biography*. Toronto: Methuen, 1985.

Dancocks, Daniel. *Spearhead to Victory: Canada and the Great War*. Edmonton: Hurtig Publishers, 1987.

Dancocks, Daniel. *Welcome to Flanders Fields*. Toronto: McClelland and Stewart, 1989.

Davies, W.J.K. *Light Railways of the First World War: A History of Tactical Rail Communications on the British Fronts 1914–18*. Newton Abbot: David and Charles, 1967.

Davis, Brian. *British Army Uniforms and Insignia of World War Two*. London: Arms and Armour Press, 1983.

Duncan-Clark, S.J., W.R. Plewman, and W.S. Wallace. *Pictorial History of the Great War: Canada's Valorous Achievements*. 4th ed. Toronto: John Hertel, 1919.

Dupuy, R. Ernest and Trevor N. Dupuy. *The Encyclopedia of Military History: From 3500 B.C. to the Present*. New York: Harper and Row, 1970.

Empey, Arthur Guy. *Over the Top*, New York: A.L. Burt, 1917.

Empire Club of Canada. *The Empire Club of Canada Speeches 1917–1918*. Toronto: The Empire Club of Canada, 1919.

Empire Club of Canada. *The Empire Club of Canada Speeches 1919*. Toronto: The Empire Club of Canada, 1920.

The Encyclopaedia Britannica. 11th ed. Cambridge: Cambridge University Press, 1910.

General Staff, War Office. *Field Service Pocket Book 1914*. 1914. Reprint, Devon: David & Charles, 1971.

General Staff, War Office. *Instructions for the Training of Platoons* for Offensive Action, 1917 Issued by the General Staff, February, 191 Reprinted with Amendments, August, 1917.* Reprint, Military History Society of Manitoba, 1994.

General Staff, War Office. *The Organization of an Infantry Battalion and Normal Formation for the Attack Issued by the General Staff, February, 1917.* Reprint, Military History Society of Manitoba, 1994.

Gilbert, Martin. *Atlas of the Great War.* Dorset Press, 1984.

Godefroy, A.B. *For Freedom and Honour? The Story of 25 Canadian Volunteers Executed in the Great War.* Nepean: CEF Books, 1998.

Goodspeed, D.J. *Battle Royal, A History of the Royal Regiment of Canada,* 2nd ed. Royal Regiment of Canada Association, 1979.

Goodspeed, D.J. *The Road Past Vimy: The Canadian Corps 1914–1918.* Toronto: General Publishing, 1987.

Gray, Edwyn A. *The Killing Time: German U-Boats 1914–1918.* London: Pan Books, 1975.

Hyatt, A.M.J. *General Sir Arthur Currie: A Military Biography.* Toronto: University of Toronto Press, 1987.

Imperial War Museum. *Trench Map Archive on CD-ROM.* Uckfield: The Naval and Military Press and the Imperial War Museum, 2000.

Kerry, A.J. *The Corps of Royal Canadian Engineers.* Ottawa: Ottawa: Military Engineers Association, 1962.

Law, Clive M. *Khaki: Uniforms of the Canadian Expeditionary Force.* Ottawa: Service Publications, 1997.

Livesay, J.F.B. *Canada's Hundred Days.* Toronto: Thomas Allen, 1919.

Love, David W. *A Call to Arms: The Organization and Administration of Canada's Military in World War One.* Winnipeg: Bunker to Bunker Books, 1999.

Mann, Susan, ed. *The War Diary of Clare Gass, 1915–1918.* Montreal & Kingston: McGill-Queen's University Press, 2000.

McKee, Alexander. *Vimy Ridge.* London: Pan Books, 1966.

McWilliams, James, and R. James Steele, *Amiens: Dawn of Victory.* Toronto: Dundurn Press, 2001.

Meek, John F. *Over The Top! The Canadian Infantry in the First World War.* Orangeville: John Meek, 1971.

Miller, Ian Hugh MacLean. *Our Glory and Our Grief: Torontonians and the Great War,* Toronto: University of Toronto Press, 2002.

Moore, William. *The Thin Yellow Line*. Ware: Wordsworth Editions, 1999.

Morton, Desmond. *Silent Battle: Canadian Prisoners of War in Germany, 1914–1919*. Toronto: Lester Publishing, 1992.

Morton, Desmond. *When Your Number's Up: The Canadian Soldier in the First World War*. Toronto: Random House of Canada, 1993.

Morton, Desmond and J. L. Granatstein. *Marching to Armageddon: Canadians and the Great War, 1914–1919*. Toronto: Lester and Orpen Dennys, 1989.

Nicholson, G.W.L. *Canadian Expeditionary Force, 1914–1919*. Ottawa: Queen's Printer, 1962.

Nicholson, G.W.L. *Seventy Years of Service: A History of the Royal Canadian Army Medical Corps*. Ottawa: Borealis Press, 1977.

Pedley, James H. *Only This: A War Retrospective*. Ottawa: Graphic Publishers, 1927.

Pope, Stephen and Elizabeth Wheal. *Dictionary of the First World War*. Barnsley: Pen and Sword Military Classics, 2003.

Rawling, Bill. *Surviving Trench Warfare: Technology and the Canadian Corps, 1914–1918*. Toronto: University of Toronto Press, 1992.

Roy, Reginald H., ed. *The Journal of Private Fraser*. Nepean: CEF Books, 1998.

Saunders, Anthony. *Weapons of the Trench War, 1914–1918*. Gloucestershire: Sutton Publishing, 2000.

Scott, Frederick George. *The Great War as I Saw It*. Toronto: F.D. Goodchild, 1922.

Shackleton, Kevin R. *Second to None: The Fighting 58th Battalion of the Canadian Expeditionary Force*. Toronto: Dundurn Press, 2002.

Simpson, Colin. *The Ship that Hunted Itself*. Harmondsworth: Penguin, 1977.

Stevens, G.R. *A City Goes to War*. Edmonton: The Edmonton Regiment Association, 1964.

Summers, Jack L. *Tangled Web: Canadian Infantry Accoutrements 1855–1985*, Museum Restoration Service, Bloomfield, 1991.

Swettenham, John. *Breaking the Hindenburg Line*. Ottawa: Canadian War Museum, 1986.

Swettenham, John. *McNaughton: Volume 1, 1887–1939*. Toronto: Ryerson Press, 1968.

Swettenham, John. *To Seize the Victory: The Canadian Corps in World War 1*. Toronto: Ryerson Press, 1965.

The Times History of the War, Volumes I–XXII. London: The Times, 1914–1921.

Vance, Jonathan F. *Death So Noble: Memory, Meaning, and the First World War*. Vancouver: University of British Columbia Press, 1997.

Vaughan, Edwin Campion. *Some Desperate Glory: The World War 1 Diary of a British Officer 1917*. New York: Henry Holt, 1988.

Weatherbe, Karl. *From the Rideau to the Rhine and Back: The 6th Field Company and Battalion, Canadian Engineers in the Great War*. Toronto: Hunter-Rose, 1928.

Wheeler, Victor W. *The 50th Battalion in No Man's Land*, Nepean: CEF Books, 2000.

Wilson, Jean Moorecroft. *Siegfried Sassoon: The Making of a War Poet, 1886–1918*. London: Gerald Duckworth, 1999.

Wolf, Leon. *In Flanders Fields: the 1917 Campaign*. New York: Ballantine Books, 1958.